Praise for *Finding Purpose Beyond Our Pain*

"Difficulties are part of life, but we don't have to let them define us; instead they can refine us. You'll find that kind of hope and help in the pages of this important book."

Zig Ziglar

"This book is a true gift for anyone who's ever asked, 'Why me?' when facing life's struggles. Dr. Meier and Dr. Henderson truly strengthen us through their wisdom and experience. It is inspiring to learn that not only does our pain matter, but it can also mature us and add more meaning to our lives for years to come."

Todd Clements MD
Author, *What I've Learned Since I Knew It All*

"We are all subject to abuses, depression, injustices, and burnout. Here is a book that can be a salve for the wounded soul. It highlights God's grace, mercy, and love as an essential component of the healing journey. Kudos to Drs. Meier and Henderson for writing this practical and inspirational guide for our emotional and spiritual health."

Charles M. Balch, MD, FACS
Professor of Surgery, Oncology and Dermatology,
Johns Hopkins Medical Institutions, Baltimore, MD, and
Former Chief of Surgery, University of Texas's MD Anderson Cancer Center

"One of the many unique features of the biblical worldview is its teaching that suffering and adversity can be ultimately redemptive. This temporal arena that we call earthly life is not an end in itself; it is a soul-forming world in which God is bigger than our pain and is able to use it to forge us into the fullness of conformity to Christ. With wisdom and precision, *Finding Purpose Beyond Our Pain* takes us on a journey through the perilous threats of injustice, rejection, loneliness, loss, discipline, failure, and death, and brings us to the other side whereby they become the stuff of redemption in the boundlessly creative hands of the living God. The rich summary insights at the end of each of the seven parts by themselves are worth the price of the book."

Kenneth Boa, PhD
Author, *Conformed to His Image* and *Augustine to Freud*
President, Reflections Ministries and Trinity House Publishers

"Drs. Meier and Henderson have accomplished a difficult task . . . that is, communicating empathy and understanding for the intimate depths of pain that are common to everyone's journey, while at the same time challenging and inspiring us to dig deeply to discover the rich treasures that can only be accessed in the midst of such pain. I love that Drs. Meier and Henderson do not shy away from the most difficult questions and painful experiences that face us all. *Finding Purpose Beyond our Pain* is the most comprehensive and courageous book available on the subject. I highly recommend it to everyone."

Dr. Charles W. Dickens
Chair and Associate Professor of Biblical Counseling,
Dallas Theological Seminary

"Hats off to Drs. Paul Meier and David Henderson! Thirty years ago Jim Houston and I formed the C. S. Lewis Institute to deal with the important questions of life, such as Lewis dealt with in *The Problem of Pain.* Now two doctors have created a sequel. What a special gift for every person seeking greater purpose in life. I loved their organization of seven major sources of pain, the great stories, practical application points, and questions to ponder. *Finding Purpose Beyond Our Pain* belongs on the best-sellers list."

Jim Hiskey
Former pro golfer; Founder, Pro Golf Bible Studies;
Cofounder, C. S. Lewis Institute; Coauthor, *Choices of Champions*

"The reality is that all of us will face deep pains as we go through life. Some deny and suppress their hurts, others self-medicate, and some will choose to grapple with their hurts honestly. In this readable book, Drs. Meier and Henderson have shed light on the purpose of pain in our lives, and how being aware of the purpose can help bring healing and comfort. Christians need to deal honestly with the reality that much of life is simply painful. This book will be a helpful guide to those searching for meaning and hope."

Scott Sonju
President, Frisco RoughRiders Baseball

"Compelling, convicting, and consoling! In a world infected with abuse, loss, and rejection, *Finding Purpose Beyond Our Pain* brings hope to the depth of our despair through unveiling the heart of a loving heavenly Father."

Nathan Bramsen
Founder, ROCK International

"As a director of women's ministry, *Finding Purpose Beyond Our Pain* is my new favorite book and recommended resource to help women deal with real-life issues. Paul and David's biblical perspective on painful circumstances we face is just the wake-up call women need. Oftentimes we (women especially) allow failure, loss, and devastation to hinder God's plan and purposes for our life. This resource gives great spiritual insight as well as practical suggestions and reflections on how to navigate difficulties and accomplish great things for God."

Debbie Stuart
Director of Women's Ministry
Prestonwood Baptist Church, Plano, TX

FINDING PURPOSE BEYOND OUR PAIN

*Uncover the Hidden Potential
in Life's Most Common Struggles*

Paul Meier, MD

David Livingstone Henderson, MD

*Ken + Bridget,
God bless you!
[signature]
7/13/2012*

THOMAS NELSON
Since 1798

NASHVILLE   DALLAS   MEXICO CITY   RIO DE JANEIRO   BEIJING

Published in Nashville, Tennessee, by Thomas Nelson. Thomas Nelson is a registered trademark of Thomas Nelson, Inc.

Thomas Nelson, Inc., titles may be purchased in bulk for educational, business, fund-raising, or sales promotional use. For information, please e-mail SpecialMarkets@ThomasNelson.com.

The names and events of certain individuals in this book have been changed to protect their identity. Their stories have been used with permission.

Unless otherwise noted, Scripture quotations are taken from THE NEW KING JAMES VERSION. © 1982 by Thomas Nelson, Inc. Used by permission. All rights reserved.

Scripture quotations marked NLT are taken from the *Holy Bible*, New Living Translation. © 1996, 2004. Used by permission of Tyndale House Publishers, Inc., Wheaton, Illinois 60189. All rights reserved.

Scripture quotations marked NIV are taken from HOLY BIBLE, NEW INTERNATIONAL VERSION®. © 1973, 1978, 1984 by International Bible Society. Used by permission of Zondervan. All rights reserved.

Scripture quotations marked NCV are taken from the New Century Version®. © 2005 by Thomas Nelson, Inc. Used by permission. All rights reserved.

Scripture quotations marked HCSB are taken from the *Holman Christian Standard Bible*. © 1999, 2000, 2002, 2003 by Holman Bible Publishers, Nashville, Tennessee. All rights reserved.

Scripture quotations marked KJV are taken from the King James Version of the Bible. Public domain.

Library of Congress Cataloging-in-Publication Data

Meier, Paul D.
    Finding purpose beyond our pain : uncover the hidden potential in life's most common struggles / Paul Meier, David Livingstone Henderson.
        p. cm.
    ISBN 978-0-7852-2922-3 (hardcover)
    1. Suffering—Religious aspects—Christianity. 2. Consolation. I. Henderson, David Livingstone. II. Title.
BV4909.M45 2009
248.8'6—dc22
                                                                        2009030448
                    Printed in the United States of America

                    09 10 11 12 13 WC 5 4 3 2

*To Angela, my most faithful friend and love; and
to my children: I will have no greater joy than to know
that you walk in truth.*

—David L. Henderson, MD

To my wife Jan: I don't deserve you, but God is gracious.

—Paul Meier, MD

Contents

Acknowledgments

You cannot write a book on pain without a great deal of encouragement and support from people who believe in its message and in you as a person. I would like to thank Paul Meier for encouraging me to pursue the idea from the beginning. I would like to thank my editor, Debbie Wickwire, and the rest of the Thomas Nelson team for jumping on board with us and working diligently to help create a manuscript that was clear, concise, and filled with hope despite the weighty nature of the material. As a first-time author, they have made me feel like one of the family. I thank God for providing a publishing company that was exceedingly, abundantly above all that I could ask or think.

I would also like to thank my parents, John and Margaret, for their earnest commitment of love and faithfulness to each other and their children over the last forty-five years of marriage—for richer and for poorer, in sickness and in health. I want to thank my siblings: Sandy for leading me to Christ, Chuck for teaching me how to share Christ, and Catherine for showing me the compassion of Christ. Thank you, Judy Primo, for raising the godliest woman I know and then allowing me to steal her away for a lifetime. Thank you, Linda and Larry Dixon, for taking us under your wing as family and encouraging us to chase our dreams. Thank you, Henrietta Thomson, for making me proud of my heritage as a Scot, an American, and a follower of Christ. Finally, thank you, Angela, for being my constant companion in this journey called life. You are my most trusted advisor and my dearest love. No matter what this life brings our way, the best is yet to come!

—David L. Henderson, MD

I want to enthusiastically voice my agreement with all the wonderful things David said about Debbie Wickwire and the entire Thomas Nelson team. David and I spent nearly two years on this project from idea stage to completion, and we have learned that when you feel led by God to help people make good sense of their pain and grow from it, God will allow you to expect some yourself so you can speak from personal experience rather than theoretically. David and I both experienced unexpected sources of pain in many of the categories we discussed lovingly in this book. But we grew. We grew emotionally and spiritually, and grew to have a deeper level of respect and concern for each other as friends.

And to my wife, Jan: through this two-year ordeal, you have been my best friend, my loyal supporter, my lover, my prayer partner, my constructive critic, and a spiritual inspiration to me. You have helped me make sense of the pains and rejections we experienced from unexpected sources. I loved you deeply before beginning this project with Dave, but I love you more deeply than ever, having experienced this journey with you this past two years.

—Paul Meier, MD

Introduction

The Light Beyond Our Seven Universal Struggles

"I will not cause pain without allowing something new to be born," says the LORD.

—ISAIAH 66:9 NCV

Edward Payson, a nineteenth-century minister in Portland, Maine, wrote the following words despite losing the use of his limbs to a debilitating illness that eventually took his life:

> If God had told me some time ago that He was about to make me as happy as I could be in this world, and then had told me that He should begin by crippling me in all my limbs, and removing me from all my usual sources of enjoyment, I should have thought it a very strange mode of accomplishing His purpose. And yet, how is His wisdom manifest even in this! For if you should see a man shut up in a closed room, idolizing a set of lamps and rejoicing in their light, and you wished to make him truly happy, you would begin by blowing out all his lamps; and then throw open the shutters to let in the light of heaven.[1]

We all have experienced, or will experience, "dark seasons" in life—times of struggle and sorrow. At times like these, we often wonder, *Does God still love me? Is there a purpose beyond my pain?* With God the answer is always yes. God can use any circumstance, even our pain, to bring about good things in our lives. The darkness may be exactly what we need in order to see the light of His presence and purpose shining all around us.

Consider how this truth is evident in the following three experiences.

Imagine yourself watching a race from the sidelines as an athlete runs toward the finish line. You can tell he is exhausted. Every muscle in his body is taut. His face is contorted into a determined but pain-stricken grimace. Sweat splashes off his body as his feet pound the pavement. As his body breaks the tape, he collapses into the arms of his coach, gasping for air. Yet with all of his energy expended and his body racked with pain, he does something rather curious. He smiles. Why? He has just won first place!

Or consider a college student, poring over her books at her desk in preparation for a final exam. She desperately wanted to go to the big game tonight with her friends, but she chose instead to study to make a good grade. For the last four years, she has spent many late nights like this, hunched over her books, her eyes blurring over, her back aching, and her mind racing with facts and figures, formulas and equations. She has often wondered if the result will be worth the sacrifice. And yet a few weeks later, she stands on the stage of a prestigious university, proudly holding a rolled-up paper and smiling. Why? That paper has qualified her to pursue her dream!

Fathers in particular will appreciate this third example. Do you remember when your wife told you it was time to go to the hospital for the birth of your first child? Perhaps you rushed her to the car and ran every traffic light on the way. Once at the hospital, you cringed as her contractions grew stronger and closer together. You watched helplessly as she cried out in pain. Suddenly, though, her cries stopped and your ears caught the sound of a very different cry—a cry unlike any you had ever heard before—the cry of your newborn child. Looking back at your exhausted wife, you noticed that she was smiling. Why? In her arms she held a new purpose for her life, and in her heart had been written a new name: Mother!

Each of these people had something in common: they realized the light beyond the darkness, the purpose beyond their pain. This is what we call consecrating pain, the kind of pain that sets someone apart for a particular purpose or plan.

What about suffering that seems to have no purpose, though, such as disease, the death of a loved one, natural disasters, wars, famines, and acts of violence and abuse? Can we find any meaning for such events? We can, but only if we look for the light beyond the darkness. It is not easy to find purpose beyond our pain in such trials, but God assures us it is there. Over and over the Bible reveals a good and loving God who allows our pain as part of His greater plan of redemption and new creation. Through the prophet Isaiah, God assures His people, "I will not cause pain without allowing something new to be born" (Isa. 66:9 NCV). If you focus on Him during your pain, it will be worth the wait.

I (Dr. Henderson) grew up just a few miles outside of New York City where the night sky flickered with streetlamps, stoplights, and neon signs. As a kid I would gaze up at night and wonder what was beyond the city's familiar glow. One evening my family took a trip into the mountains, far from the city. The steady stream of bright, red taillights tapered off until our family station wagon was the only sign of life on the quiet country road. Only then, as I looked into the darkness, did I discover the most beautiful lights imaginable in the night sky. Though they had been obscured by man-made imitations, the stars became more brilliant the farther into the darkness we drove.

Pain Is Not the Enemy

We are living in an age of hurting, cynicism, fear, and doubt. More than ever, people are looking for the light beyond the darkness of their pain. According to the World Health Organization, depression is the leading cause of disability and the fourth leading contributor to the global burden of disease.[2] Suicide, a risk of untreated depression, is the eleventh leading cause of death in the United States, accounting for thirty thousand deaths each year.[3]

As physicians we have dedicated our lives to the relief of suffering: physical, mental, emotional, and spiritual. Though we consider it a great privilege and responsibility to help those who are hurting, we also believe that the goal of our lives should not be to avoid pain altogether. Pain-free living is impossible this side of heaven. We will never find a magic pill to prevent suffering or sorrow.

What if, instead of chasing after a pain-free life, we realized that pain is not the enemy? In fact, pain can be our ally if we allow it to lead us away from danger and toward the healing power of Christ. After all, most people do not go to a doctor unless they are aware that something is wrong. Just as physical pain alerts us to our need for physical healing, emotional pain can work the same way. How many times have you talked with people struggling with empty places inside their hearts that they desperately want to fill? Though those unfulfilled longings may be painful, they can spur us on toward finding the true source of joy and fulfillment.

For those who have already found the source of all joy and comfort— namely, Jesus Christ—the painful circumstances of life prove how powerful His joy and comfort can be. The apostle Peter puts it this way:

> Be truly glad. There is wonderful joy ahead, even though you have to endure many trials for a little while. These trials will show that your faith is genuine. It is being tested as fire tests and purifies gold—though your faith is far more precious than mere gold. So when your faith remains strong through many trials, it will bring you much praise and glory and honor on the day when Jesus Christ is revealed to the whole world. (1 Peter 1:6–7 NLT)

Why Can't We See the Light?

There are three reasons we often miss the light that shines beyond the darkness that comes during our times of struggle. The first is our misplaced *focus*. In times of pain we tend to focus on our circumstances rather than on God. We get so caught up in our pain that we either do not see or do not search for the purpose behind it. How many athletes do you know who exercise because they like pain? Not many—and those who *do* should probably see a psychiatrist. No, athletes know there is a purpose behind their physical pain. They are training for something higher. It is at the precise moment when an athlete begins to focus on the pain rather than the prize ahead that his or her performance declines. This is not easy! It is a constant battle that rages in the mind, especially when we cannot see the finish line. Yet we must maintain that proper focus if we are to keep pressing forward.

The second problem is our misguided *fear*. In the 1990s, "No Fear" T-shirts were the rage. On the back of each shirt was a slogan, such as, "No Scars, No Scrapes, No Proof . . . No Fear" or "If you're not living on the edge, you're taking up too much space . . . No Fear." These are the kind of inspiring expressions a coach might use to motivate his players before a big game, but having no fear is not the answer for overcoming real-life challenges and hurts. We must instead supplant our fear of pain with a healthy fear of God. The more we get to know Him and the more we stand in awe of His mighty presence in our lives, the less frightening our circumstances become. In their book *The Cry of the Soul*, authors Dan Allender and Tremper Longman wrote, "The fear of God overcomes our fear of the world."[4] When we have a proper understanding of who God is, our fear of temporary pain slowly dissipates and allows us to push through it toward greater, eternal gains.

The third problem that keeps us from seeing the light of God's purpose beyond our pain is our minds' *forgetfulness*. When we are in the midst of pain, we tend to forget how God has been faithful to us in the past. If we take time to look back, most of us will realize that God has been working through the pain to produce something amazing in our lives.

We also tend to forget that our pain is temporary. Peter says, "You have to endure many trials *for a little while*" (1 Pet. 1:6 NLT; emphasis added). When we are in the midst of a painful situation, it does not feel like "a little while." In fact, sometimes it feels like an eternity! But for those of us whose lives are submitted to the purposes of God, even lifelong suffering is temporary when compared to eternity.

"So be truly glad," Peter said (v. 7). Can we really be glad amid our suffering? One of the most irritating things people say to us when we are hurting is, "Cheer up; it could be worse." That is the only hope of a world without Christ. For them pain is meaningless. But Peter can confidently say to us who believe in the power of God, "Cheer up; it will get better. Infinitely better. Just wait and see."

To paraphrase the apostle Paul, "We are persuaded that the darkness of this present time is not worthy to be compared with the light that will be revealed in us"—if not in this life, then in the next (Rom. 8:18). Don't forget it!

The Light Beyond Our Most Common Struggles

In this book we will take a long, hard look at seven struggles we all have experienced, or will experience, at some point in our lives: injustice, rejection, loneliness, loss, discipline, failure, and death. Because these circumstances are unavoidable, we will show you not only how to endure them, but how to even embrace them as gifts from God meant to equip you for a greater purpose.

- When we live through the heartbreak of *injustice*, we will learn to trust God's sovereign control in bringing about our good.
- When we accept the darkness of *rejection*, we will be free to live in the light of transparency and find true acceptance from God, from ourselves, and from others.
- When we know the pain of *loneliness*, we will truly appreciate the healthy and loving relationships in our lives (the most important being a relationship with Christ).
- When we experience the deep shadows of *loss*, God will illuminate the most valuable possession we have, one that we will never lose—our inheritance as God's children.
- When we subject ourselves to the dark pain of *discipline*, we will grow strong physically, spiritually, and emotionally.

- When we allow God to shed light on our *failures*, we will understand true success.
- When we are reminded of the reality of *death*, we will be better equipped to focus on fulfilling our true purpose for living.

This book will challenge and encourage all of us who want to discover the light of purpose beyond our most common struggles. Each section stands alone, so if you would like to read the ones that most readily apply to your current circumstances first and then revisit the others at a later time, feel free. As we face these dark moments in life, if we allow God to teach us through our pain, we will rejoice as the dawn of His purpose rises before our eyes.

This dawning itself requires a change in our focus. Light, even more than darkness, can blind us if we are not used to its brilliance. Those who have stepped from a darkened hallway into the bright sunshine of a summer day will understand this truth, especially if they have forgotten to wear sunglasses! If you will allow your spiritual eyes to adjust their focus as you read this book, you will also experience what Edward Payson described as the shutters being thrown open in the dark places of your life "to let in the light of heaven."

Part 1

INJUSTICE

*"You have struggled with God
and with men and have prevailed."*

—GENESIS 32:28 HCSB

1

Beyond Injustice

Though the autumn day was unseasonably warm, even by South Carolina standards, Debbie Townsend moved like a weary traveler caught in a snowstorm. As she followed me (Dr. Henderson) to my office, her head was bowed and her shoulders hunched forward. Her arms crossed her chest, gripping her sides as if to prevent an already broken spirit from crumbling into pieces. With a stone-cold face and a lifeless voice, she began to share her story. As she did, it became apparent that Debbie was carrying on her shoulders the weight of injustice.

Ten years ago at the age of thirty-five, Debbie was in bed when she heard someone breaking in through her front door. She was living alone with her three young children after divorcing a man who had been physically and emotionally abusive. The decision to leave him had been difficult. She was pregnant with their fourth child and had no money. She and the kids had lived at a domestic violence shelter on the outskirts of Columbia for a few months until she found a job and was able to get a place of her own. Now, with a home in the suburbs, she thought she would finally get some relief from the abuses that had plagued her marriage, but she was wrong. Huddled beneath the covers, she saw the silhouette of her ex-husband appear in the doorway. He was intoxicated and enraged. After violently beating Debbie, he left her unconscious and bleeding on the floor.

When Debbie finally regained consciousness and called 911, she was taken to the hospital, where the emergency room doctors told her she had miscarried her fourth child as a result of the attack. She was overwhelmed with grief. To add insult to injury, she discovered that her ex-husband negotiated his way out of jail time and, instead, got off with a few months on probation. Her physical wounds eventually healed, but her emotional wounds had festered, eating away at her soul.

As she sat in my office ten years later, she began to open up about the pain:

> I can't sleep, I can't eat, and I keep having flashbacks, panic attacks, and blackouts. I'm so angry! Yet I also feel overwhelming guilt, like maybe there was something I could have done to prevent the attack. For years I've tried to smile and pretend that everything is all right, but I just can't do it anymore. Normal, everyday activities take all my strength, and familiar sounds—like the opening of a door or a car pulling into the driveway—make me jumpy and suspicious. I avoid my bedroom and often sleep on the couch at night. I can't work or take care of my kids. I don't want to die, but if this is what life is going to be like from here on, I really don't want to live either.

Debbie is just one of thousands of people who have faced the injustice of physical, sexual, or emotional abuse. The symptoms she described are what psychiatrists call post-traumatic stress disorder (PTSD). Risk factors for PTSD are not entirely clear, but they generally include the length of time a person is exposed to a traumatic event, prior emotional or psychiatric conditions, and/or lack of support from family or friends. The greatest obstacle to overcoming PTSD is a sufferer's perceived sense of injustice.

Any pain, whether physical or emotional, is harder to overcome if it is viewed as injustice. Studies have shown that perceived injustice (as in the case of a car accident or work-related injury) is a potential risk factor for problems recovering from musculoskeletal injuries. An individual's perception of injustice is likely to affect the severity of physical pain, the frequency of thinking about the pain, and feelings of being helpless to overcome it.[1]

If this is true, then imagine how important it is to deal with the pain of injustice as we strive to overcome other types of pain. If we are unable to move past the pain of injustice (even if the injustice is real), then we will never find purpose beyond our losses, our failures, or our experiences with death, loneliness, rejection, and discipline. We must overcome the sense of the unfairness of our pain before we can move forward to see the meaning beyond it.

Who's to Blame? No Comparison

We hear about corporate corruption, sexual abuse, and mistreatment of innocent children, and we rightly cry out for justice. But we also see friends who never smoked a day in their lives get lung cancer, couples who would make great parents unable to conceive children, and promising young athletes crippled by injuries that shatter their dreams. Are these injustices? If so, to whom do we attribute blame?

It is easy to compare our lives to others' and wrongly perceive injustice. Jesus told the parable of the generous employer and the hired hands to illustrate this fact (Matt. 20:1–16). The first group of employees came early in the day and agreed to work for a specified price. They were satisfied with this agreement until they found out the employer had also decided to pay latecomers the same amount for fewer hours of work. Outraged, one of the employees objected that equal payment for unequal work was unjust!

The employer answered them, "I haven't been unfair! Didn't you agree to work all day for the usual wage? Take your money and go. I wanted to pay this last worker the same as you. Is it against the law for me to do what I want with my money? Should you be jealous because I am kind to others?" (vv. 13–15 NLT).

Comparing our circumstances to others' and calling it injustice will not bring relief from pain. It only makes it worse.

Equal treatment does not automatically represent what is fair and just. For example, two teenagers with differing IQs do not need to be treated the same in order to be treated fairly. Equality would demand that parents spend the same amount of time helping each child with his or her home-work, but that would not be fair, because the needs of the one are greater than the other. Likewise, if both teenagers work hard to get into college, but only the smarter of the two gets a full scholarship, the parents would be perfectly justified in spending more for tuition on the child who struggles academically. The provisions are based on need, and though they are not equal, they are most certainly just.

Not only do we struggle to define injustice, but we also have a hard time determining what actions to take when rectifying the wrong. Letting the punishment fit the crime is a murky business at best. As imperfect beings we often deal out imperfect justice. Who knows how many people are in jail for crimes they did not commit? How many people have escaped just punishment because of a technicality? We try our best to be fair, but even the most righteous judges in our courts are susceptible to subtle influences, shifts in mood, misinformation, or lapses in judgment.

What about punishment? Is a quick death at the hands of an execu-tioner a fair punishment for the torture and murder of a helpless child? Is a two-hundred-dollar speeding ticket as equal a deterrent for a billionaire as it is for a third-grade teacher? Can we ever find a punishment that will satisfy the pain of our own personal injustices?

The more questions we ask, the more we realize how little we under-stand about justice. Yet as we wrestle with our frustrations with God and with others, the dawn will break, we will open our eyes, and we will realize that we have prevailed over the pain!

2

Entitlement Versus Truth

Our intellectual acknowledgment of society's injustices can quickly turn to visceral emotion when we are the ones facing it personally. I (Dr. Henderson) remember acknowledging the frustrations my patients had in dealing with their insurance companies. With a calm, sympathetic nod, I would utter a few condolences and then quickly change the subject to "more important" matters—that is, until I experienced those same frustrations firsthand.

Our daughter, Victoria, has had a number of health problems since her birth. After putting her through thousands of dollars' worth of medical tests and treatments, we received a letter in the mail from our insurance provider stating that they had rescinded her from our policy due to a technicality in her medical records. When we recovered from the initial shock, my wife and I were incensed. How could they do this to us, to our innocent little girl? How were we ever going to afford to pay all those medical bills on our own? After two months of phone calls, requests for medical records, conversations with lawyers and doctors, and long letters of appeal, the insurance company finally reversed their decision. Though we were so grateful to God for answering our prayers, it was hard not to feel resentment for the two months that we had been put on hold, both literally and figuratively. After all, we had done nothing wrong, but we had spent hours working to fix the mistakes of others. Our sense of injustice had been heightened because of our personal experience with it.

Whether our injustice is as little as being put on hold for hours waiting to speak with customer service, or as severe as being injured by a reckless driver, being overlooked for a promotion because of company politics, or being accused of a crime we did not commit, our perception of the injustice determines how we handle it. This is why we must properly define *injustice* before we can deal with it in a healthy way.

The problem is that our perception of injustice is so easily distorted by our sense of entitlement. Before we can distinguish between injustices that are only perceived and those that are actually real, we must first whittle away our sense of entitlement and uncover our true rights as human beings. After all, the more we feel we deserve, the deeper our sense of injustice will be when we do not receive these things.

Entitlement is believing that somehow what we deserve is special or above others, that our rights as individuals or as a group are more important than the persons or groups around us. Conversely, our sense of entitlement tells us that we are less deserving of mistreatment or pain than those same persons or groups. The biblical worldview, however, tells us that this is not true. The Bible says that God "sends rain on the just and on the unjust alike" (Matt. 5:45 NLT). Even if we are upstanding, law-abiding citizens, we are not entitled to have everything go our way.

If you find this reality uncomfortable, it would be wise to remember C. S. Lewis's words. In short, he said that if we look for comfort instead of looking for truth, we will end up with neither![1]

Too many people suffering from the pain of injustice enter psychiatrists' offices looking for comfort apart from truth. They are often disappointed, even angry, when medicines or therapy fail to provide that comfort. Though medications and therapy can help, we often have to educate patients about their roles in the recovery process. If there are underlying psychological, social, or spiritual issues that are not being truthfully addressed, doctors can only provide symptomatic relief, not long-term healing. To overcome the pain of injustice, we must seek truth above all else. In doing so we put away the false idea that we have a right to a comfortable, easy life.

Can You Handle the Truth?

So what *are* we entitled to in this life? The real answer, whether you believe in God or not, is nothing!

Some of you may read those words and respond, "Nothing! Come on, you can't be serious. After all, I work hard. Don't I deserve a day off now and then? I'm a nice person. Don't I deserve to find someone who will love and care for me each day? I eat healthy foods and exercise. Don't I deserve to live a long life free from heart disease and joint pain?"

We hate to be the ones to break the news, but the answer is no. Here's why.

An atheist believes that life is a chance phenomenon. To survive we need to be the fittest, the smartest, and quite frankly, a bit lucky. To a person who views life this way, natural disasters and random catastrophes are simply part of a meaningless existence. There is no justice in the world other than the contrived justice that societies impose upon themselves in their effort to survive. We obey rules only as long as they keep us safe and comfortable. If they fail to do so, then we change them. In the words of Friedrich Nietzsche, "There is no eternal justice."[2] The ramifications of this belief exclude any notion of rights.

Without God in our lives, we are selfish creatures. Why in the world would we follow Jesus' teachings, such as love your enemies, do good to those who hate you, bless those who curse you, and pray for those who hurt you? That would be absurd. There is no justice in behaving that way.

If there is no absolute standard of justice, then rules are meant to be broken. We should do whatever can give us an advantage over others to survive. An atheist can become angry over the pain of life, but he has no one to blame. He has no rights beyond what he can take and hold by force. Entitlement for him is nothing more than what Sigmund Freud called *wish fulfillment*—the satisfaction of a desire, need, or impulse through a dream or other exercise of the imagination.

In contrast a theist's sense of injustice can be harder to curb because he does have someone to blame for all of his problems: God! After all, if God created human beings, then isn't He responsible for our pain? We ask, "How could God let this happen to me? Why didn't He stop me from getting hurt?" To answer these questions, we must recognize the sense of entitlement that drives them.

Why Blame God?

If you believe God created you and He is a personal being, then you must also believe that He has a definite purpose for your life. To ask, "Why was I ever born?" in an accusatory way is to question God's right to create whoever and whatever He wants. "Who are you, a mere human being, to argue with God? Should the thing that was created say to the one who created it, 'Why have you made me like this?'" (Rom. 9:20 NLT).

To know God correctly, we must know Him completely. We cannot expect Him to leave us alone in the good times and to step in during the bad. We cannot break His rules and then demand that He rescue us from the consequences. We have no rights except those that come from God—and even those are gifts.

Unfortunately, we have taken the privileges we have in a free society and turned them into rights. Where once we believed in legitimate rights—the right to life, liberty, and the pursuit of happiness ("rights" endowed for us by our Creator)—we now have added to these a laundry list of other desires: the right to choose life or death, the right to security and comfort, and the right to instant gratification. We expect to have satisfying nine-to-five jobs, hassle-free health care, guaranteed retirement at sixty-five, and three weeks of paid vacation each year. We expect our marriages to be effortless, our children to raise themselves, and our elderly parents to age gracefully in a plush retirement community. All of this is in addition to our having the latest fashions, the sportiest cars, and the fanciest homes.

Our society's sense of entitlement has even changed the way we practice medicine. Because of advancements in technology, people not only expect to be made healthy again through medical treatment, but they expect to be made better than normal! Parents, college students, and business professionals are flooding psychiatrists' offices and requesting stimulants in an effort to get ahead of the curve. More and more athletes are getting caught using steroids to win in their respective sports. While in other parts of the world people are struggling to obtain basic health care, people in the United States are spending millions of dollars on cosmetic surgeries to achieve physical perfection.

With all of this power and control, that we are often blindsided by injustice is no wonder. Though as a culture we have become desensitized to such things as violence, sexual immorality, and hedonistic pleasures, we have become overly sensitized to the pain of injustice. We are so accustomed to having things *our way* that we are shocked, overwhelmed, and enraged when they are not. In our anger we look for someone to blame. When we find no human scapegoat, we turn our anger toward God.

3

The Light of Perspective

Imagine being born blind and living in total darkness. Others try to describe to you the colors and shades of things you can only sense with touch. Words such as *light, dark, shiny,* and *color* have no real meaning to you. Descriptions of sunsets and mountain ranges have no tangible experience for you. How would it feel to know that everyone else around you is experiencing what you cannot—that because of your disability, much of the beauty of life is passing you by?

Now imagine, having lived in darkness all of your life, your eyes are suddenly opened. All of your questions about the visual world are answered in one overwhelming panorama. And then, while you are still trying to fully comprehend the miracle of your physical sight, you are told that the reason for your blindness is that God chose *you* to reveal His power to the world. Would the years you spent in darkness, waiting, have been worth that one amazing moment in time?

For the blind man Jesus healed in the gospel of John, chapter 9, the answer was an emphatic yes. When the disciples saw this man begging on the side of the road, they asked Jesus whose sin had caused his blindness—his parents' or his own? They assumed his disability must have been a punishment for sin.

Jesus gave a different reason, though. He replied, "It was not because of his sins or his parents' sins. This happened so the power of God could be seen in him" (John 9:3 NLT). With that, Jesus healed the man.

Then He asked the man one question: "Do you believe in the Son of Man?" (v. 35).

What would your answer have been? If you knew that ten, twenty, maybe fifty years down the road of life God was going to make known to you the purpose for your pain and reveal His power to the world through the injustices you will have faced, would you be more willing to face it and believe in Him? Would the time you spend waiting be worth it?

At this very moment, we may not be able to understand the pain we have suffered, but God *has* given us several truths on which to cling while we wait for the answers to life's injustices.

Life Is God's Gift

The first truth is that life, no matter how painful, is God's gift to us. It does not always feel that way, but it is nonetheless. As long as you have breath, you have the opportunity to know love, joy, hope, peace, purpose, and fulfillment. The fact that we take life for granted robs us of its simple pleasures. As Daniel, a Hebrew slave, reminded the king of Babylon, "God . . . holds your breath in His hand and owns all your ways" (Dan. 5:23).

Ironically, it is often the most traumatic experiences that remind us of how precious life is. Josh Turner realized that while serving during the Iraq War. While leading a convoy carrying medical supplies to a nearby town, his vehicle was hit by a roadside bomb that injured Josh and killed several others on board. The images of death and destruction Josh witnessed on that day and at other times during his service left an indelible impression. Instead of embittering him to the injustices of war, the tragedy made him appreciate how precious life is. When he returned to the States, he made up his mind that anything short of the trauma he experienced in the service was not going to get him down. Now he tries to appreciate every moment. Even in the tough times, he is quick to verbalize his thankfulness for life and his acceptance of each day as a blessing from God.

If only we could realize this same truth without having to experience what Josh did. Instead of cursing God for the injustice that this life can bring with it, we could be thanking Him for the many blessings He provides amid the pain.

God Defines Justice

The second point to remember is that God defines justice. As our Creator, He makes the rules that govern our lives, and any rights we have as humans are ours only because He has given them to us. Some of the rules God has established are natural laws. For example, if you jump off the Golden Gate Bridge, you had better know how to swim. The law of gravity is in effect. If you want to enter a building, you do so by the front door, not by walking through brick walls. The laws of matter are controlling us. No one would argue that falling or breaking your nose as a result of ignoring these laws is unjust.

God has also established absolute moral laws of right and wrong. These laws have been instilled in us as His creation. Even though we "suppress the truth in unrighteousness" (Rom. 1:18), ignoring the moral laws of God does not make the consequent suffering unfair. This would be like saying that ignoring the laws of gravity should make it easier for us to fly.

The Ten Commandments are a perfect starting place for learning the absolute moral laws of God. He did not establish them to punish us, but to give us a fulfilling life here on earth. Psalm 112:1 says, "How joyful are those who fear the Lord and delight in obeying his commands" (NLT). Disobeying them not only separates us from God but also leaves us feeling miserable. Read through the Ten Commandments and ask yourself how you or a loved one has been hurt by someone breaking these moral laws.

For example, failing to take a day of rest has led many people to nervous breakdowns and chemical addictions as they try to keep up in a fast-paced society. The effects are also multigenerational. Workaholics leave children feeling neglected and lonely. They often grow up suffering from severe anxiety and perfectionism.

Disrespecting our parents, no matter how much we may resent their imperfections, will only make life worse for us in the end. Scientists have shown that the two extremes of anger—explosive fits of rage and suppressed seething bitterness—increase an individual's risk for heart disease and stroke. And beyond the physical consequences of disrespect, our children will observe how we treat our own parents, and they will learn from our examples. "Do to others what you would want them to do to you" (Luke 6:31 NCV) is a multigenerational command. If you want your kids to honor you when you are old, you might want to demonstrate that same honor for your parents. Also, if we can learn to honor our parents, it will serve us well when we have to deal with others who are in positions of authority. So much of life is doing things that those in authority tell us we have to do. Why not learn to accept this early on in life? The Bible goes so far as to say that this will actually increase the quality and length of our lives (Eph. 6:2–3).

What about committing adultery? It not only damages your relationship with your spouse and forces your children to take sides, but it also breeds a crippling form of paranoia that will interfere with your future relationships. After all, if the person with whom you cheated was willing to hurt others to be with you, how can you ever be sure that he or she will not hurt you someday in the same way?

Do you know people who are prone to exaggeration? They become so used to stretching the truth that they begin to believe their own tall tales. Then they wonder why they are the laughingstock of everyone who knows them. Those who lie repeatedly can never relax or let down their guards. They become so obsessed with covering their tracks that they miss out on the peace and joy of an honest life.

As Christian psychiatrists we see many individuals who are suffering from the consequences of ignoring God's moral laws. We try to point out the destructive nature of their choices in a loving and compassionate way, but it can be hard to do if the individual does not believe in an absolute standard of right and wrong. In our if-it-feels-good-do-it society, most people do not want to be told that their actions have consequences. But you must know truth before you will ever find comfort! If you want to do what is just, you have to know God's Word.

The Bible teaches us what is right and wrong. Without the Scriptures as our guide, our minds will become "dark and confused" by the seeming injustices we suffer (Rom. 1:21 NLT).

God Is Good

The third point to remember is that God is good. He is not the author of evil. Though many people like to blame God for sin, the apostle James said it best when he wrote, "God is never tempted to do wrong, and he never tempts anyone else. . . . So don't be misled. . . . Whatever is good and perfect comes down to us from God our Father, who created all the lights in the heavens. He never changes or casts a shifting shadow" (James 1:13, 16–17 NLT). If this is true, then the *real* injustices we experience are not from God. He may not intervene when we get caught in traffic, in order to help grow our patience, or He may allow a scenario that keeps us from getting a coveted promotion in order to teach us contentment. But God never causes a father to abandon his family or a pedophile to molest innocent children. That is never His will. Jeremiah says that God's plans are "plans for good and not for disaster, plans to give you a future and a hope" (Jer. 29:11 NLT).

It is here, then, that we discover the true meaning of injustice: it is any act committed against another person that seeks to violate God's good and perfect will for that person's life. Though God's ultimate plans for us will never be thwarted, the free will of man can temporarily suspend them. Does this mean that God's power is limited? Absolutely not. There is nothing amazing about the sovereignty of a God who has to cause everything that happens in this world. In fact, that kind of a God would be dreadful at best. As we have said before, God does not cause evil. What is truly amazing is the sovereignty of a God who can make room for the free will of humanity and still be in complete control of the final outcome.

God Is Love

Some might ask, "If God is all-powerful, then why does He allow injustices to occur? Why doesn't He stop them before they happen?" The answer is that a world that makes no room for injustice is a world that shuts out unconditional love. As beings created in the image of God, we have a will that enables us to obey or disobey His commands.

All of us at some time in our lives have hurt or been hurt by the people we love. The pain is excruciating, almost unbearable, but whatever pain we experience, we must realize that God feels it even more. An injustice against God's creation is an injustice against God Himself. True justice demands retribution, but love patiently endures the pain because it realizes a higher purpose. Even Jesus said, "If you love only those who love you, what reward is there for that? . . . If you are kind only to your friends, how are you different from anyone else? . . . But you are to be perfect, even as your Father in heaven is perfect" (Matt. 5:46–48 NLT).

The greatest injustice in this world was the crucifixion of Jesus. Christ did not deserve to die, nor did He *have* to die. Out of that injustice, however, came the most perfect act of love this world has ever known.

Jesus asked the apostle Peter the night He was betrayed, "Don't you realize that I could ask my Father for thousands of angels to protect us, and he would send them instantly? But if I did, how would the Scriptures be fulfilled that describe what must happen now?" (Matt. 26:53–54 NLT). Jesus was willing to suspend justice even at the cost of horrific suffering in order that he might fulfill a higher purpose and secure eternal life for us. That is true love!

The Bible says, "Love suffers long" (1 Cor. 13:4). What injustices have you had to endure for the sake of love? How long is your love willing to stay retribution in order to accomplish something even greater? Perhaps you are a counselor or a pastor, pouring out your life to individuals who never show their appreciation for your efforts. Maybe you are a single parent spending countless hours training young children. It could be that you are a businessman who has been fired for the mistakes of a fellow employee, a victim of a drunk-driving accident suffering from intractable pain, or a young adult healing from an abusive childhood. Whatever your situation, be encouraged. You have a promise from the One whose love for us endured more pain than we will ever know or understand. "Love never fails" (1 Cor. 13:8). As long as you are willing to wait for justice, there is time enough to see the power of love heal broken relationships, tear down walls of bitterness and discrimination, and restore the peace that passes all understanding.

Will you claim this promise as your own? Do you believe that God can take any problem or trying circumstance in your life and turn it into good? If so, then turn that circumstance over to Him. You'll be amazed at how your long-suffering leads you to find the joy that only God's love can bring (1 Peter 1:6–9).

4

All Things Made Right

As we wrestle with the pain of injustice, we must remember that God is faithful. Justice deferred is not justice denied! Someday every injustice will be made right, whether in this life or the next. A classic example of God's faithfulness in righting what is wrong is the Old Testament story of Joseph, a man whose life was riddled with injustices. He was the son of Jacob, the father of the nation of Israel, and his early life story could easily be titled "A *Real* Series of Unfortunate Events."

As a child Joseph was a product of favoritism. His father loved him more than any of his other children, because Joseph had been born to Jacob in his old age. Jacob was more like a grandfather to Joseph, spoiling him with special attention, favors, and gifts. The most famous of these gifts was his coat of many colors (Gen. 37:3–4).

No wonder Joseph's eleven brothers hated him. The surest way for parents to stir up feelings of injustice within their children is to show favoritism. This does not mean that every child must be treated exactly the same, but it does mean that parents should invest an equal effort in displaying love and attention to each of their children. Making comparisons can create animosity between siblings. Statements like "Why can't you be more like your sister?" or "You should learn from your brother" do not bring siblings together. Jacob's favoritism was intended as a blessing on Joseph, but it turned out to be a cruel curse. It was this special treatment that fueled his brothers' seething jealousy and led them to sell him into slavery.

That experience alone would have been enough to consume him with bitterness, but Joseph's bad breaks were just beginning. When he came to Egypt, he was sold to a high-ranking official by the name of Potiphar. Instead of succumbing to the meaningless existence of a slave's life, Joseph worked hard at what he was given to do and succeeded in winning his master's favor. He finally landed a very responsible job, only to have it stripped from him when Potiphar's wife falsely accused Joseph of attempted rape. To prison Joseph went.

Again Joseph refused to wallow in his pain. While in prison, he worked hard and became a favorite of the prison warden. He continued to seek out the purpose beyond his circumstances, and when an opportunity arose to help one of Pharaoh's most important servants, he did. This servant was Pharaoh's chief cupbearer and, like Joseph, he had been thrown into prison on a whim. In fact, their common experience may have moved Joseph to help him. One night the cupbearer had a dream that Joseph wisely interpreted to mean that the cupbearer would soon be released. In exchange for easing his fears, Joseph asked the cupbearer to petition Pharaoh to have him released also, "For indeed I was stolen away from the land of the Hebrews; and also I have done nothing here that they should put me into the dungeon" (Gen. 40:15). The cupbearer, however, "did not remember Joseph, but forgot him" (v. 23).

Strike three for Joseph. For the next two years, he sat in prison, waiting to hear from Pharaoh, and every day for two years he was disappointed. Have you tried putting yourself in Joseph's shoes? Two years in prison! We struggle to wait ten minutes in line at a grocery checkout. Two years in prison just isn't fair! What kept Joseph from being consumed by the pain of injustice? There is only one answer: the Lord was with him (Gen. 39:2, 21, 23).

For Joseph to move beyond the pain of these real (not just perceived) injustices, he had to believe that God had not abandoned him, that there must be a purpose beyond the pain, and that someday God would be faithful in revealing that purpose to him. Joseph was not disappointed.

After two years the cupbearer Joseph had helped finally remembered his promise. Pharaoh had two dreams (more like nightmares). One was of seven fat cows being eaten by seven sickly cows. The other was of seven plump heads of grain being eaten by seven thin heads. No one in his royal entourage could interpret what the dreams meant; no one but Joseph could ease his troubled mind. You can imagine the tagline for the cinematic production of Joseph's life: the favored son who became a slave, the slave who became a prisoner, the prisoner who saved an empire!

Joseph's God-given ability of interpreting dreams gave him the opportunity to stand before Pharaoh and warn Egypt of a seven-year famine that would come after seven years of plenty. This knowledge allowed Egypt to store food in preparation for the upcoming famine, thus saving many lives, including Joseph's own brothers—the ones who had sent him there against his will in the first place.

In order to appreciate how important each of Joseph's injustices was in bringing him to his final position of power, we must work our way backward. Joseph would never have had the opportunity to interpret Pharaoh's dream had he not been sent to prison. The Bible says that while he was locked up, he noticed the pain of others. He saw that the cupbearer was sad, and he took the opportunity to help. This connection eventually led him to Pharaoh.

But what about all that time in between? The years Joseph spent as a slave and a prisoner gave him the experience necessary to manage complex networks of people and resources. These skills were essential to him as Pharaoh's second-in-command. It is also interesting to note that Joseph's dreams were what got him into trouble at the beginning of his life, and dreams were what saved him in the end.

Now Joseph had come full circle. Because of his wisdom and fortitude, he had risen to the position of second-in-command under Pharaoh himself. With his newfound power, his chance to take revenge on those who had mistreated him had come. However, Joseph's trust in God's faithfulness and power overwhelmed any sense of injustice or desire for revenge he may have had. His words have gone down in history as one of the most powerful testimonies of God's sovereign ability to work all things together for good.

Weeping not with sadness but with great love and joy, he embraced his brothers who had come to buy food and said, "You meant evil against me; but God meant it for good" (Gen. 50:20).

Many people are destroyed by their desire for revenge, because it pulls them into a vicious cycle. Our sense of injustice intensifies our anger, anger intensifies our pain, and our pain leads to a deeper sense of injustice. As human beings our natural tendency is to seek retribution, but in doing so we get stuck in our own pain. We want the perpetrator of injustice (whether real or perceived) to suffer just as much as we have, or else we are not satisfied. But how much is "just as much"? How do you measure that? Pain is subjective, and no pain is as intense as the pain we experience personally. We can try to imagine what others are going through, but we can never know for sure. Therefore we can never be satisfied that their suffering is truly enough.

This is why God says, "Vengeance is Mine, I will repay" (Rom. 12:19). Justice is too big for us. It overwhelms us like Frankenstein's monster unchained. If we put justice in God's hands and let Him take care of it, then we can focus on healing from our pain instead of inflicting more. Then, when He finally reveals the good works He has accomplished through the experience, we, like Joseph, will forget about revenge and focus on rejoicing!

This is why our goal for those who have experienced physical or emotional trauma is to have them reach the point of accepting the injustice of it. The trauma is now a part of their life stories. They cannot run from it, and they cannot change it. They have to face it. Only then can they begin to move forward in recovery.

Many people enter therapy in denial. The shock that life could be so cruel is too overwhelming. We want them to open up about their pain, express their anger, their frustration, and their sadness, but we also do not want them to remain stuck in their situation. The key to moving forward is acceptance and forgiveness, and the key to these is *faith*—faith that there is a God who can take any painful situation out of our control and turn it into something good.

The Rest of Debbie's Story

Debbie Townsend, the woman suffering from PTSD, chose to confront the injustices she had faced in her past. Instead of succumbing to her pain, she was determined to discover the purpose beyond it. After three weeks in an intensive outpatient program in Columbia, South Carolina, her outlook changed dramatically. She later described her experience in a letter to her therapist:

> I spent the first two days here bundled up, both outwardly and inside emotionally, but I listened to Bible studies, Christian life workshops, and other patients tell their stories, and I thought, *This is my chance to ask the hard questions about God and get on a solid foundation once and for all.*
>
> So I did. . . . I wrote my story, shared it in my group, and for the first time I started to release my pain. I got answers to hard questions, reestablished a belief in God, and eventually came to grips with the abuses that had been haunting me. I realized that through the pain God had made me strong. Not only that, but God cared enough about me to take my pain and use it to conform me closer to his image. . . . Wow!
>
> Because of my pain, I have been able to help others. When I bought my first home after the divorce, I wanted an extra bedroom so that I could offer a place to anyone who was in a similar situation. By the grace of God, I've already been able to help someone, and that alone has been worth the pain. Whoever it is out there, I want them to know that there is peace. Healing is in the pain. They can face it and win with God's help!"[1]

Finding Purpose Beyond Your Injustices

Now that we have discovered all that God can do through even the most painful injustices, we want to give you five practical application points to strengthen and encourage you as you search for the purposes beyond your own injustices.

1. *Remember your status.* No matter what injustices you face in this life, if you are a child of God, He is always with you. An injustice against you is an injustice against Him, and He always fights for His children! (Rom. 8:31; Exod. 14:14).

2. *Always give thanks.* No matter what you are experiencing, there is always something for which you can thank God. Giving thanks during times of injustice can sometimes feel like pouring alcohol on an open wound. It may be good for us, but it surely isn't fun. As we get used to saying thanks, however, it becomes a salve that soothes our injustices, re-focuses our perspective, and helps us to relax even during some of the most stressful periods of our lives (Phil. 4:6–7).

3. *What you see is not all you get.* Don't be too quick to judge your circumstances. What you perceive as an injustice may actually be the working out of God's blessing in your life (Gen. 50:20).

4. *Justice deferred is not justice denied.* Never give up hope. God is just and will make all things right someday. We cannot lose hope in this promise, even though our circumstances seem to disprove it (2 Peter 3:9).

5. *Keep a record of rights.* The Bible says we should not keep a record of wrongs done to us, but we can certainly keep records of the circumstances in our lives that have been made right. Consider using a journal to record the injustices that have worked out for good in your life, or even purchase some decorative stones on which you can write God's blessings. Take them out each year and read them with your family. Let this give you courage for the future trials you may face (Josh. 4:5–7).

Set aside some personal time to consider your own situation in the light of these truths. Then answer the following questions truthfully in order to establish the groundwork for overcoming the injustices in your life.

1. What are my entitlements, and how necessary are they for my happiness in life?

2. In what areas of my life can I thank God for His blessings? How can I remind myself of these blessings during moments of injustice?

3. How have past injustices in my life been made right? In what ways can I use these examples to trust God in my present and future injustices?

4. While I wait for God to make things right, what actions are under my control as I fight against injustice?

5. What principles from this chapter might help me deal with the other pains we discuss in this book: rejection, loneliness, loss, discipline, failure, and death?

Part 2

REJECTION

He made us accepted in the Beloved.
—Ephesians 1:6

5

Beyond Rejection

Carlos Rivera was thirteen years old when his parents sent him to soccer camp. Though he was excited about the opportunity to improve his athletic skills, he was nervous about meeting new people. He was an introvert and especially had difficulty talking to girls, even though like most teenage boys, he was "girl crazy" in the truest sense of the term.

Carlos would never forget the first day of camp, the day he saw Suzanne for the first time. The very air seemed to part in front of her as she walked. Slender and athletic with long, dark hair and dark eyes, she seemed like a Greek goddess to him. The fact that she was three years older secured his infatuation. He determined then and there to do anything he could to get her attention. (Except, of course, talk with her directly. He wasn't that crazy!)

That week he played the best soccer he could, always keeping an eye out to see if Suzanne was watching. He dove recklessly for headers, made daring slide tackles, and ran circles around the defenders. Off the field he was just as diligent. He showered sometimes three times a day, making sure his hair was perfectly styled and his aftershave liberally applied. He even did push-ups before going to the lake to swim in hopes that what few muscles he had would look a little bit bigger. But as much as he tried, Suzanne never seemed to notice him.

One morning, as the cabin groups were lining up for breakfast, he saw his chance. "All right," the camp director said, "it looks like Cherokee has cleaned up nicely. You guys can head in first." *This is it*, he told himself. As he paraded past Suzanne's cabin with the other boys in his cabin, he knew she would have to notice him. He decided that this time he would look straight into her eyes and say hello. But before he got the chance, he overheard her talking to her friends.

"I can't believe Cherokee gets to go first. I mean look at them. That guy's shirt is untucked, that one's hair isn't even combed, the hat he's wearing is crooked. . . ." And so began a running commentary of each boy's appearance as he passed by her critical eyes. When Carlos got close enough for her to notice him, she paused for a brief moment, as if she could not think of anything to criticize. His heart swelled. *Maybe I've finally succeeded in making an impression*, he thought.

"And he . . . he's got zits all over his face!" she finally blurted out.

Carlos's cheeks reddened with embarrassment as the girls' laughter trailed behind him. The pain of those words hurt more than any kick in the shins he had endured that week at soccer camp.

Most of us have had similar experiences with rejection as kids. Looking back, we can sometimes shrug our shoulders and laugh as Carlos did when recalling this event many years later. At other times it is all we can do to keep from crying. The pain of rejection is a common experience, and whether we admit it or not, it hurts. We all long for acceptance. We try very hard to make ourselves acceptable to God, to ourselves, and to others, which is why, when we do get rejected, we feel so bad. But is being rejected by others always bad? Can we ever find purpose beyond the pain of being overlooked, excluded, ignored, or openly rejected?

What Is Rejection?

What does it mean to be rejected? In the medical community the term refers to an immunological response that refuses to accept into the body substances or organisms that are recognized as foreign. This is a healthy response when that substance or organism is dangerous. In the case of an organ transplant, however, the body may actually reject something that is good and necessary for its survival.

As people in relationships with other people, we can view rejection in a similar way. We tend to push away those who appear foreign, dangerous, or unacceptable to us in some way. At times the rejection is appropriate. For example, a professor who refuses to allow a disruptive student to continue attending his class is practicing a healthy form of rejection. At other times the rejection is unwarranted, even cruel, as in the case of a person who takes pleasure in ridiculing people with physical or mental disabilities. Being on the receiving end of rejection, no matter what the cause or motivation, is painful. It would be nice if we never had to experience it, yet rejection is not only unavoidable but often necessary for us to grow spiritually, mentally, and emotionally.

The problem for those who have not experienced the pain of rejection by others is that they are never forced to learn how to accept themselves as unique individuals. How does this process work? Rejection is the catalyst that drives us toward introspection; and introspection, if practiced properly, leads us to deeper levels of maturity and self-acceptance.

Identifying the Source of Rejection

In the midst of rejection there are two important questions we must ask ourselves. The first is the more obvious: why have we been rejected? The factors that lead to rejection are varied and numerous. They include the personalities, emotions, biases, and maturity levels of each person involved as well as the timing and circumstances surrounding the rejection. Sometimes we deserve to be rejected. People who are arrogant and feel entitled may need a healthy dose of rejection to wake them up to the pain they have inflicted on others. But even if you are the most genuine, gracious, honest, and loving person in someone's life, he or she may still reject you.

As professors at Dallas Theological Seminary (DTS), we have taught future pastors and Christian counselors the importance of a proper perspective when facing rejection. I (Dr. Meier) warn them to expect automatic rejection from about 10 percent of the congregation, no matter what. The

10 percent of the congregation who had the most dysfunctional families of origin and was hostile toward one or both parents will transfer much of that repressed hostility to authority figures in their adult lives. Pastors and counselors can be convenient scapegoats for the pent-up feelings of rejection we experience but of which we are completely unaware.

Since there are so many reasons people will reject us, and because it may never be possible to know the motivations of someone else's heart, our perceived reason for the rejection may be more important to examine. Though perception is not always reality, it does teach us in what areas of our lives we are most sensitive to the pain of rejection. This perception is influenced by several factors. Parents can have a significant influence as they instill in us values we carry with us into adulthood. For example, a young girl who has to win the acceptance of emotionally distant parents through her academic achievements will be more sensitive as an adult to the rejection of other authority figures who are also insensitive to her efforts to please. This woman's perceived reason for rejection is, "I am not good enough."

Society also has a profound influence on our perceptions. A man who is inundated with messages from a sex-crazed media may believe that his wife's rejection of him sexually is because he doesn't have six-pack abs, when in reality her rejection stems from her being physically exhausted, having worked or taken care of the kids all day. The pain of rejection can alert us to the sensitive spots in our lives, areas on which we may have placed too much or too little value.

Identifying Our Response to Rejection

Once we have identified the source of our pain, we must ask ourselves a second important question: how will we respond to it? There are a number of ways to respond to rejection, but most people lean toward one of two extremes: those who build walls in their relationships and those who dig wells. Either extreme can be unhealthy. Someone who tries to dig a well too deep too quickly by being open and transparent with everyone they meet runs the risk of being taken advantage of or hurt by those who are not ready to go deep themselves. A person who builds up walls, however, will suffer from the pain of loneliness, which we will discuss in a later chapter. The key is to find a healthy balance; and in order to do this we must be honest about our emotional responses to rejection. Let's look at some of the ways people respond to rejection.

Falling in the Well

We all want to go deep in our relationships, but we often make the mistake of digging too deep too quickly. Relationships take time to develop. They do not happen overnight. On the contrary we often sabotage their development when we try to rush them. We are setting ourselves up for rejection if we do not take the time necessary to invest fully in healthy, well-grounded relationships with others. There are two types of wells that we must dig slowly and carefully. It may take longer to get there, but it will save us a great deal of pain in the long run.

The Well of Physical Closeness

Our society is notorious for encouraging couples to explore physical intimacy long before they develop any kind of commitment to one another, let alone marriage. God created sex to be the most intimate physical, emotional, and spiritual connection that a man and a woman could have. A great deal is wrapped up in that one act. It represents in a physical way all that we value in a relationship—openness, vulnerability, trust, self-esteem, pleasure, security, confidentiality, leadership and submission, sharing—it is all there. Yet we have taken this sacred act that the Bible depicts as two people literally becoming "one flesh," and we have pretended that it is nothing more than entertainment. But if that were so, then why have so many people been broken by the pain of infidelity and promiscuity? Why do so many men and women have severe insecurities about their physical appearance and their ability to remain attractive in the eyes of their mates? The more we expose ourselves indiscriminately in this way, the more we will face rejection.

Physical closeness is more than just sexual, though. It can mean the people with whom we desire to be close—the first person we call to go out to eat or have coffee, those we choose to associate with on a regular basis. Some kinds of physical intimacy are unavoidable, such as interactions at work or at home. If we constantly spend time with people who are manipulative, uncaring, or abusive, we will easily fall apart. That is why the Bible encourages us, as Christians, not to forget to spend time with one another (Heb. 10:25). We must be intentional in choosing with whom we spend time.

The Well of Emotional Transparency

Emotional transparency is the ultimate goal in any relationship, but it also doesn't happen overnight. Many people who have not developed a healthy response to rejection dive headlong into new relationships just to ease the pain from the ones before. They convince themselves that they cannot survive on their own, and so they search frantically for someone to fill the void. Usually they have not taken time to process the reasons for the original falling out. Instead, they bring their open wounds with them into their new relationships. Because they have not dealt with their own pain, it pours out in their conversations, attitudes, and actions with the persons they have just met. These newfound "friends" respond in one of two ways. If they are healthy emotionally, they will pull away to create some distance to process all that is being dumped on them. After all, they want to protect themselves from a person who might be unreasonably needy or overbearing.

If, however, this new individual has less than noble intentions, he or she might seize the opportunity to hurt or take advantage of someone so vulnerable. This scenario becomes a revolving door wherein the rejected persons, by nature of their responses to that rejection, repeatedly attract people who will continue the cycle. This not only occurs in romantic relationships but with friends, family members, business associates, and acquaintances. It does not matter. Trying to make up for lost time in one relationship by digging too deep too quickly in another will only poison the waters of your wells.

It is also true that you can try to maintain too many wells at once. If you try to go deep with everyone you meet, you will eventually hurt someone when you fail to live up to their expectations of intimacy. We must prioritize those relationships in which we invest the majority of our time. Those on the top of our list should be our spouses and children. Avoiding rejection in these relationships should be more important to us than with a casual acquaintance.

Protecting Your Wells

In the Middle East, especially during biblical times, water was a precious commodity. If a man drank from someone's well without permission, he needed to be prepared to fight for his life. Armies attempting to subdue their enemies might try to poison the enemies' water supplies. In the wilderness, well water had to be protected. Moses, after fleeing from Egypt, heroically stood up to a group of shepherds who were keeping the daughters of Reuel, the priest of Midian, from watering their flocks (Ex. 2:16–17). This was serious business.

The same is true with our hearts. Proverbs says, "Above all else, guard your heart for it is the wellspring of life" (4:23 NIV). This is true in our relationships. We cannot and should not let just anyone draw deeply from the well of our souls. You must develop trust in a relationship before deeper intimacy can be attained. This takes patience and constant effort to achieve. There are always setbacks when people hurt us or let us down, but eventually we get deep enough to enjoy the cool waters of intimate friendship, having carefully dug through the layers of trust, commitment, and forgiveness that lead us there.

Walling Off the World

Each of us has a level of intimacy with which we are comfortable. This level of comfort is influenced by many factors, including our genetics, our culture, and the choices we have made. Many of us hit a ceiling of intimacy in our relationships. We are afraid that closeness will uncover ugly secrets about ourselves and the people we love. Maybe that is why

Shakespeare's quote is so memorable: "All the world's a stage, and all the men and women merely players."[1] We play a part for the people in our lives in order to avoid rejection. There are at least three kinds of walls people build to protect themselves.

The Wall of Self-Centeredness

The first is the wall of self-centeredness. A self-centered person tells himself, *I'm not going to care about other people, because that would mean I would have to care about what they think about me. That is too painful.* As a result these individuals seem arrogant or aloof. They talk a lot about their accomplishments in front of others and put others down to make themselves feel better. Instead of approaching relationships based on unconditional love and acceptance, they limit their interactions to those relationships that will provide them some material or emotional gain. They see all people, including their mates, kids, parents, friends, business partners, and others as objects. By making people less human, they do not need to consider others' emotions or opinions; nor will they have to feel bad if they are rejected. These individuals choose not to invest anything in their relationships that will not produce equal or greater returns for them personally. That way, if the relationship fails, they either break even or take more than they have lost. In the long run, however, this mentality creates more pain. The barriers they have erected shut out all love and leave them completely alone.

The Wall of Superficiality

The second kind of wall that individuals build is superficiality. Though they may seem friendly and engaging, they never go deep in their relationships. Because of their craving for acceptance, however, they must compensate for their lack of depth in some other way. They may act inappropriately seductive or provocative, often using their physical appearance to draw attention to themselves. Their mannerisms are flamboyant and overexaggerated. They are easily influenced and often conform their opinions to the views of others in order to maintain someone's acceptance. Should anyone try to get too close, however, they will break off the relationship. They think if anyone finds out who they really are, they will suffer the pain of rejection.

The Wall of Self-Deprecation

The third wall that people often erect to protect themselves from rejection is self-deprecation. Instead of building themselves up and putting others down like the first group of people, they do the complete opposite. They put themselves down. Inwardly they are craving approval and acceptance, but they are unwilling to get involved with people unless they can be certain of being liked. They believe the only way to know this for sure is to lay out ahead of time all the faults and problems they think others will find out with time. They denigrate themselves, hoping that by doing so they will attract sympathy instead of criticism, acceptance instead of rejection. They believe they can preempt the pain of rejection from others by rejecting themselves first.

Many teenagers who do everything they can to look different, such as dressing in all black or piercing every piece of cartilage on their entire body, are in this category. They think, *If I make myself look as odd or unattractive as possible, then people will reject me only for my outward appearance and not for who I truly am inside.* At first this may work. The doting they receive for "being too hard on themselves" feels great. But if the self-denigrating continues, people begin to avoid them altogether. We call this the "negative charge effect."

My (Dr. Henderson's) son started playing with Thomas the Tank Engine toys at the age of two. Each train car has a positively charged magnet on one end and a negatively charged magnet on the other. When turned in the right direction, each car attracts another car to its front and back ends, forming a train with which even Daddy enjoyed playing.

I sat watching him play one evening and could not help but laugh at his confusion as he tried to force two negatively charged ends of the train together. The more he pushed with one car, the further away the other one rolled. Suddenly it dawned on me: many people do exactly the same thing in their relationships. They may be kind and loving, but they push people away with their incessant self-deprecation and negative thinking.

The Bible encourages us to dwell on things that are positive. "Whatever things are true, whatever things are noble, whatever things are just, whatever things are pure, whatever things are lovely, whatever things are of good report, if there is any virtue and if there is anything praiseworthy— meditate on these things" (Phil. 4:8). This includes those qualities and attributes with which God has blessed each of us. A realistic but positive sense of self is not only healthy; it is godly. It takes time to develop, but you will soon find that your positive thinking in Christ will attract others who will appreciate you for who you are.

Living Healthily Transparent

Living transparently is not spilling out all our problems and flaws to everyone we meet. It is rather a willingness to open up and be vulnerable as we work toward deeper relationships with the people in our lives. Transparency is a risk because it could lead to rejection, but the rewards it can bring are even greater. One reward is that it leaves no room for unhealthy relationships. I (Dr. Meier) had a pastor friend who was dealing with an extremely critical church member. Sadly, this individual was able to convince twenty other members that he could do a better job of leading the church. Without warning, the entire group left the church to start their own.

I told my friend, "Well, Pastor, if you don't pull the weeds out of your garden, God will be kind enough to do it for you. I think we should celebrate that God graciously removed these negative influences from your church, rather than grieving about their lack of confidence in you. Just think how much better off your church garden will be without them." When the pastor saw it from that perspective, his tears turned to smiles, and we celebrated all the free gardening the church had received from God Himself.

Transparency allows us to live loving, moral, open, honest, fair, and productive lives without fear. We can focus on doing our best with what we have been given and not worry about whether people hate or love us for it. With transparency comes freedom—freedom to have healthy relationships based in truth, not lies. Lies tie us down and chain us, but "the truth shall make you free" (John 8:32).

No More Pedestals

The pain of rejection hurts the worst when we place others on pedestals. When we overvalue the opinions of any one person, we set ourselves up for rejection. This is why Proverbs tells us, "In the multitude of counselors there is safety" (11:14). It is important to prioritize the opinions of others, the most important being God's opinion of us. (We will discuss this in the next chapter.)

In order to feel valuable, many people believe they must find acceptance in the eyes of an idealized relationship. That relationship may be with a parent, a spouse, a child, a coworker, a boss, or even a celebrity. If those relationships fail, they come to the very faulty conclusion that they are worthless, insignificant, and unlovable. They never stop to ask if their idol's opinion of them is accurate or important.

This is why surrounding ourselves with wise counselors, who will lovingly and honestly advise us, is often the best way to soften the pain of rejection. They will help to show us where we can grow and change, but they will do so out of genuine love and concern for our good. They also will not abandon us because of our flaws. Knowing this allows us to be transparent without fear.

Idol worship is practiced in many romantic relationships. Couples do everything they can to become what they think will secure for them the acceptance of their partners. Instead of practicing transparency, they hide behind masks, but as soon as the marriage vows are said, those masks begin to crack. The marble statues with which they initially fell in love crumble into pieces, causing more damage than imagined. Honest exposure early on might bring immediate rejection, but finding acceptance based on truth will be worth the pain.

It's Not All About Me

Why is it that when we are rejected we assume that it is all about us? Often we don't realize that the rejection we experience from others has more to do with their issues than ours. If we call a friend and she forgets to call us back, do we immediately assume she doesn't want to spend time with us, or do we take time to consider how overwhelmed she might be feeling with life right now? When our neighbor yells at us for accidentally parking in front of his mailbox, do we give him the benefit of the doubt and realize he may be venting on us the frustration of a hard day at the office?

Even when rejection is about us, it is not always *about us*. People tend to transfer their negative experiences with others onto their present relationships. You might look, sound, or act the way someone's abusive stepfather did. So every time he interacts with you, he is unconsciously reminded of that negative relationship. An intense dislike for you will then develop even if you are the nicest, most loving person on the planet. This transference influences the way people view any number of characteristics: your height, weight, religion, skin color, geographical origins, political leanings, or clothing choices; your posture or the way you hold your head; your body language; your education level; or your level of sincere godliness. If you take it personally, you will experience a lot of unnecessary pain.

The Sources of Our Acceptance

Maybe after reading this chapter you identify with one or more of these responses to rejection. We all have areas of our lives where we are more or less sensitive to rejection. As we face rejection, a little introspection will help us discover how we respond to it. It will also force us to determine the sources of our acceptance. The following chapters will lay out answers on how to find acceptance from God, from within ourselves, and from others. We have put them in this order because we will never find acceptance from others if we do not learn to accept ourselves. Likewise, we should never try to accept ourselves without seeking acceptance from God first.

6

Acceptance from God

God is all about acceptance. That's why He sent His Son, Jesus. But while He has His arms wide open, ready and willing to accept us if we come to Him, that coming must be on His terms, not ours. He has established through His Word, the Bible, clear guidelines for becoming "acceptable" in His eyes, and that acceptance requires complete transparency from us. For many people this process is just too painful. They are afraid that if they expose their darkest thoughts and actions to God, He will reject them just as others have rejected them. Nothing can be further from the truth.

The Birth of Rejection

Adam and Eve, the first man and woman, were created to have a transparent relationship with God. There were no secrets between them in the beginning, but that was about to change. Look at the Genesis account to see what happened (Gen. 1–3).

Eden was a perfect place: a beautiful garden in which Adam and Eve could find fulfillment and purpose. They lived in the presence of God and could openly communicate with Him and with each other without any shame. They were totally exposed—physically, emotionally, mentally, and spiritually—and had no fear of rejection. They were perfect in their form, in their thoughts, and in their relationship with each other and with God.

The only command God gave them was not to eat of one tree, the tree of the knowledge of good and evil. This command was meant to establish trust, the essential element necessary in any loving, healthy relationship. Adam and Eve were meant to trust God's goodness, and God expected Adam and Eve to be obedient to Him, thus demonstrating their love. Sadly, this trust was broken. Satan tempted Adam and Eve to question God's goodness and to reject His plan for their lives in the garden (Gen. 3:1–8).

After Adam and Eve ate from the tree God had commanded them to avoid, several things happened. First, Adam and Eve recognized their sinful actions and were ashamed. The Bible says, "They knew that they were naked" (v. 7). They realized they were completely exposed. This led to a second action. They sought to cover the nakedness they themselves had exposed. In doing so they not only hid themselves from God, but they hid their nakedness from each other. Their sin and shame not only destroyed the purity of their relationship with God; it weakened the relationship they had with each other as well. The seeds of rejection had been planted.

For centuries since that time, men and women have sought to hide their true selves. Because of Adam and Eve's choice in the garden, we now know good and evil. The exposure of such truth is painful because we realize that we are that "evil" and God is that "good." That is why we see the illustration of darkness and light throughout the Bible. The light that exposes our evil is painful. Many people choose to avoid it altogether. Ironically, to have a healthy relationship with God (and with others), exposing ourselves to the light is an absolute must. God forced that exposure in the garden of Eden by searching for and calling Adam and Eve.

Many people believe that the actions God took next were a form of rejection, but in reality everything God did was part of His plan to make Adam and Eve acceptable again in His eyes. First God covered their nakedness. Covering and hiding are two different actions. Most people try to hide their shame from God and from others as Adam and Eve did, but they never succeed. God sees everything. He does not want to hide our shame. He wants to remove it. He wants to expose our nakedness so that He can clothe us with His mercy and grace. The skins Adam and Eve wore were a continual reminder of their rejection of God's original plan, but because of His forgiveness, they no longer needed to be ashamed. He gave them a new plan and purpose no less glorious. In the act of clothing them, God demonstrated what He would one day do with His very own Son in shedding His blood to cover our sins.

After God clothed Adam and Eve, He banished them from the garden of Eden. In this second act, God again seemed to be rejecting Adam and Eve, but He was not. True justice demanded that Adam and Eve live with the results of their sinful actions for the rest of eternity, and that is exactly what would have happened had they eaten from the tree of life. God's banishment protected Adam and Eve from such pain and would ultimately allow them to return to the place where they were in His presence once more.

Because of Adam and Eve's sin, humankind has inherited that which should fill us all with shame: a sin nature. When we step out of the darkness of sin and examine ourselves in the light of God's holiness, we come to realize that all of us deserve rejection. The Bible says, "All have sinned and fall short of the glory of God" (Rom. 3:23). God cannot, by nature of who He is, associate with someone who is anything less than perfect. That should destroy any pride we have (no matter how "good" we may think we are), knowing that we will never be good enough in and of ourselves for God.

What gives us power in the realization of this deserved rejection is that God wants to accept us *despite* our undeserving selves. In fact, He has even provided a way for us to gain acceptance again in His eyes. When we completely expose ourselves to Him (our faults, our sins, our insecurities, our fears, our desires); when we admit to Him what we truly are and ask for His love and forgiveness; when we ask for Him to cover us with the blood of Jesus Christ that was shed for that very purpose, He accepts us unconditionally!

"For you know that God paid a ransom to save you from the empty life you inherited from your ancestors. And the ransom he paid was not mere gold or silver. It was the precious blood of Christ, the sinless, spotless Lamb of God" (1 Peter 1:18–19 NLT).

There is a freedom that only comes from exposing ourselves to the light of God's love, accepting His gift of acceptance through Jesus Christ, and knowing that He will not reject us no matter how ugly or unworthy we may feel. If God is waiting and willing to do this, then how can we not do the same for ourselves?

Accepted Children of God

For those of us who have exposed ourselves to God and asked Him to come inside us and cleanse us with the blood of Christ, the Bible says we have become children of God: "How great is the love the Father has lavished on us, that we should be called children of God! And that is what we are! Dear friends, now we are children of God, and what we will be has not yet been made known. But we know that when he appears, we shall be like him, for we shall see him as he is" (1 John 3:1–2 NIV).

For those of us who grew up with fathers who were abusive or absent or overly critical, picturing God as a father figure may not be a comfort at first. But God is a far better Father than even the best of dads here on earth. Imagine what it would be like to have a father who lavished love on you, unconditionally, no matter how many times you messed up. Not a spoiling kind of love or a pretend love motivated out of guilt, but an unselfish love that was willing to do anything necessary to see you make the most of your life.

We have such a heavenly Father, and that gives us power to grow up as spiritual adults in the safe, secure arms of God. We can be confident in our position as children and heirs to our Father's inheritance, no matter what others may say, do, or think about us. Now we can be real with the people we meet. We can expose ourselves as we are without shame. We can be transparent. The pain of rejection loses its scariness when we know that the most important person in our lives loves us unconditionally, accepts us as we are, and wants to train us patiently to become like Him.

The timeless story *The Prince and the Pauper* illustrates this point perfectly. Written by Mark Twain, it is the story of two boys from two completely different backgrounds who meet by chance and switch places. The one boy is Prince Edward, the son of Henry VIII of England. Used to all the privileges and power that royalty affords, he decides to put on the rags of his newfound friend, Tom Canty, a lowly street urchin who had made a living by begging on the streets. In doing so, Edward gets a taste of the rejection Tom has grown up with all his life. Unlike Tom, however, Edward remains confident in his true status as the prince of Wales and refuses to subject himself to such treatment. He spends a good portion of the story trying to escape from a scoundrel who believes Edward is *his* son. This fiend has no idea that the boy he is mistreating is the son of the king! As much as Edward appears on the outside to be Tom Canty, the simple pauper of Offal Court, inside he is true royalty. This gives him a confidence that his friends admire and his enemies despise.

Tom, however, is not so confident in his new role as the prince. Though he wears the proper clothes and even plays the part fairly well, his anxiety overwhelms him because he knows he is just pretending. As desperately as he tries to prevent exposure, his words and his actions soon betray the common peasant that he is.

It is the same for us. All of us start out like Tom Canty. We are born paupers, stained and dirty from the filth of sin. Some of us try to dress ourselves in royal robes. We do what we can to look and act the part of righteous, good people, but deep inside we know that we will never measure up. Until we expose ourselves for who we truly are (unworthy peasants in the presence of a holy and powerful King), we will never be at ease. The King to whom we must expose ourselves is not, however, Henry VIII, who many scholars say was an absolute madman! No, He is the perfect King, just but also merciful and gracious, ready to make all who accept His gift of salvation His children. As such we can walk confidently through the darkest neighborhoods of rejection and smile, knowing our true position in the kingdom. It is an amazing feeling that no amount of rejection can steal.

How Far Will His Acceptance Go?

In my psychiatric practice, I (Dr. Henderson) had the opportunity to evaluate a known sex offender. Though he had never acted on his urges,

Jack had spent a great deal of time looking at pornography and chatting online. He believed that by doing this he could hide from others his sinful desires, but he soon found himself in a downward spiral of addiction.

After years of deluding himself into thinking that he was strong enough to resist the temptation to act further, he finally gave in and arranged to meet a thirteen-year-old girl he had been chatting with online. Fortunately, the "girl" turned out to be an undercover police officer, who promptly arrested Jack.

I interviewed him as well as his wife, who tried to remain supportive despite her utter disgust at what she now knew about her husband. Neither of them could make eye contact with me. The shame and embarrassment were too great. The hardest challenge for both of them was that Jack would now have to be registered as a sex offender. He would then be exposed to everyone in his community as a criminal and have to accept the hard reality of the rejection that would inevitably follow.

I must admit that like most people I was initially repulsed by Jack. I thought about all the children he might have abused had that police officer not been doing his job. But then I realized something very sad. Jack, too, had been a little boy once. No police officer was around when Jack's father forced him to do things no child should ever have to do. Jack's eyes welled with tears as he told me about the shame he had covered up all of his life. His hiding went far beyond his current sexual activities. He was hiding his past as well. If only that shame had been exposed earlier to someone who could have helped him, maybe Jack would not have been in this situation.

His biggest question at this point was, "What purpose and acceptance can I possibly find in life now?" My mind quickly returned to the story of King David. I told Jack about all the things that David had done. He, too, had given in to the lust of his flesh and committed adultery with Bathsheba. But he did not stop there. He then had her husband murdered to keep from being exposed. What a scumbag, right? And yet God called David "a man after my own heart" (Acts 13:22 NIV).

David, despite his sins, desperately wanted to know God and His love. Though David suffered greatly from the consequences of his sins, God never stopped loving him. He never rejected him. When David finally admitted his sin and exposed himself before God and the nation of Israel, he experienced a profound sense of relief and power. Take some time on your own to read Psalms 32, 38, and 51, and reflect on his words as he exposes himself to God and then experiences God's forgiveness.

Not only did God use David again *despite* his sinful past, but God used him *because of* his sinful past. The power David experienced in God's forgiveness compelled him to proclaim it to everyone around in words and in song. This actually caused other sinners to come back to God. And King David's poetry and songs have been preserved in Scripture and have taught millions of people through the centuries about the goodness, mercy, and grace of God. Does that not send chills up and down your spine?

As Jack and I talked, he acknowledged that being placed on the sex offender's registry might be the best thing for him, as painful as that might be. Finally, the shame of his past would be exposed, and the healing process could finally begin. He could also continue to find meaning and purpose in life. No one told him it would be easy. Rejection is difficult to bear! But many, like Jack, have found great gains through their rejection. By exposing themselves completely for who they are, they, like David, have turned others to God.

Not everyone struggles with a sin so openly abhorred by our society, but we all have secret insecurities we are afraid to expose. Sasha, outwardly, was the image of perfection. She was a self-made woman. Having obtained a business degree from Penn State University, she had successfully developed and sold a chain of beauty salons that raked in several million dollars in profit. Not only was she successful, but she was gorgeous to boot. Her friends used to joke with her that if the business world ever got too rough, she could easily become the next top model! But even with all she had going for her, Sasha harbored a dark secret: she struggled with anorexia. The purging had started in high school after being out sick for two weeks with pneumonia. She had lost ten pounds due to the illness, and when she returned, everyone told her how amazing she looked. Though she loved the attention, it also put her in a bind. What if she gained the weight back? Would people notice her "getting fat" again? She determined in her mind that she could not let that happen. She regimented her mealtimes, limited her portions, and exercised vigorously, and if ever she ate too much, she would simply excuse herself and head to the bathroom to purge. This went on for many years, undetected by her family and friends. She became a master of deception, keeping her secret safe behind her perfectly applied makeup and designer outfits, but her shame and insecurity could not stay hidden forever. One evening at her health club, Sasha lost consciousness and had a seizure. She was rushed to the hospital, where the doctors discovered that her electrolytes were depleted due to malnutrition. She was told to see a psychiatrist.

In the end she discovered through therapy that her perfectionism developed at a very early age. Her parents, though very loving, often smothered her. They controlled every aspect of her life and were always pushing her to excel. She grew up believing that acceptance from God, from herself, and from others could only be obtained through perfection, and anything short of that deserved rejection. Only when she learned to accept her failures and imperfections did her weight slowly return to a healthy norm. Finally, she could relax and enjoy her many successes as gifts from God.

All of us wrestle with shame. Some people are scared that if their church finds out they take medicine for depression or anxiety, they will be seen as lacking in faith. Others believe that if they tell their spouses about the mistakes of their pasts, they might use it against them in the future. Many people worry that God cannot see past their doubts, their anger, their addictions, or their stubbornness. If David could find acceptance from God and even be used by Him despite his past, then so could Jack and Sasha. And so can you!

In the following chapters, we will discuss how to be transparent with ourselves and with others. But do not move on until you have been transparent with God. Put down this book, get on your knees before Him, and ask with a humble and willing heart how you can become acceptable to Him. We promise you from personal experience: *you won't regret it*!

7

Acceptance for One's Self

Everybody knew that Ian Glendale loved to have fun. He was the life of every party, known for his wild antics (most of which he could not remember the following morning). Though he could outdrink any guy twice his size, he never saw his alcohol use as problematic. Even after his first DUI, when friends began to caution him to take it easy, he laughed it off as a bad coincidence.

He said, "Everybody drinks and drives at some point. I was just unlucky enough to get caught."

His situation worsened, however, when the weekend partying started earlier each week: first on Friday, then Thursday, and, on occasion, even Wednesday nights. Getting to work in the morning became difficult, and he regularly called in sick, but it was not until he had to be rushed to the emergency room for detoxification that he was finally willing to admit to himself, *This has got to stop.*

It was not easy. After three years in Alcoholics Anonymous and several early relapses, he explained why:

The hardest obstacle for me to overcome was admitting that I had a problem. The second hardest obstacle was admitting my problem to others. I thought for sure that I could keep my struggle with alcohol to myself. I tried to go to the same parties and be the same old Ian, but I couldn't . . . not without alcohol. When I did not drink, people kept asking me what was wrong.

"You don't seem yourself tonight," they said.

But they were wrong. This was the real me, and the real me was totally insecure without alcohol. It had been my mask for so long that I felt exposed without it. Suddenly people would see me as I really was (or as I thought I was) . . . boring! It took me a long time to get comfortable in my own skin and realize that I did not have to be drunk to have fun. When I finally told people I could not drink anymore, a lot of my friends *did* stop hanging out with me. They were not willing to accept the new Ian, but I've found new friends who accept me as I am, and this has given me confidence to believe that I can have an identity free from alcohol!

Transparency feels awkward and unnatural at first. It does not matter if we have been hiding behind alcohol, perfectly applied makeup, a successful career, or a religious facade. We may have found acceptance from God, but we struggle to be honest with ourselves and with others. We might be fine opening up to God about our hurts, our struggles, and our desires, but extending that transparency beyond the confines of our relationship with Him scares us to death. This is because we have not learned to accept ourselves as He does. The more we work at accepting ourselves as God does, the more we will trust that others' acceptance of us is genuine. It will also make the pain of rejection easier to bear, having developed a confidence in ourselves that is no longer solely dependent on the views of other people. Below are several steps we must practice in order to reach that point in our lives.

Learn to Let Go

Often as we have counseled patients, we have heard them say, "I just can't live with myself!" They spend their entire lives with guilt that cripples them.

We are not saying that we should feel no remorse for our sinful behaviors. When we live transparently, much of the pain comes from what we know needs to change inside of us. What we fail to understand is that when we invite God into our lives, He gives us the power to change. We do not have to labor alone. Too often, however, we try to take that power into our own hands. We set out to fix all of our faults and forget that God has to help us in the process. And God is not in a hurry. He is patient with us, more concerned about the relationship as we grow closer to Him. We have all of eternity to be perfected. Unfortunately, many individuals get in a rush and burn out. They still cannot let go of their guilt even after they have repented and been forgiven. They feel the need to punish themselves relentlessly.

However, the Bible tells us that when God forgives us of sin, He removes it from us "as far as the east is from the west" (Ps. 103:12 NIV). But what do *we* do with our sin? We hold on to it. We wallow in it and let it hold us back from fulfilling God's plan for our lives. Because sin is so often described as dirty, filthy, and disgusting to God, we have tried to think of the most disgusting scenario to illustrate our point.

Have you ever walked into a public bathroom stall and discovered that the person before you failed to flush? Talk about nasty, right? Now imagine doing the same thing in your own home. Have you ever thought about "fasting from flushing" for even just a week? Have you ever been forced to because of a clogged septic tank? Anyone in his right mind would be on the phone in a heartbeat, calling a plumber and urging him to come immediately to fix the problem. Why, then, do we fail to do this with our sin, which the Bible describes as "garbage"—a Greek word that literally means "dung" or "excrement" (Phil. 3:8)? If we are being too crude, good! We want you to understand how God views our clinging to the guilt and sin that clogs up our lives, sin from which He has already cleansed us.

Rejoice in Your Weaknesses

Another reason why we fail to harness the power of transparency is that examining our own lives shows us how weak we really are. Have you ever said anything like the following? "I've failed. I'm a nobody—nothing special. I've got no talent. I'm just an average Joe. My past is too screwed up.

I'm not smart enough, rich enough, attractive enough, fit enough . . ." Well, don't worry. You are exactly what God is looking for:

> Think of what you were when you were called. Not many of you were wise by human standards; not many were influential; not many were of noble birth. But God chose the foolish things of the world to shame the wise; God chose the weak things of the world to shame the strong. He chose the lowly things of this world and the despised things—and the things that are not—to nullify the things that are, so that no one may boast before him. (1 Cor. 1:26–29 NIV)

When was the last time you picked up your Bible and read about the "great" men and women God has used? Let's see. Noah got drunk and passed out; Abraham was a liar and a coward; Jacob was a deceiver; Jephthah, a great judge of Israel, was an illegitimate son; David was an adulterer and murderer; Solomon was a sex addict (come on . . . a thousand wives?); Peter was headstrong and impatient; and Paul, by his own admittance, was a bad public speaker.

What about the women? Sarah, the mother of the nation of Israel, was a doubter; Rahab was a prostitute who ended up in the lineage of Christ; Ruth, a foreigner, was the great-grandmother of David, also a part of Jesus' family line; Martha was a workaholic; and Mary, the mother of Jesus, was an insignificant teenager before His birth. This is just the short list. There are countless stories in the Bible and throughout history of God using "the foolish things of the world to shame the wise" and the "weak things of the world to *shame* the strong" (1 Cor. 1:27 NIV). Transparency requires us to admit our weaknesses and foolishness, but in doing so we join a long line of weak and foolish people whom God uses to do amazing things for Him. That is reason to rejoice!

Get Pride out of Your Way

Ironically, it is often our overconfidence that gets in the way of God's using us to fulfill His purposes. Transparency teaches us not to think of ourselves more than we should. Before we can rejoice in our weaknesses, we must acknowledge that we have them. We are works in progress, and though we do not wallow in our sins, we continue to be mindful of the fact that we *are* sinners. It is our humility that keeps us from being crushed by rejection. It also reminds us to practice daily dependence on God for our strength.

I (Dr. Meier), in the 1990s, had an extremely successful mission trip to Russia and, sadly, let it all go to my head. As I lay alone in my hotel room overlooking the Baltic Sea, I fell asleep thinking about how lucky God was to have Paul Meier, the Christian psychiatrist, doing His work for Him there. I woke up that night from a horrible nightmare. All my past major sins had flashed before me in sequence. I sat up in bed, weeping, remembering that God had called me to serve Him not because of my "greatness" but because of my simple beginnings. I apologized to God for thinking so arrogantly of myself, and His Spirit comforted my own spirit clearly with the words *My strength is made perfect in weakness* (2 Cor. 12:9 NIV).

The next morning I kept my nightmare to myself and went to our mission team's daily devotions. A businessman from Chicago led by sharing that God had showed him a verse the night before: "My strength is made perfect in weakness" (2 Cor. 12:9). I was amazed and humbled, but the feeling lasted for just a short period of time.

Two years later I had an even more spectacular mission trip to Cuba, even getting the opportunity to appear on Cuban television and radio and lecturing on Christian psychiatry to a thousand Cubans, including some of Castro's leaders. Can you guess what I was thinking at the end of the ten-day trip? Yep, how lucky God was to have me. I had already forgotten the lesson I learned two years earlier in Russia. So that night (you guessed it), I had another nightmare similar to the one I had before. Once again I apologized to God for my arrogance. Again the Holy Spirit spoke clearly to me within my own spirit, saying, *I like to use the foolish things of this earth to confound the wise, Paul, and that is why I chose you—so I could get the glory.* The next morning I again kept my humbling experience to myself and went to breakfast with our medical team.

A medical missionary from Ethiopia led our devotions at breakfast. He had changed his talk from what he had originally prepared to a verse that God had showed him the night before—you guessed it—"God has chosen the foolish things of the world to put to shame the wise" (1 Cor. 1:27).

I wish I could say that I finally learned my lesson once and for all, but I must admit that God still has to humble me periodically. As much as I'd like to be proud of my accomplishments, He will not let me get cocky. He won't let you either!

Look for the Extraordinary in the Ordinary

God does not always use us for tasks the world would think spectacular, powerful, or significant. At times our very actions, not just our persons, seem foolish or worthless and will go unnoticed. This should not be discouraging. You never know how God will use the foolish or weak or mundane tasks we do to accomplish His purposes. But first we need to be willing to do them. We need to keep our eyes open for these everyday opportunities God has waiting for us. They usually are not readily noticeable. Not everyone is called to build an ark or conquer Jericho. Do you remember the Israelite slave girl taken captive by the nation of Aram? You can read about her in 2 Kings 5:2–4. Her whole life is summed up in three measly verses, but God used her one small act of faithfulness to impact an entire nation, not only in her generation but also in generations to come.

What did she do? She simply told her mistress, the wife of a general named Naaman, a man who had leprosy, about the prophet Elisha and his power to heal people. The wife told her husband, and he in turn went to Elisha for healing.

After being healed Naaman declared to Elisha, "There is no God in all the earth, except in Israel" (2 Kings 5:15). He took his newfound faith and the proof of his healing back to Aram, where hundreds, perhaps thousands, of people witnessed the power of God in his life. We do not even know that young girl's name, but God used her simple act of faithfulness in a mighty way.

Conquer Core Beliefs

Sometimes people do not even realize they have problems with accepting themselves. They only experience the emotions that come when particular circumstances trigger unconscious, negative "core beliefs" as we call them in psychiatry.

Robert LePaglia was a very successful software company executive. Everyone who knew his work was amazed at his abilities and told him so. But Robert could not believe them.

He experienced an overwhelming fear of failure every time he started a new project. He also described feeling like a little kid when talking to his boss and other high-end executives with whom he worked. The anxiety and depression that resulted were crippling. When he finally discovered the source of these deep-seated emotions through therapy, Robert began to get better.

He told a story that summarized the source of his core belief. When he was in junior high school, he had the opportunity to take a mission trip to Peru with his youth group. When he asked his dad about it, his dad promised Robert that if he could get straight A's on all his report cards for the year, he would pay for the cost of the trip minus any support money Robert could raise. After an entire school year of studying hard and raising support, Robert returned with half of the money for the trip and a 4.0 average for all three of his report cards, but his dad, who acted surprised, refused to fulfill his end of the bargain, and Robert's friends had to leave him behind.

"I didn't think you'd ever be able to earn that much money, so I really had no intention of helping in the first place," his father admitted.

Robert's dad was acting out of his belief that his son would never amount to anything. After years of hearing the same message, Robert began to believe it himself. When he finally realized this, he was able to begin the process of changing his core belief. Through a great deal of counseling, prayer, and practice, he worked hard to see himself, not as a hopeless failure, but as the intelligent, skillful, successful businessman God had allowed him to become.

What is it about yourself that you cannot accept? Whatever it is, take the steps necessary to get help in overcoming the obstacles. After all, if God can love you and use you knowing everything He does about you, isn't it time you learn to do the same? The power is there. You just have to start using it. Are you ready to begin?

A New Way to Love

In the following chapter, we will take a good look at how to be transparent with others and find the right kind of acceptance. But be warned that you will never find acceptance from others until you have learned to accept yourself. When the Bible says to "love your neighbor as yourself" (Matt. 19:19 NIV), there are two people in the passage who are in need of love. If you have not learned to see yourself in the light of God's love, the second greatest commandment, "Love your neighbor as yourself," will be difficult. How will you possibly love others "as you love yourself" if you do not love yourself first?

Practicing transparency may be painful. Your spiritual eyes may feel strained and sore as your focus changes from the darkness to the light. It may be necessary to unlock some dark closets and pull out hurts and rejection you have buried in the past. You can't do it alone. If you haven't already, find someone you can trust to help you: a friend, a relative, a pastor, a counselor, or a psychiatrist. God wants you to tap into His powerful plan for your life. It is time to let in the light!

8

Acceptance from Others

Whenever two people meet, there are six people present—the two as they see themselves, the two as they see each other, and the two as they really are. Life would be a whole lot simpler if only the last two people stuck around, but this requires transparency on the part of both individuals, which can be scary. The key to overcoming this fear is to realize that transparency with others is not practiced to gain their acceptance. If we have followed the lessons learned in the previous chapters, we have already found the acceptance we need in our relationship with God and ourselves. The acceptance we get from others is only the icing on the cake. True freedom comes when we can enter relationships, not for the acceptance we can gain but for the acceptance we can give. This is where the light of joy shines the brightest.

Some people will turn away from us because of our transparency, but if we are secure in God and in ourselves, that will be okay. Their rejection may still hurt, but we no longer have to fear the pain. Instead of shutting down and hiding behind walls of self-protection, we will continue to seek out people who need us.

In our relationships with people, we usually tend toward one of two extremes. We either work too hard at staying true to ourselves and fail to "try to find common ground with everyone" (1 Cor. 9:22 NLT), or we compromise completely and throw aside our relationship with God to obtain relationships with others. Take the following two stories as examples.

Tony Mitchell had grown up in a very strict household where innocent questioning of authority was met with sharp rebuttals and even physical punishment. He was expected to accept rules and regulation without reason or explanation, even as a teenager.

If ever Tony tried to express his opinion on an issue, his dad would berate him. Because of this Tony became a very good debater. Soon Tony's dad began to lose arguments with his son. Tony took the opposing side of an issue just to make his father mad. He had become a "monster of logic" with an ingrained contempt for those who were unable to stand against his words of reason. His debating skills followed him into other relationships.

His wife, for one, was no match. She always walked away knowing she was right but feeling she was wrong. She soon stopped trying to communicate at all. His boss had had enough of Tony's incessant infusion of his opinions into their weekly staff meetings. Even Tony's kids avoided him. When challenged, he responded by saying, "Hey, this is just the way I am. If they can't deal with it, too bad."

No wonder Tony was now sitting in a psychiatrist's office, depressed and alone. His uncompromising stances on even the most trivial of issues had pushed away everyone in his life who cared about him. If Tony had been living transparently with himself and with others, he would have been able to see that his pride and his fear of losing control were keeping him from developing intimacy. True transparency requires us to admit that we do not know it all. Tony was more concerned about hiding his insecurities than he was about being open with those he loved.

Sometimes people do the opposite. They try to find common ground with everyone but wind up compromising their own moral convictions in the process. A high school girl named Louisa Yang experienced this firsthand with her boyfriend. She said she trusted God to lead her into right relationships, yet instead of waiting for Him, she decided to take matters into her own hands by practicing the all too common act of "missionary dating." Her boyfriend was the star of the football team, good-looking, and charismatic. He treated Louisa like a princess, and she decided it would be okay to date him. After all, if she set a good example and prayed for him, she might be able to lead him to Jesus, right?

So she went with him to all the football after-parties, cruised with him in his sports car, and even smoked a joint or two just to show she was not a total "good girl." One night after a few too many beers, she found herself justifying his sexual advances. "It's because he loves me that he wants me like this. I want him to know that I love him back. Anyway, he has promised to marry me and even start coming to church."

She dreamed of the family they would one day have together. But his spiritual interests were self-serving and insincere. They did end up having a beautiful little girl, but unfortunately he did not stick around for the birth. Louisa was left to raise her daughter alone, feeling confused and rejected. Instead of being transparent about her convictions, she hid them, fearing her boyfriend's rejection. In the end she was still rejected, but instead of losing just a boyfriend, she lost a great deal more.

Find the Balance

So how do we find balance between becoming "all things to all men, that [we] might by all means save some" (1 Cor. 9:22), and remaining true to our convictions and God's purpose for our lives? Here are a few practical tips.

Do Your Homework Ahead of Time

The Bible has some very clear guidelines on where we can compromise in our relationships and where we must stand firm. We have to do our homework to know the difference.

We must stand firm in our quest for purity. First John 3:3 tells us to purify ourselves, just as our heavenly Father is pure. As His children, we should want to become like Him, but that will not happen until we take a good look at ourselves in light of His love letter to us and determine where we need to grow and strive for purity. Transparency helps in this process. When we strive for openness, God can use others' rejection to show us the areas of our lives that need work. This is why it is so important to surround ourselves with godly people. Our transparency will allow them to see and point out areas where we need to change, and we, in turn, can trust that their doing so is motivated out of genuine concern for our well-being.

Proverbs 6 is a good place to start in evaluating our relationships. It gives us a list of seven things we should always avoid when relating to others. No compromising here!

1. *A proud look.* When we look down on people because of flaws in their personalities, physical appearance, or even because of particular sins with which they have struggled, God gets upset. Why? He has forgiven and accepted us unconditionally, and He expects us, His children, to do the same for others, no matter how difficult.

2. *A lying tongue.* This, as we have said, includes lying to ourselves. We call this *rationalizing*. We can come up with any number of excuses to justify our negative thoughts and behaviors, but God says, "Don't do it." Be honest with yourself and others. Life is so much simpler that way.

3. *A hand that kills the innocent.* If you think you have managed to avoid this one, remember that Jesus said hating your neighbor in your heart is the same as murdering him.

4. *A heart that plots evil or revenge.* It is easy to feel angry when someone has rejected us. We want to get back at them, make them realize just how much they have hurt us, but as we learned in the section on injustice, this attitude will consume and overwhelm us because it does not satisfy. Better to do as Romans 12:20 tells us: "If your enemy is hungry, feed him: if he is thirsty, give him a drink; for in so doing you will heap coals of fire on his head." The confidence that comes from transparency will allow us to do this without regret.

5. *Feet that race to do wrong.* We need healthy boundaries in our lives, lines in our relationships that we refuse to cross. These standards

are meant to protect us from harm, not to spoil our fun. Sometimes what is wrong can often seem right at first. Instead of rushing in to a new scheme or venture, we need to demonstrate self-control and discernment. Even when the act itself is not bad, we need to stop and examine our motivations behind it so that we can be sure we are doing it for the right reasons.

6. *A false witness or gossip.* Gossip is often motivated out of a desire to see someone else rejected. If we talk poorly about someone else, we feed a false sense of superiority. This is an unhealthy way to feel better about yourself, and it usually backfires when people realize that you cannot be trusted to respect their transparency with you.

7. *A person who creates discord in a family.* The family is meant to be the primary source of love and acceptance for individuals. God has established it this way, and He becomes very angry when people try to destroy that basic foundation of security. A large majority of the patients we see have psychiatric illnesses that have stemmed at least in part from problems with their families of origin. Satan knows the very best place to stir up trouble in the present and for generations to come is in the family. We must be sure we are working hard to develop an atmosphere of harmony in our own families and keep from creating discord in others.

Interestingly, avoiding these actions will not only please God but will give you deeper, more intimate relationships with those around you.

So what about areas where we *can* compromise? Anything that fosters a spirit of love, joy, peace, patience, kindness, goodness, faithfulness, gentleness, and self-control is acceptable. The Bible says, "There is no law against these things!" (Gal. 5:23 NLT). There is never a time when these attitudes and actions are forbidden. They are always permissible when seeking acceptance in our relationships. Sometimes we refuse to practice the fruit of the Spirit because we fear that it will backfire on us. "I don't want to love my wife unconditionally because I'm afraid she might hurt me too deeply if I do." "If I practice being joyful during difficult seasons of life, I might lose the help and attention I normally get from those who pity me." "If I am too kind to my employees, they might take advantage of me." "Why make the effort to honor my word when my friends already accept that I'm forgetful?" Notice that all these excuses revolve around the fear of how others will respond to our love, joy, peace, patience, kindness, and goodness. But if we have found a healthy self-acceptance and true acceptance from God, others' responses to the fruit of the Spirit manifested in us will not matter.

The real problem is that sometimes we practice false or "rotten" fruit when our motivation is the approval or acceptance of others. We may practice rotten kindness with coworkers because we want them to take up the slack on a project we have failed to complete. We might practice rotten patience with a lazy husband who refuses to help at home, because we are afraid he might leave if we put our foot down. If we like to flaunt our piety or superiority, we might practice a rotten form of self-control, hoping that we can manipulate others by making them feel guilty for not measuring up to our standards.

On the flip side we might avoid the "ripe" fruit for the same reason. True kindness may require us to fire lazy employees so that they learn the consequences of poor work ethics. True gentleness may mean punishing our children severely in order to prevent them from worse pain in the future. The fruit of the Spirit will not always be pleasant, but it will always be good for you and good for your relationships.

God is clear that, even when we practice all of these principles, there will still be times when others reject us. Jesus warned his disciples, "If the world hates you, remember that it hated me first" (John 15:18 NLT). We have known people who honestly believed that, if they just lived out fully the love of Christ in their lives, people could not help but love them back. Not according to Jesus. After all, He was God incarnate, and God is love. But that did not stop the people who knew Him from abandoning Him when times got tough, even crucifying Him. If someone is rejecting you because of your love for Christ, the Bible goes so far as to say you should rejoice about it. The apostle Peter said, "Even if you should suffer for righteousness' sake, you are blessed!" (1 Peter 3:14).

Does this mean we should instigate suffering by stirring up trouble for ourselves? Not at all. But we should "be ready to give a defense to everyone who asks [us] for a reason for the hope that is in [us], *with meekness and fear*" (v. 15; emphasis added). If others reject you because of such convictions, take comfort in the fact that you are not really the one being rejected; Jesus is. So you are in good company.

Meet with Your "Professor" for Supervision Daily

Sometimes we do our homework by knowing God's Word, but we have questions about specific situations with difficult people. We need to ask God for the strength necessary to show love to the unlovable and the wisdom necessary to discern healthy compromise from unhealthy compromise. This requires two important kinds of conversation with God: routine prayer and crisis prayer.

Routine prayer occurs at a specific time and a specific place. One of my (Dr. Henderson's) closest friends and mentors is a professor at Columbia International University in Columbia, South Carolina. We used to meet regularly at a local café to catch up, share our struggles, and pray for one another. Both of us practiced transparency, and we always looked forward to these meetings as a time of refreshment, encouragement, and growth.

As valuable as these scheduled times for relationships are, our physical bodies and the time-constraining universe in which we live puts limitations on where and when we can meet. Not so with God. There is no excuse for not meeting with Him daily over a cup of coffee and allowing Him to fill us up with the power of His Spirit. These meeting times usually work best in the mornings—at the beginning of a new day—but anytime will work as long as you are consistent.

We can use these meetings to pray about specific people we might encounter, asking God to prepare our hearts and their hearts for the mutual interaction. These meetings will give us patience "with each other, making allowance for each other's faults because of your love" (Eph. 4:2 NLT).

The second kind of praying is the crisis prayer. One of my (Dr. Henderson's) wisest counselors has been my father. I keep his contact numbers in my cell phone on speed dial. When a crisis arises that requires some godly counsel, I can almost always get in touch with my dad, even if it is just to ask for prayer. My father knows this kind of call because it usually starts out with, "Hey Dad, it's me. Real quick . . ."

For me calling my father is an instinct—an automatic response to situations that feel out of control. Why? Because my father knows me better than anyone else, and I trust his counsel. Many of you reading this do not have an earthly father like that, but you have something infinitely better.

Is God, your heavenly Father, on your speed dial? Do you have His number memorized? How often do you remember to call out to Him in times of stress? For example, let us say that your boss calls you into his office unexpectedly. Your first thought may be to panic or become defensive. Instead, you can quickly whisper, "Lord, give me peace." He will!

How about this scenario: you run into an annoying coworker in the hallway, the one who likes to corner people with mindless conversation. Your initial emotion may be irritation or anger, but you call out to God instead and pray, "Please, Lord, help me to be patient."

What about when your husband leaves the cap off the toothpaste for the hundredth time, and you want to lash out at him for the oblivious slob that he is? "Please give me your kindness, Lord."

Everyone has immediate thoughts and emotions that pop into their heads, especially when encountering difficult people and situations. In psychiatry we call them "automatic thoughts and emotions." Sometimes these thoughts can be so automatic that we are not even conscious of them. We just react instinctively. It takes practice to prevent them from escalating into unwanted behaviors—behaviors that can have painful effects for everyone around. God can help us to overcome these "automatic thoughts" that have been ingrained in our minds as a result of past experiences, but we need to get in the habit of speed dialing Him in times of crisis.

Show Up for Test Day

Ultimately we will never learn to overcome the pain of rejection unless we are tested. This means we have to get out there and begin to do life with people. We can start anywhere: at home, our church, with old friends and new acquaintances. Wherever you begin, remember that we will all make mistakes. No one scores a perfect 100 percent on this exam, but that is not the goal of transparency. The goal is to show progress in our ability to be honest with God, with ourselves, and with those around us. People will get hurt along the way, but it is a pain with a purpose beyond it.

The Reward for Transparency

Do you remember Carlos from the opening chapter? Years after the embarrassment of soccer camp, he recalled the first time he saw Amelia, his future wife, in college. He was struck by her beauty. He felt nervous to approach her, but unlike his experience with Suzanne, he decided not to let his fear of rejection keep him from being transparent. He decided to take things slowly and see what would happen as they got to know each other. He knew where he was willing to compromise and where he would stand by his convictions, and he was secure in the fact that God loved him and wanted the best for his life, so he could afford to risk the pain of rejection for the potential reward God might have in store.

The more Carlos got to know Amelia that fall semester, the more attractive she became to him. She was honest, passionate about the Lord, an encourager, kind, outgoing in an unassuming way, and full of joy despite some very tough life experiences. Most importantly she was transparent.

After three years of dating, Carlos and Amelia were married. They have known each other for a long time now. Their faults, their hurts, their imperfections, and even their sins are perhaps just a little more apparent now than when they were in college. (Okay, a lot more apparent.) Transparency has not been easy, but the rewards have been far-reaching.

They continue to accept each other as they are, knowing that for both of them their chief desire is to become more like Christ. Carlos has often expressed how thankful he is for the pain of rejection from girls before college. Those experiences have made him so appreciative of the treasure he has in Amelia. The season of rejection can be painful, but if it brings us into a deeper, more meaningful relationship with God and with others, then the purpose is worth the pain.

Finding Purpose Beyond Your Rejections

As you reflect on how much we can grow through the pain of rejection, use these practical application points to find meaning and purpose beyond your own experiences with rejection.

1. *Mind your wells and walls.* Every relationship requires depth and transparency, but this is a continual process that calls for a great investment of time and energy. To avoid unnecessary rejection, do not dive into relationships too quickly. Pray about the people God brings into your life, and ask Him to lead you toward healthy relationships with others. Also ask yourself what walls you have erected to protect yourself from further pain (Prov. 12:26; 17:17).

2. *Consider the source.* Rejection can be the gauge that helps us determine where and how we find acceptance. We can be sure that the more sensitive we are to rejection in a particular area of our lives, the more value we have placed on that area to guarantee our self-acceptance. The same is true for people. The more we are hurt by the rejection of a particular person, the higher the level of importance we have placed on his or her opinions of us. Remember, we can never find acceptance from others if we haven't learned to accept ourselves, and we cannot do this until we have found acceptance from God first (1 Thess. 2:4).

3. *Look for the extraordinary in the ordinary.* Self-acceptance comes when we realize we do not have to be Superman to be loved. God uses the weak things of the world to shame the strong, and the foolish things of the world to shame the wise. This is true for the inner workings of our daily lives. You do

not need to be the most talented, beautiful, intelligent, or important person in the world's eyes in order for God to do great things with your life (1 Cor. 1:27–31).

4. *It is not always about you.* When you do face rejection in your life, take time to consider that it may not always be about you. We all have areas in our lives where we need to improve, and rejection can help us see those areas more clearly; but often the rejection we face from others has nothing to do with us, and everything to do with them. If we can remind ourselves of this fact and put it into practice in our relationships, we will be less likely to be hurt by their rejection. The next time you feel rejected by people, ask yourself how much of this is about you and how much of this is about them (John 15:18–19).

5. *Success is not perfection.* Let's face it: no one is perfect. Not even you or me! So give yourself a break and stop pretending to be. Allow yourself the freedom to make mistakes in your relationships. Seek forgiveness and strive for holiness, but do not let false guilt and fear of rejection beat you down. Ask yourself how you can allow yourself the same mercy and grace you are working to provide for others (Phil. 3:12).

Set aside some personal time to consider your own situation in the light of these truths. Then answer the following questions truthfully in order to establish the groundwork for overcoming the rejections in your life.

1. Are you a well digger or a wall builder? How are these wells or walls preventing you from developing new relationships in your life or maintaining established ones?

2. In what areas of your personality, physical appearance, or abilities are you most sensitive to the pain of rejection? What is the most important and lasting source for your acceptance?

3. Look around you. What ordinary things do you do on a daily basis that could be used to accomplish amazing things for God?

4. Think back to the last time you were rejected. What were the specifics of the experience, and why might the rejection have been more about them and less about you?

5. When was the last time you accepted someone despite his or her faults? When was the last time someone did that for you? What would life be like if you did the same for yourself?

Part 3

LONELINESS

"I will never leave you nor forsake you."
—HEBREWS 13:5

9

Beyond Loneliness

Lori Halowitz left everything she knew in Michigan—her family, all her friends, and the church where she grew up—when her dream job at a prestigious consulting firm transferred her to the West Coast. She knew it would take time to adjust to her new surroundings, but nothing could have prepared her for the overwhelming loneliness she was about to endure.

Except for a few weekly meetings at the corporate office, Lori was able to do much of her work from home. Though this seemed like a perk at first, she quickly began to feel isolated from the outside world. Her new boss was more demanding than she expected, and nonnegotiable deadlines kept her working late into the weeknights and even on weekends. The cost of living was much higher in California, and the troubled economy kept spending money tight. She was often exhausted from the pressures of her new job, and that made what little social life she did have even harder to manage. She longed to be back home, surrounded by people who knew and loved her.

Almost compulsively, she began checking her mailbox, her cell phone messages, her e-mail, and her Facebook account, hoping for some small affirmation that her friends back home were thinking about her. More often than not, she was disappointed. She tried taking the initiative to call them herself, but there was only so much catching up she could do before the awkward pauses in the conversation became unbearable. She knew there wasn't much they could do to soothe her loneliness, living so far away, but a growing fear began to take hold of her that "out of sight was truly out of mind." At times her fear turned to sheer panic as she imagined everyone around her moving in fast-forward while she remained stuck in the freeze-framed walls of her apartment.

Lori tried to meet people where she lived, but she discovered that breaking into well-established circles of friends was not easy. Her co-workers could not seem to talk about anything except company politics, and the several churches she had managed to visit seemed more interested in her wallet than her soul. The whole culture in California seemed so foreign compared with the slow, steady pace of her hometown, and she got the distinct feeling that she didn't belong. She was always taking the initiative to connect with others, and because she was not naturally outgoing, every attempt zapped her energy, especially if she felt rejected. This became her excuse to retreat further and further into isolation. Before she knew it, Lori was severely depressed.

When Lori tried to remember the last time she had felt so alone, a memory from her childhood came back to her as if it had happened yesterday. When she was four years old, her father had taken her with him to the grocery store to get some supplies. Because it was a really short list, he decided to leave Lori in the car while he ran in and out. She would never forget his words to her before he left: "Wait right here, honey, and don't open the door for anyone. I'll be right back!"

She did wait. She waited a long time, but he never showed up. He had had a massive stroke inside the store and was unable to tell anyone that his daughter was just outside waiting for him. It was not until the police called Lori's mother at home that they realized where she was. Even then they had to break into the car to get her. She was too scared to open the door herself. What always amazed Lori about that day was that for the hour or so she spent alone, sobbing in her daddy's car, people passed by every few minutes. Some even made eye contact with her, but for whatever reason, no one tried to help.

Lori was a grown woman now, but the pain of loneliness made her feel four years old once again. Here she was separated from everyone and everything familiar, staring out from her window on the world, where no one seemed to notice, and she was too scared to step outside herself.

Aching Loneliness

If rejection is the sharp stabbing pain of a heart attack, the pain of loneliness is the insidious gnawing of starvation. The two pains usually go together. We often experience loneliness as a result of others' rejection, but even more often we experience loneliness as a result of our efforts to avoid rejection altogether.

Sometimes loneliness develops not as a result of *rejection* but as a result of *loss*. When we lose the most significant relationship in our lives, the loneliness that results can be acute. Unfortunately, the potential for lost relationships is ever present. Whether through death, physical separation, or altered circumstances, relationships in this life come and go. The night season of loss is a natural part of these relationships, and so is the pain that results. But the potential for finding light beyond the darkness of such pain is also close at hand, if we only look around to befriend others who also may be lonely as we are.

Our question is this: how can we take the loneliness in our lives and use it to create meaningful relationships with those around us? Our goal is to answer this question in the following chapters, but first we must define some terms.

Defining Physical Loneliness

Before we can experience the great gains that can come by working through the pain of loneliness, we must first understand how to define it. There are two states of aloneness: the physical state of being alone (solitude) and the emotional state of being alone (loneliness). Solitude is not always painful. In fact, it may be quite pleasant for those who are confident and comfortable with themselves, and who understand that it need not be a permanent experience. More than just for pleasure, daily time alone is necessary to maintain a healthy lifestyle. Even Jesus, though He was God incarnate, needed times of solitude to rest and recuperate, in order to continue an effective earthly ministry. His solitude allowed Him time to meditate, focus on the tasks ahead, and seek help from His heavenly Father. Sometimes we think that because Jesus is God, He was invincible to fatigue and mental exhaustion while on earth. But the Bible is clear that Jesus needed rest just as everyone else does. A stable balance between solitude and time with others is necessary for mental and physical well-being.

Sadly, most people, depending on their personality types, go to one of two extremes. Introverts may feel they are immune to the pain of loneliness and do not require intimacy with others to be happy. (To determine if you are an introvert or extrovert, ask yourself this question: if you go to a party with lots of people you know and with whom you are very close, do you come home exhausted or energized? If you said exhausted, chances are that you are introverted at your core.) An introvert who enjoys quiet moments alone to reflect, daydream, unwind, and recuperate must guard against too much of a good thing. He may have to break out of his comfortable easy chair, put down the book with which he had engrossed himself, and call someone up just to chat. If he does not, he will wake up one day and realize that he has been starving himself of much-needed relationships.

Unlike introverts, extroverts may avoid solitude at all costs. Being with people is their way to unwind, express themselves, and find love and acceptance, but they also can experience too much of a good thing. By surrounding themselves with people, no matter how superficial the relationship, they, too, think they are immune to the pain of loneliness. But loneliness can haunt even the extrovert. It can attack at any stage of life, on any step of the social status ladder, and in any physical location. It is better for extroverts to become comfortable being alone on their own terms by making time for solitude than to have it forced upon them by the unavoidable circumstances of life.

Even when we are forced to be alone, knowing that someone is with us in spirit helps. How powerfully dispelled is loneliness by the knowledge that at the very moment of our solitude, special people are thinking and praying for us. A young child who is lost but knows his parent is searching for him is less afraid than a child who thinks he has been forgotten. The knowledge that others have remembered us, that we are occupying the thoughts of others even as we face the most desolate of circumstances, can bring comfort to our troubled souls. Conversely, a crowded mall or stadium packed with thousands of people may only make the pain of our loneliness worse if no one notices our presence or fails to care. This is the difference between solitude and loneliness.

While planned time for solitude (including self-reflection) is eye-opening and enlightening, loneliness can blind us. Loneliness deceives us into thinking we are the only ones, no one else understands, and no one can help us. By getting caught up in these negative emotions, we fail to notice that the person sitting next to us is suffering from the exact same pain, that the opportunity for healing both wounds can be found by removing the scales from our own eyes and focusing on the loneliness needs of others.

Unfortunately, the dark scales of emotional loneliness are extremely thick and difficult to remove. One need only look at the statistics for suicide to know this truth. The highest rate of suicide in the United States is not among teenagers, but widowed elderly white males. At first you might think this is counterintuitive. After all, men at this age are supposed to be the toughest of the bunch. They have weathered all sorts of pain in their lifetimes. Why would they bail out on life when they are so close to the finish line?

Men who have grown up without solid training in relational intimacy find themselves in the later stages of life suffering from suicidal depression and loneliness. Our culture has not helped this trend much. The underlying message in our society is that "real men" do not seek emotional intimacy. The tough guy is the one who goes it alone, not the one who reaches out for support and love. When we add in the basic personality and genetic factors that can make emotional intimacy harder for men than women, the toxic concoction for suicide becomes most potent.

There is hope. If we can open our eyes to the true circumstances behind the pain of loneliness—that it is more an emotional state of mind than a true physical reality—we can begin to understand the purpose beyond its pain.

Defining Emotional Loneliness

We have made a distinction between the physical state of being alone, called solitude, and loneliness, the emotional state of being alone. But before we move on, we still need to clarify exactly what it means to be alone emotionally.

To begin with, loneliness is not simply feeling unloved (although without any significant love relationships in your life, you will most certainly be lonely). Even in loving relationships, people can still experience loneliness. Take Jessica as an example.

As a single woman, Jessica suffered severely from the pain of loneliness, even though she had a large family of siblings and parents who loved her dearly. Being the youngest at family get-togethers, she watched her older, married siblings interacting with each other and their children in a way that made her feel left out. Though her parents, siblings, nieces, and nephews loved her completely, her inability to relate to their common experiences made her feel lonely, so much so that she often avoided such gatherings. Only after Jessica married did she begin to feel connected with her siblings again.

Another person, Marty, suffered from the syndrome that says, "I love you, but I really don't like you." Marty was a pessimist, a gloom-and-doom kind of guy. Though his family and friends were always willing to help him out of a bind and genuinely had his best interests at heart, because of his personality, no one ever wanted to be around him. Love was not the problem. It was the *liking* that got in the way. It turned out that Marty had a chemical imbalance. He suffered from a condition called *dysthymia*, a longstanding form of depression that never gets to the point of suicidality but is crippling nonetheless. Many medical illnesses, such as hypothyroidism and even medications like beta-blockers for blood pressure can cause such symptoms. It was not until Marty received treatment that his affect brightened and people began to enjoy his physical presence once again.

There are many reasons for the "I love you, but I don't really like you" syndrome. Perhaps we do not understand someone's personality, sense of humor, hobbies, or personal interests. Maybe we feel uncomfortable or helpless when faced with the reality of a particular pain or loss in that person's life. It is easy to feel awkward around the unfamiliar. In these instances we usually do not dislike the individual. We just dislike the misunderstanding, the discomfort, helplessness, and awkwardness we experience when we are around this person. Instead of giving in to the all-too-tempting urge to avoid these individuals, we should determine first if our own negative feelings are keeping us from relating. We are commanded to love, but following that commandment is a lot easier if we work at liking and relating, no matter how awkward it may feel at first.

On the other hand, the only true way to demonstrate love in some relationships is to subject the loved ones to the very pain they would most like to avoid. Forcing them into a state of loneliness can bring healing to a life destroyed by abusive behaviors. The parents who allow a drug-addicted son to live under their roof to help him save money think they are showing him unconditional love. In reality they are enabling his addiction. The woman who stays in a physically abusive relationship is not loving her husband; she is hating herself. Unconsciously she plays the part of the martyr, thinking she deserves such treatment or she will be able to take pride in having fixed what is broken. The best thing she could do for her man is to leave him lonely until the day he realizes his need to change. If that day never comes, at least she will have worked through her own pain of loneliness, the very pain that might have driven her into such an unloving, unhealthy relationship in the first place.

Loneliness is not simply the absence of love, nor is it simply the absence of communication, though this, too, can contribute to loneliness. Take Janice and Jim Fredricks as examples. For twenty years they raised a son with muscular dystrophy. Day in and day out, they communicated. They communicated about who would take Barry to his next doctor's appointment or who would make dinner for the family while the other paid the medical bills. They talked about Barry's progression over the dinner table and before they went to bed at night. In short, their whole system of communicating revolved around their son. When Barry passed away at age twenty-one, suddenly Janice and Jim realized that for more than two decades the only thing they had had in common was Barry. There communication was constant, but it did not foster closeness between them—only with their son. When they realized they had nothing left to talk about, they both suffered tremendously from feelings of isolation and loneliness. Why? They now lacked the one important ingredient essential to any relationship: relatedness!

Relating to Others

What is relatedness? *Relatedness* is the sum total of all spiritual, emotional, experiential, and physical connections that draw two individuals together for their common good. Realize that relatedness is not sameness. Opposite charges attract through magnetism. Puzzle pieces fit together not because they are the same shape, but because they are pieces to a bigger picture. The Bible uses the metaphor of iron sharpening iron: two rough edges rubbing together to create smooth, sharp surfaces that can become effective tools for the master builder to use (Prov. 27:17). The term *relate* is where we get the word *relationship*. It is impossible to have a relationship with someone if you cannot relate to him or her in some way.

It is only after we understand this definition that we can understand the true definition of *loneliness*: the perceived inability to relate to those around us. Discovering how to relate to others is the key to working through the dark pain of loneliness. It sounds obvious, but the more people to whom we can relate, the more numerous our relationships will be. Likewise, the depth and scope of our relating will determine the intimacy of our relationships.

There is a hierarchy to relatedness. Some forms of relationships are more important than others. Just because two people enjoy shopping at the same bookstore does not mean they enjoy reading the same books or drinking the same coffee. Statistics show that men and women who take time to determine the level of their spiritual and emotional relatedness prior to marriage are more likely to avoid divorce. Businessmen who establish a common vision and purpose for their companies before they join together in partnership usually avoid lawsuits and bankruptcy.

At times this hierarchy gets turned on its head. Instead of seeing the deeper relationship and connection we can have with those around us, we get caught up in petty differences, such as the color of our skin, the place of our birth, even our loyalties to different sports teams. Our superficial preferences keep us from going deeper with those who otherwise might sharpen us as iron sharpens iron. If we choose to associate only with those who fit within our preconceived notions of commonality, we will miss out on some incredible opportunities for relatedness. If we head into any situation assuming that we cannot relate, chances are we will not. The severest form of discrimination comes whenever we use the expression "I am the only one who . . ." (you fill in the blank). Whenever any aspect of our lives is preceded by those words, we essentially exclude everyone else from relating to us in that particular way. Unfortunately, the more time we spend reflecting on how different we are from others, the more likely we are to be lonely. If, instead of eliminating and discriminating, we were to invest in maximizing and capitalizing on our relatedness to others, loneliness might soon cease to be a pain worth mentioning.

Finding true relatedness with those around us can be complex, because intimacy in relationships requires honest communication of thoughts and emotions with love and acceptance of each other as we really are, not as we pretend to be. In the next chapter, we will review the obstacles that keep us from this kind of relating.

10

Obstacles to Relating

I just can't relate!""You just don't get it, do you?" "You will never under-stand." Have you ever caught yourself making any such statements? The obstacles to relatedness are numerous. If we are not careful, we can allow these obstacles to separate us from relationships that are meant to steer us through the pain of loneliness. In this chapter, we will describe a few of the subtler obstacles that can often take us by surprise.

Modern Comforts

There is nothing wrong with enjoying comfort. Modern technology pro-vides us things of which other generations could only dream. Can you imagine getting a root canal without Novocain or watching one of your children die of an infection because you did not have antibiotics? The epidural has done wonders for easing the pain of childbirth, as have laparo-scopic surgeries for shortening the time of recovery after an operation. Airplanes have allowed us to travel around the world, not in eighty days, but in twenty-four hours or less.

Advances in communication have paralleled, if not surpassed, those in other fields of science. The Internet allows us to exchange information, pic-tures, videos, and ideas with people around the globe in a matter of seconds. Cell phones give us instant access to friends, family, and business associates. Caller ID allows us to prioritize calls based on importance and urgency. We communicate with each other on social Web sites like MySpace, Facebook, Twitter, and others. In this way we have been able to maximize our time and energy to pursue the kinds of relationships we deem important and necessary for healthy living. In this sense modern comforts are blessings for which we should thank God.

In the midst of our comfort, however, we must be careful not to forget one very important fact: relationships are not always comfortable. In fact, a relationship that becomes too comfortable can be at risk for falling apart. Healthy relating requires a constant investment of time and hard work. It requires self-sacrifice, even a healthy dose of pain now and then. If we seek out relationships only when they are convenient and easy, our tolerance for pain will drop well below what is necessary for healthy relating. If a bodybuilder lifts only the amount of weight that feels comfortable for him, his muscles will not grow. In fact, they might actually shrink. Bedridden invalids will notice their muscles begin to atrophy. Our minds are also organs that need constant stimulation. Men and women with higher levels of education, who continue to work even after retirement, are less susceptible to the effects of Alzheimer's disease. "Use it or lose it." The same is true in our relationships. We must work hard to maintain them, or eventually they will die out.

Modern advances in communication have the potential to create two problems. The first develops when we let our modern comforts interfere with the depth of our relating. If we allow it, technology can become a barrier, not a pathway, to deeper, more intimate relating.

Take Randy Phillips as an example. Randy came into my (Dr. Henderson's) office extremely depressed and lonely, but he could not understand why. "After all," he told me, "I've got lots of friends."

"Really? Who are your closest friends?" I asked.

He proceeded to name off several individuals with whom he communicated on a regular basis. It did seem strange that someone with so many friends could be so lonely.

"How did you meet them?" I probed further.

"I met them online," he said matter-of-factly.

"Oh, that's a great way to meet people," I assured him. "Did it just so happen they lived near you?"

"What do you mean?" he asked, looking confused.

"You know, that you were able to get together with your friends for dinner, movies, coffee, parties, and such."

"Oh, well . . ." he shifted in his chair. "I've never actually met them in person. We just chat online. Play video games and stuff."

It turned out that all of Randy's "relationships" were over the Internet. He stayed in his apartment, communicating in a way that was most comfortable to him, but his relationships were limited to his computer screen.

"It's much easier this way," he explained. "I like to be able to really think about what I want to say. Sometimes I will write a sentence and edit it several times before I send it. That way I'm sure I've communicated my thoughts clearly and effectively. In face-to-face relationships I usually end up saying things that are stupid or offensive. This way I don't have to worry about it."

The Internet allowed Randy a virtual perfection he could not know in real life. But by remaining in his comfort zone, he had starved himself of well balanced relationships much like an anorexic woman who deprived herself of most of the major food groups. This is not healthy, no matter how comfortable it feels. Healthy relating pushes through the pain of inevitable mix-ups and misunderstandings, hurt feelings and disagreements. Like a bodybuilder lifting more and more weight, we must push through the pain of relating in order to find a deeper, truer intimacy with those around us. This cannot be done if we choose to remain comfortable.

Limited Scope

Not only can we let modern comforts interfere with the depth of our relating, but we can also allow them to limit the scope or breadth of our relating with groups of people. In theory modern communication has made relating to larger groups of people easier, but it has also made avoiding larger groups of people easier as well.

In the old days, if your annoying neighbors showed up at your house to borrow a rake or some sugar, your only options to avoid them were to slam the door in their faces or pretend you were not home. Yet in today's culture we have established effective barriers that can shield us from such unwanted interruptions. We have become more sophisticated in our ability to make communicating with those less desirable as impersonal as possible.

Those we would rather not see in person, we can call on our cell phones. For those we would rather not speak to at all, we can send text messages or e-mail. We can just stick those who are not worthy of the time it takes to send an individual text or e-mail, on a bulk e-mail list. If this is still too time consuming, we can just send them an open invitation to visit our blog and read about our lives as they would a biography from Barnes and Noble. Please understand that these are all great ways to keep people up to date with us and save time in the process. However, the more impersonal our communication becomes, the less we are practicing true relatedness. We may be able to *keep in touch* with more people, but unless we are also *keeping in depth*, we may actually be limiting the number of intimate relationships in our lives, not expanding them.

Because technology affords us opportunities to pick and choose the individuals with whom we interact, we must be aware of the potential dangers. What will be the cost of our comfort? You may ask, "If the modern conveniences of life allow me to stay connected with my best friend, who meets and fulfills all of my relationship needs, what is the point of trying to work on less intimate friendships? If technology allows me to stay connected with the people I know, why should I make an effort to reach out to strangers?"

The answer is twofold: First, putting all our eggs in one basket is dangerous. Not only does this put a tremendous amount of pressure on the individual we hope will meet all our intimacy needs, but it will also leave us very lonely when that individual can no longer perform in that capacity. Second, many people who might otherwise have benefited from our investment in their lives will also have one fewer friend on whom they can rely. We all need an intimate support *group*, not an intimate support *person*.

We should consider this daily as we make use of the comforts of modern technology. For example, I (Dr. Henderson) stood in line at a grocery store and watched a woman placing her items on the conveyer belt for the cashier to scan. At first I thought she knew the cashier personally, because she was staring right at him and carrying on a full-length conversation totally unrelated to groceries. It was not until she turned around and I saw the Bluetooth headset in her ear that I realized she was talking on her cell phone. Physically she was present, but mentally she was far away, talking to one of her close friends. It was as if the cashier behind the counter did not even exist. She was simply staring right through him.

That scene struck me, and I began to take more notice of people interacting around me. On a recent plane ride to Dallas, the gentleman beside me listened to his iPod and scrolled through the latest stock prices on the Chinese market. The only time he looked up was to let me pass as I took my seat next to the window. Physically we were so close our arms were touching. Mentally he was in another country thousands of miles away.

I wondered how often I had been guilty of the same mental and emotional detachment. How many opportunities had I missed to relate to those around me because I had chosen to limit the scope of my relationships to a self-centered virtual reality?

Technology itself is neither good nor bad. However, anything that allows us the opportunity to feed our self-centered and self-focused tendencies can become an obstacle to finding relatedness. By retreating further and further into our own comfort zones, we may not only miss the opportunity to heal someone else's loneliness, but we may find we are that much closer to experiencing it ourselves. The deepest pit of loneliness is dug by those who shut out the largest number of people around them. Don't let the convenience of modern comforts do this to you. Make the effort to be conscious of your surroundings. Take time to look for the opportunities to connect with those around you. It might just be the key to solving your own struggles with loneliness.

Objectification

Objectification is a self-centered form of relating that views other people as static, unchanging objects necessary only to fulfill our personal needs and wants.

Unfortunately, our society's measure of success propagates objectification. Success to the world is determined by what we accomplish for ourselves, not for other people. We see others simply as a means to help us achieve our own ends.

The truth is we shift roles and positions in life frequently. Relationships are fluid, and we must treat them as such. The parents who continue to view their grown sons or daughters as children will miss out on the opportunity to relate to them as adults or friends. The boss whose employee has been promoted above him will not keep his job if he cannot conform to the change in their relationship. Loneliness develops when we try to fit others into one particular mold and then realize it is impossible.

People who seek to change for the better encounter this rigidity in others all the time. Whenever they begin to make strides toward their goals, friction develops in their relationships. In our psychiatric practices we try to warn people about that. If one person bends, the people closest to them must bend also; otherwise the relationship breaks. This is particularly true in families. Many individuals work hard to become mature adults only to find they revert to previous childhood roles whenever they get together with their families. The unhealthy roles are so well established that change comes slowly. But these changes are necessary for continued relating.

In some ways married couples must remarry each other psychologically every decade or so. This is because neither of you is the same today as you were ten years ago. People do change, hopefully for the better. Ten years from now the new them will need to recommit to the new version of their mate. Relationships take work and adjustments, even over long periods of time.

Striving to see people as individuals and not as objects does not come naturally. Objectification is an obstacle we must scale to find true relatedness with the greatest number of people.

Pride

Remember that in chapter 9 we defined loneliness as our perceived inability to relate to those around us. In an extreme sense our perception is reality. We cannot relate to anyone completely. If we could, we would cease to be individuals. In order for me to understand you completely, I must *become* you, but that is obviously impossible. Because we are individuals, we never experience life in completely the same way. As a group of fathers watch their children walk across the graduation stage, they will experience different emotions, depending on their relationships with their children, and they will express these emotions uniquely based on their different personalities. The graduates themselves, though obtaining the same degree, may place different meaning upon their achievements, depending on their personal life experiences.

The same is true for suffering. No other human will ever be able to relate completely to your pain, because it is unique to your personality and circumstances.

Many people in therapy put up resistance to the therapist's attempts at providing counsel for this very reason. They exclaim, "How could you possibly understand what I am going through? You've never experienced what I have!" Many times they are right. But even if the therapist had experienced the same thing, he or she still could not completely relate because the therapist is not *them*!

We may not be able to completely understand what it is like for our friend to lose a spouse to death, let alone what it is like to lose his or her particular spouse at that particular time in his or her life. In that sense we cannot relate. But should that completely negate our ability to find relatedness? Ask us if we have ever experienced the specific pain of divorce, and we may say no, but ask us if we have ever experienced the more general pain of abandonment, and most of us who have lived long enough can say yes. We all may not have experienced the pain of losing a job, but most of us have experienced the pain of loss.

With this in mind, our loneliness usually develops not because we cannot relate to others but because we will not relate to others. For some people being alone in their suffering is important to their pride. Why? Because they think admitting that their suffering is common to humanity trivializes their present pain. In a way we can understand their dilemma. What kid, suffering from a scraped knee, wants his father to say, "Deal with it, Son . . . Life will only get worse from here on"? What woman in the throes of labor wants a nurse, who is patronizing and flippant, to say, "Oh, honey, it's not that bad. Why, I pushed out five thirteen-pound boys, and I never complained like you are now!" These statements, no matter what the intention, are not comforting. In fact, the intention usually is to build up the pride of the person speaking. We want people who can relate to our pain, not play one-upmanship with us.

In reality the commonality of human suffering does not trivialize our own individual pain. It instead signifies the incredible opportunity for us to relate to one another as humans and as spiritual beings. In 2 Corinthians the apostle Paul said that God "comforts us in all our troubles, so that we may be able to comfort those in any trouble" (1:4 NIV) When we get too caught up in our individual pain, we miss out on this opportunity in a big way.

I (Dr. Henderson) recently submitted some research findings to a national psychiatric organization for presentation at their annual conference. I was overjoyed when I received a letter from the president of the organization, asking me to consider submitting a written form of my work for publication.

My joy dampened somewhat when I realized one of my colleagues had received a similar letter. My excitement continued to dissipate as I found out that everyone who submitted research findings to the conference received the exact same letter. It was nothing more than a formality. There was nothing unique or worthy about my research that warranted special attention or favor. In my disappointment I failed to see the opportunity that such a letter opened up for me. I had been invited (no matter how many others had also been invited) to share my research with my colleagues for the mutual advancement of our education.

The same is true in our suffering. Somehow we think that the more remarkable our pain, the more right we have to complain, to demand sympathy from those around us, or to be proud of our endurance through it all. Unfortunately, our pride and/or our self-pity get in the way of relating and sharing in each other's suffering. This sharing and relating are what ultimately bring healing, but if, in our pride, we choose to be alone, that is exactly how we will remain.

Segregation

Segregation goes much deeper than the color of our skin. We segregate based on denomination, age, gender, styles of music, dress, stages of life, education, jobs, family backgrounds and upbringing, financial standings, and many other things. Segregation is sometimes necessary and helpful. When we segregate children based on their academic performance, it allows us to cater more easily to their educational needs. Segregation becomes a problem when we choose to avoid opportunities to relate with those who stand outside of our preconstructed circles.

Many churches are guilty of fostering segregation. We have done so much to organize our congregations into neat, well-defined groups that we have created barriers against our ability to relate to a diversity of experiences, ages, and cultures. Contemporary versus traditional services makes the first division. Then we create Sunday school classes that are so specific you have to fill out a detailed application before gaining admittance. If you are single, under twenty, in college, and dating, you get sent to the "Under Twenty Singles Class #2," which just happens to be studying the manual on "biblical dating." If you are a married female with one child who is not potty trained, they send you to the "New Moms Class #3," which is conveniently studying the manual on "potty-training your toddler with patience." There is a place for these specific classes, but there needs to be a balance. Singles can witness commitment from couples who have been married many years, and new parents can benefit from the experiences of those who have successfully survived the child-rearing stage. We need interactions with people outside of our own peer groups.

Social segregation does two things: it limits the diversity of our relationships, and it excludes those who do not "fit in" anywhere. For example, the elderly have lost their connection and relevance to the younger generations because we have separated them. Older couples with adult children have lost their connection with young families because they only associate with other empty nesters. We have tightened our circles of relatedness so much that there is little room to grow. It is no wonder that unity among all Christians (not just denominations) seems to be wishful thinking.

Time

Time is necessary for intimacy. Unfortunately, even with all our advances in technology, time does not move any slower. It can be a sacrifice to schedule in time to have relationships, especially when society pressures us to accomplish other, "more important" things. The less time we spend on our relationships, the more superficial they become. Superficiality is safe. If we stay superficial, we never have to worry about getting hurt too badly in our relationships. *A flesh wound is better than a shot through the heart,* so we think. Staying busy allows us an excuse from going deeper with others, but in the end, we still suffer.

If all you have time for in a relationship is the occasional "Hi, how are you?" you will never really get to know someone. Likewise, the longer you go between times of connecting with others, the longer it takes to get past those superficial conversations that occupy so much of our time. It is like cleaning your desk. The longer you wait, the more papers accumulate. Before you can work on the desk itself, you have to wade through the growing stack.

Just think how much better off the church would be if we made more time for relating. It is so amusing, yet sad, to visit churches that designate thirty seconds during the service to "greet one another." Those thirty seconds allow us just enough time to state our names to the people next to us and then promptly forget theirs before the music starts up again. What if we sang one less song, the pastor preached ten minutes less, and we took that extra time to ask our neighbor, "How can I pray for you right now?" And then we actually did it. Maybe if we cut out all the fluff and spent our time ministering to each other as the body is called to do, we might find the kind of spiritual growth no church building could contain.

This, we believe, is one reason people have become disillusioned with organized religion. We have gotten so organized that the relational aspects of church have been pushed aside. James 5:16 tells us to speak the truth *to each other*, exhort *one another*, rebuke *one another*, help *one another* with overburdens, and confess *to each other* in order to experience healing. Notice the verse does not say that it is the sole responsibility of the pastor to speak the truth, exhort, rebuke, help, and take confession. We are to do it to and for each other. If we do not make time as individuals and as a church body for this kind of relating, we may grow in numbers, but we will never grow closer to one another.

A Change in Mind-Set

We have discussed just a few of the obstacles that prevent us from relating, but keep in mind that none of them is necessarily bad in and of themselves. They only become so when we use them to avoid relating. Ultimately the biggest obstacles are ourselves: our comfort, our success, our pride, our preferences, and our time. The key word is *our*. To conquer the pain of loneliness, we must seek relatedness, but this requires us to change our mind-set and focus on what is best for the relationship and not the individual. This can be painful because it requires self-sacrifice, and by nature we are selfish beings. But if you can push through the pain, the light of healthy relatedness to others will far outshine the darkness of loneliness in our lives. Count on it!

11

Never Really Alone

N o matter what obstacles we may face in our quest for relatedness, no matter how many people reject us or turn their backs on our pleas for a relationship with them, no matter how acute the pain of our loneliness becomes, there will always be at least one person who can relate to us—the One who created us—God Himself.

In order to fully accept this fact and begin a relationship with God, we must accept one of two premises: either we believe that becoming gods ourselves is possible (many people do), or we believe the reverse—that God must have become human like us. If this second premise were true, He would need to experience life just as His creation does: face the same challenges, pains, and hardships. If God could accomplish this, then any of us, His created beings, could have the awesome opportunity to form a lasting relationship with Him.

What Did Jesus Suffer?

God did become human in the person of Jesus Christ, but what was Jesus like? And did He experience enough during His time here for Him to identify with my problems today, two thousand years later?

Isaiah 53:3 says that Jesus was a "man of sorrows." The literal translation of *sorrows* is "pains." He knew all human pain intimately. He knew hunger from a fast that lasted forty days and forty nights. His feet got sore and calloused from long walks over the rugged Judean countryside. His arms probably grew tired from working hours on end as a carpenter. As a human He aged just as we do. His nerve cells sent the same pain signals to His brain as ours do when we cut or burn ourselves. His death on the cross was just as physically agonizing to Him as it was to all the others who died that way. He can relate to our physical pain!

And yet Jesus experienced much more than physical pain. Isaiah tells us that He was acquainted with the "deepest grief" (v. 3 NIV). Jesus wept bitterly at the loss of His friend Lazarus. He felt intense anger with the Pharisees, who were always trying to thwart Him. After long days of preaching, He experienced physical and mental exhaustion and needed to get alone by Himself to recuperate. He even needed sleep, an essential requirement for mental and emotional well-being.

On top of all of this, Jesus dealt with the ever-present and plaguing knowledge that His ultimate destiny was to suffer death by crucifixion. As that time drew closer, His anxiety became progressively worse until it reached a peak in the Garden of Gethsemane. He pleaded with His Father to save Him from the pain: "Let this cup pass from Me!" (Matt. 26:39). He knew it was not possible, but in the asking He demonstrated to us the depths of His inner turmoil.

Jesus was even tempted by sin, just as we are today (Heb. 4:15). This has allowed Him to relate to *our* struggles against sin. He is our "great High Priest," whose understanding enables us to come "boldly" before Him where "we will receive his mercy, and we will find grace to help us when we need it most" (vv. 14, 16 NLT).

Did Christ become lonely? Of course He did. Loneliness afflicted Him because He knew that even though He could relate to our humanity, we could not relate to His deity, nor could we understand the sacrifice He had made in leaving His heavenly kingdom to live as a man for thirty-three years.

On top of all this, most of His followers were not interested in a relationship with Him. They were preoccupied with what Jesus could do for them, rather than what He could be for them. Can you imagine how lonely this must have made Him feel?

As soon as Jesus stopped meeting the crowd's material needs and started focusing on their more important spiritual needs, they left Him and moved on in search of the next big miracle man. Talk about painful! The twelve disciples who remained were faithful to a point, but even they abandoned Jesus when He needed them most.

As the religious and Roman authorities dragged Jesus to the cross, the most excruciating pain of loneliness came when Jesus cried out, "My God, My God, why have You forsaken me?" (Mark 15:34). In those few moments on the cross, Jesus suffered an eternal weight of loneliness apart from God that we will never know.

Because of Jesus' sacrifice, we can now have a relationship that dispels all loneliness. He has become the "friend who sticks closer than a brother" (Prov. 18:24). He knows us, not just intellectually but experientially, and we can know Him the same way. We can trust Him because He has suffered everything we have and more, and he has lived to tell us about it. He wants to walk beside us in life, guiding us through our own pains with His gentle arms around us. To think that all of this pain was not for His gain, but for our own, we need never be lonely again.

How do we respond to such a desire on God's part for a relationship with us? Do we shrug our shoulders and ignore Him, or do we seek out a relationship with Him wholeheartedly? Remember: a relationship with God requires just as much work, if not more work, than any human relationship. Unlike others with whom we are in relationships, God does not force Himself upon us. He waits patiently for us to seek Him. When we do, the gains will far surpass any other. His is the only relationship that can completely satisfy our loneliness. Before we can find fulfillment in relating to people, we must experience relatedness to God.

Think about your relationships with people. Where does God fit in? Imagine your relationships as concentric circles, like ripples spreading out from a stone thrown into a lake. The outer circles represent strangers and acquaintances. The nearer to the center you move, the more intimate the relationships become. These more intimate relationships will be different for each person, but for all of us, in the very center should be our relationship with God. What happens if we try to fill that void with someone else? The emptiness becomes like a drain that sucks away all our other relationships, leaving even more emptiness and pain.

You will never find complete relatedness in anyone else but God. He is the only one who can relate to us completely and who can heal us of the pain of loneliness. The indwelling of Christ into our humanity is what completes us, making us whole. Ironically, this is the starting point for developing healthy relatedness to others.

C. S. Lewis used the term *over-longing* to illustrate the destructive kind of relating called "enmeshment." Like a starved beggar, who inhales a filet mignon without relishing the taste, our over-longing for relationships often prevents us from finding true joy in them.

Take Jesse Mansfield as an example. Jesse came from an unloving, dysfunctional family. He had no friends and no relationship with God, and he was starving for relatedness. As a result he rushed into a marriage with Cameron Anderson, whose own dysfunctional relating rivaled Jesse's. They thought they could heal one another's pains, but instead, they tore each other apart mentally and emotionally. Their hunger went unsatisfied until one day Jesse attended a Celebrate Recovery meeting. Slowly he began to replace his over-longing for Cameron with a true relationship with God. As he did, he developed a deeper, more lasting love for Cameron, which he gave to her freely without expecting anything in return. She could see the change in Jesse's life—how satisfied he had become through Christ—and soon she wanted to know where she could get some of the same. The love of Christ filled them up so completely that they were finally able to savor the love they shared with each other and with their families.

The solution to the painful starvation of loneliness is to take our over-longing to Christ and let Him fill us up. When we satisfy our own gnawing loneliness in a relationship with Him, we become free to relate to others in a way that brings pleasure and power to everyone involved. That is the kind of relating we can get excited about. He enables us to love and be loved much better than we possibly can without Him.

Relating to God

When we realize all that God did to relate to us, a longing should well up inside of us to relate to Him. Instead of our pain creating a sense of loneliness, it will create an instant connection with the One who suffered for us. We have an exciting opportunity to identify with His pain and through that identification experience tremendous joy.

The apostle Paul desperately wanted to experience this kind of relationship with Christ: not just the power of Christ's resurrection, but "the fellowship of His sufferings" as he put it (Phil. 3:10). To gain this experiential knowing, Paul considered everything else in life as worthless.

There is a camaraderie that comes from our common experiences. Before my (Dr. Henderson's) wife, Angela, had our first child, she had always enjoyed people. She led Bible studies through programs such as First Place and Fellowship of Christian Athletes. She worked as a personal trainer at the local gym and enjoyed active involvement in church. One of her biggest fears as a new mother was that she would lose her connection with the outside world—that her scope of relating to people would be significantly limited.

Nothing could have been further from the truth. The first day she took our infant son out for a walk, she realized she had an instant connection with women who otherwise would have remained strangers—women of all ages, backgrounds, and cultures.

When considering the connection people develop through mutual experience, many men's minds turn quickly to the camaraderie of battle. Some of our favorite stories in the Bible are of David's mighty men of valor. They were the faithful ones who stuck by David not just when he was king, but when he was nothing more than a fugitive running from Saul. Their mutual experience of pain formed a lasting bond that united them through thick and thin. That is what we can have with Jesus whenever we suffer from the unavoidable pains in our lives.

What we must do when that unavoidable pain arrives is embrace it with a proper perspective, knowing that we are experiencing just a small glimpse of what Christ experienced for us. We are drawn closer to Him, and whatever other pain we suffer, we do not have to be alone.

12

Know Yourself

According to Pausanias, a famous Greek traveler and geographer of the second century AD, the expression "know thyself" was inscribed in the courtyard of the temple of Apollo in Delphi. The Greeks felt that knowing oneself was paramount for establishing healthy relationships with others. We would add that people can never fully "know themselves" until they "know God"—for He is our Creator and, as we learned in the previous chapter, can relate to us more than any person on earth. As we begin to know God, we discover His plan and purpose for our earthly relationships and His expectations concerning our treatment of others. In short, we begin to see others through the eyes of Christ. The next step is to know yourself.

God-knowledge and self-knowledge, obtained through both intellectual and experiential learning, become the foundation for healthy knowing and relating to others. After all, Jesus is the one who told us that if we obey the two greatest commandments—"Love the Lord your God with all your heart, with all your soul, with all your mind, and with all your strength" and "Love your neighbor as yourself" (Mark 12:30–31)—we will obey all of His other commandments. As psychiatrists we believe you can love others on a deep inner level only as much as you learn to love yourself in a healthy, humble way. In this chapter we will explain why self-knowledge is so important for relating and give you some practical tips to help you "know yourself."

Taking Inventory

Think of establishing relationships like constructing a building. Once we have established God as our foundation for relating, self-knowledge becomes the bricks and mortar we use to build strong relationships with people. If our self-knowledge is weak or broken (our actions and attitudes are driven by unconscious motivations), our relationships will be weak and broken as well. When the proverbial rains come tumbling down, as they certainly will, since all relationships have conflict, the relationship may itself survive, but the storm damage will require a lot more time and effort to repair. This is why it is so important for each of us to understand what we bring to the table (good and bad) in every relationship we have. Do we have enough to build a sturdy relationship? What areas of the building might need strengthening? Where might we need to draw on the other person's resources, and where will we have to invest more of ourselves? Doing this will keep us from being overwhelmed by the floods of emotions (good and bad) that well up inside us when we interact with people.

In marriage therapy we often use the term *baggage* to represent the spiritual, emotional, and physical flaws brought into the relationship, but this term need not have such a negative connotation. Picture a newly married couple moving into their first home. Each has acquired furniture and other personal belongings they will take with them into the new house. Prior to moving in, they take stock of what they own and what they need to purchase to make their home comfortable and inviting for each other and their guests. They also get rid of those personal items that do not fit with the décor of their new home. If couples were as concerned about taking an inventory of their respective personality traits, emotional states, and spiritual maturity as they are about material items in their homes, marriages might last longer than they do today. If we all were to do this, every relationship we have would be lasting.

One of my (Dr. Henderson's) professors in medical school, a rheumatologist with a thorough understanding of internal medicine, used to tell us, "What the mind knows, the eyes see!" In other words, the more diagnoses and presenting symptoms you have studied ahead of time, the likelier you are to notice them while examining your patients, and the more effective you will be at treating them. This is true not just for the physical body, but in our relationships as well. Knowing ahead of time the potential obstacles and problems that can arise in our relationships because of who we are as individuals will prepare us for and even allow us to preempt potential conflicts.

But there is another benefit. Developing a strong foundation of self-knowledge allows us to focus more on others, their needs, their insecurities, their desires and loves. We become less defensive and more proactive in loving and ministering to people. We can know them more fully because we have already taken the time to know ourselves.

Most people, however, do not spend enough time pursuing self-knowledge. We seem to care little about *knowing*: knowing God, knowing ourselves, and knowing others. Instead, we want to be *known*! We want to be seen and heard. We want our pictures in a hall of fame. We yearn for, even expect, the world to notice us, experience us, understand us, and accept us as we are, even though we rarely take the time to notice, experience, understand, and accept ourselves. The result is the knowledge that might have been a tool in our relationships now becomes a concealed weapon that sabotages every interaction we have with people.

For example, a young woman walked down a busy city sidewalk, wearing a tight, hot-pink T-shirt with the words *Notice Me* emblazoned across the front. She got noticed all right, but did she know the kind of attention she was attracting? More important, had she considered the reasons she wanted that kind of attention in the first place? Probably not. As it stood, her motivations laid the groundwork for attracting unhealthy relationships with men based purely on sex.

Projection is another example of what poor self-knowledge can do to our relationships. It is the unconscious act by which our own traits, beliefs, and emotions are attributed to someone else. For example, have you ever been around people who, no matter how nice you are to them, always interpret your actions as mean, condescending, or manipulative? You smile at them to be nice, and they shout, "Are you laughing at me?" You feel as if you are walking on eggshells around them, because one wrong glance or comment will set them off. Don't worry; it's not you. These individuals are practicing projection. They cannot stand themselves but refuse to admit it. It feels better to accuse others of inflicting on them the painful emotions they cannot handle in themselves. Because of it, they push others away until they are completely alone. Their poor self-knowledge has crippled their ability to relate.

The Importance of Self-Knowledge in Selfless Relating

Another problem with having poor self-knowledge is that it propagates self-centeredness in our relating. Without self-knowledge we look to others for validation. We seek out relationships that make us feel special or significant. As children this was very important for our development. Parents represented the sole authority in determining our identities at this young age. If they were godly parents, we obtained a godly understanding of ourselves through their training and care. If not, our views of the self become distorted. Many individuals require therapy because they believed lies from an early age: "You're unlovable. You're not worth my time. You're bad, a mistake, a disgrace." Or maybe they were told the opposite: "You're God's gift to the world. You deserve everything handed to you on a silver platter. You can do no wrong." Both types of messages are wrong, but simply stating this to these people does little to fix the problem. They run from relationship to relationship, trying to get back what they lost in childhood. It takes a great deal of work on their part to change such faulty self-knowledge, but it can be done. These adult children need someone to come alongside them, start from scratch, and train them to develop the healthy self-identity their parents never provided. Depending on the severity of the situation, they may need professional counseling to regain a healthy sense of self. Until this happens, their relating will be very self-centered, because they need more than they can give.

As we grow into our teenage years, we who have had healthy childhoods begin to build on our identities by seeking relationships outside of our parents. We want to see if others' opinions of us are the same as or different from our parents'. It is at the beginning of this stage of independence that we turn to our peers for help. We may not be as selfish or needy in our relationships as we once were, but we still need validation as we seek to "know ourselves."

Ask any teenager why he hangs out with a certain group of friends, and the usual response will be, "Because my friends understand me." In reality, however, this teenager does not want his friends' understanding as much as he wants their acceptance as he seeks to understand himself. His friends are the ones who will support and encourage him through the process. Unfortunately, many teenagers give too much weight to the opinions of others in their quest to answer the question, "Who am I?" They stumble through their junior high and high school years defining themselves solely based on the perceptions of others.

Amanda imagines, *If Rebecca comments on how amazing I look in my new outfit, I will consider myself a beautiful person. But if I am made fun of because of the blemish on my nose, I must find a friend who will reassure me of my beauty. Otherwise, I will think I'm the ugliest girl who ever lived.*

Robert thinks, *If the coach praises me on Monday but lays into me on Thursday, my self-worth will be restored only if I can regain his praise again on Friday.*

In short the teenagers think (albeit subconsciously), *I am what my friends believe me to be.* They substitute the opinions of their parents with the opinions of their peers. If, in the process, they fail to develop their own self-knowledge, their emotions as adults will be ruled by the emotional states of the people around them. They become extremely dependent and needy in their personalities. They struggle to form their own opinions and are easily swayed by the influences of others.

The ultimate goal as we mature is to become self-defined adults (self-defined meaning our knowledge of self, which is grounded in a deep relationship with God, is consistent and stable despite the fluctuating moods and opinions of others). We no longer rely on human relationships to define us or validate us. They become the natural result of who we are already! Now we have enough confidence in our position before God and the knowledge of ourselves to be completely selfless in our relating. We can fully obey Philippians 2:3–4: "Don't be selfish; don't try to impress others. Be humble, thinking of others as better than yourselves. Don't look out only for your own interests, but take an interest in others, too."

That's the goal, but let us be frank: none of us is there yet. Ask the modern love-struck Hollywood couple to describe what attracted them to each other, and you will be surprised at the unoriginality of their responses. After you hear about how smart, funny, and good-looking their mate is, you will most certainly hear them say, "He/she always seems to *know* exactly what I need!" or "He/she *knows* me better than I know myself." In other words, "How could I not love them? Look at what they do for my ego!" We are all guilty of this selfishness in our relating at some level.

Only Jesus was perfectly self-defined. He knew exactly His relationship to God and His purpose on earth, and He was not swayed by the opinions of others. He did not need validation. He could dine with the rejects of society without a twinge of fear or guilt concerning what the religious people would think. Likewise, He was totally selfless. Everything He did was for the good of others.

Improving Relationships with Others

All of us need human relationships to survive this life. God, after all, created us to need one another. We need friends who will steer us in the right direction, hold us accountable for our actions, and encourage us when we are doing what is holy and right. Likewise, we can experience tremendous joy in knowing that we are doing the same for others. However, if we look solely to others for validation, to define who we are as individuals or to fill an inner need to be known or noticed, we must ultimately be disappointed. The key to good relationships is not to seek from others that which can be found only in God and in ourselves. Instead, we must first seek to know God and ourselves. Then and only then can we truly enjoy knowing and being known by others. None of us has completely arrived at this level of relating, but we can and we ultimately will if we are willing to step through the darkness of our loneliness into the light of self-knowledge. The following are some practical steps for knowing ourselves and using that knowledge to improve our relationships with others.

Avoid Complacency in Your Relationships (or Seek Healthy Relationships)

No relationship is perfect. As hard as we try to find people who will make us feel good, even the best of relationships will make us feel bad at times. Likewise, the most challenging relationships can actually be the catalyst that drives us to grow in our relating. Unfortunately, most people believe that healthy relationships are synonymous with comfortable relationships. This is faulty logic. If you always stick with people who chant, "I'm okay, you're okay, we're all okay," you may not experience pain, but you will also not develop intimacy. People who follow this mantra never get close to anyone for fear of what they might find in others and in themselves. The closer you get in your relationships, the more you realize, "Okay . . . they're not okay. They've got problems just like everyone else." What is more important is that you will realize the same thing about yourself. The key to successful relating is to use the problems in our relationships to look inward, not outward, to increase our self-knowledge. Every challenge we face in relating is another opportunity to grow as an individual. The healthiest relationships are those we have with individuals who refuse to let us remain as we are. They are always challenging us to be better than we are right now.

Remove the Plank in Your Eye First

Many people who darken the door of a therapist's office initially come to learn how they can "fix" someone else. They are usually able to admit they feel bad, but the causes are always outside themselves. "How can I get my husband to take responsibility in our relationship?" "My wife is such a nag; she's driving me crazy! Is there a way I can fix her?" "What can I do to get other people to treat me better?" "I can't stand my boss . . .

If only I didn't have to work in such a stressful environment, I could be happy again." These individuals might be willing to *do* anything to change their relationships, but asking them to *become* anything other than what they are is where the challenge lies. It is true for all of us. Let's face it: no one wants to admit that the potential solution to a relational problem lies within oneself. In fact, we become downright defensive when someone suggests anything of the sort, but after careful reflection, we can always discover some area where we could improve. We cannot easily change our circumstances, but we can often change our attitudes about them. Using difficult relationships to grow and mature personally is a tremendous opportunity we cannot afford to miss.

Change the Focus of Your Prayers

We have all felt frustration in our relationships. We see what we would like to change in an individual and then become angry when our efforts fail. We even approach prayer with this same "fix-them" mentality. We pray, "Lord, please help so-and-so to repent of his sin and accept You as his personal Lord and Savior," instead of praying, "Lord, show me how I can be more like You, so that so-and-so will see your love through me and will want it for himself." Instead of praying, "Lord, teach me to be a wise, gracious, and merciful parent," we pray, "Lord, help my kids to shape up and be more obedient." It is not wrong to pray these things. In fact, it is very right! The Bible encourages us to pray for others' salvation and for their continued growth and change. But what if that person for whom you have prayed or worked so hard to fix never changes? Before we can grow in the strength of our relating, we must accept this possibility. What then? Was it all a waste? It was if your only motivation for relating was to change them and not yourself.

In any relationship the question we should ask God is, "What can I do for this person?" not "What can I do to them?" Likewise, in regard to ourselves, we should ask, "What can I learn about myself through this person?" not just "What can I get for myself from this person?" This is when we really begin to see God at work in our lives and in the lives of others.

Turn Conflict into Opportunity

The key to discovering healthy relationships in our lives is this: when problems arise, instead of asking, "What can I do to fix this?" we might ask, "Who can I become to fix this?" The more annoying our coworkers are, the more opportunity we have to become patient people. The more insulting our enemies, the more opportunity we have to work at developing kindness and godly self-confidence. It is the friction of these relationships that alerts us to the areas in our lives that need work. Your greatest conflict could become your greatest opportunity to grow.

Look to the Future Reward for Your Pains

When we realize that God can use the most trying of relationships to sharpen us personally, we must also remind ourselves of the ultimate purpose for this experience. God wants to prepare us for the perfect kind of relating we will experience in heaven one day. Even if certain people with whom we relate never change, the sharpening that takes place in our own hearts as a result of the friction will drive us into deeper, healthier relationships with those who are willing to change along with us. These relationships will also protect us from being hurt by those who are unwilling to change. Ultimately all those individuals who have chosen to "become new creations" through the power of the Holy Spirit and the sharpening of believers and nonbelievers alike, will enjoy relating to one another in perfect smoothness. No more rough edges. No more scraping or filing. Like priceless gems polished to perfection, so shall our relationships be in heaven. Every time we participate in this perfecting process here on earth, we take one step closer to that kind of heavenly relating. That's exciting!

Be Encouraged by What You Learn About Yourself

If this heavenly relating is the reward for our work, then why are most of us so resistant to change? The first reason is that the process is painful. When we get used to interacting with people in a comfortable but destructive pattern, it takes time and energy to modify that interacting. The second reason is that most people believe that admitting the need for change or growth is somehow the equivalent of surrendering in a battle or losing a war. We beat ourselves up every time we "fail" in our relationships, but this is the wrong attitude to have. Introspection should lead us not necessarily to ask, *Where am I at fault?* (although this may be revealed to us if we look openly and honestly at the situation). Instead, we might simply ask ourselves, *Where am I in my maturity, and is there room to grow through this situation? Where am I able to compromise, and where must I stand on my convictions? Where am I needing to be more patient, more merciful, more accepting, more discerning, or more understanding? What is keeping me from reaching that next level of relating in these areas?* These questions should encourage us and motivate us to grow. Remind yourself that "He who has begun a good work in you will complete it" (Phil. 1:6).

Be Teachable

Our culture has taught us that to be happy we must be "true to ourselves," no matter what the cost to others. This is a lie. Being true to self is simply a euphemism for selfishness. It is the refusal to allow the rough edges in others to sharpen our own. "Hey, this is the way I am. If people don't like it, then they can just get lost!" This attitude will not bring happiness in the long run, only deeper loneliness and isolation. There will always be areas in our personal lives where we can grow. We just need to be willing to learn through the tough times in our relationships.

This unteachable attitude is why many people avoid a relationship with God. He knows us and loves us as we are, but His love will not allow us to remain the way we are. He wants us to grow in our maturity and our relating, but sometimes that requires painful interactions with Him and with others. God can use those challenges in our relationships to teach us things about ourselves that we would never have seen otherwise.

When Clyde Neisman, a pastor of a large church in Des Moines, Iowa, found out that his wife had been having an emotional affair with a man from the church, he was devastated. He and Nancy had been together for fourteen years, and now he felt completely alone and abandoned. Despite his grief, he refused to talk about his feelings with Nancy, who had already admitted she was wrong, ended all contact with the man, and desperately wanted to work through the difficulties in their own relationship.

"This is exactly the problem," she said, exasperated. "You never open up to me. I want to be a part of your life, but I always feel like I'm on the outside. You're always so involved giving yourself to your ministry that there's never anything left over for your family! How can we possibly have a relationship if you won't ever tell me what you're feeling?"

Clyde knew she was right. He had been too busy, neglecting the most important ministry God had given to him: his role as a husband and father. He had been stubborn. He knew how important communication was to Nancy, but he just took for granted that she would always put up with his "strong, silent" personality. Looking back, he had refused to change. Now God had gotten a hold on him through the pain of Nancy's drifting, and he began to work on expressing his thoughts and feelings in their relationship. As he did, Nancy found the intimacy she needed and was never again tempted to search for it elsewhere.

Just as God taught Clyde through the difficulties in his relationship with Nancy, He wants to teach us as well. If we will get alone with Him and take an honest look at our relationships and what we can learn about ourselves through them, we will be able to return to the world of relating, more fully equipped to go deeper with people. This is a continual process. When practiced, it will lead us to the pinnacle of Christlike relating. Here we will find joy as never before. No longer will we just see and be seen. We will know and be known in the healthiest and most truthful way.

The Rest of Lori's Story

Lori suffered for some time in her loneliness after moving to a new state, but eventually she determined that she could either continue in that loneliness or use her solitude to draw closer to God. Whenever she began to feel alone, she would talk to Him, sharing her fears and pain and asking Him to reveal the purpose beyond her loneliness. As she did, the Lord taught her a lot about herself. Her fears had kept her sheltered in a deeply rooted comfort zone. This move had forced her to see how much she relied on others for her happiness. She had an over-longing that could only be filled by God, but it required her to move halfway across the country to see it.

Now that she was alone, she treasured her times with God. One evening, while studying her Bible, she came across a story in the Old Testament that she had never noticed. It was about a servant of a great prophet who found himself surrounded on all sides by a vast army bent on destruction. The servant was very afraid, feeling cut off from the rest of the world, but his master assured him, "Don't be afraid, for those who are with us are more than those who are with them." Then his master prayed that the servant's eyes would be opened, and suddenly he saw chariots of fire waiting on the mountains all around to save them (2 Kings 6:16–17).

Lori was amazed by the story. It rang true with her experience in California. She had thought she was alone in her pain, but she knew there had to be others around her with the same problem. She just had to open her eyes and see them! She got down on her knees right then and prayed, "Lord, help me to see those people surrounding me who are with me in my struggle against loneliness. Help me to share with them the love that You have shown me in this difficult season of my life. Amen."

Six months later Lori was having Thanksgiving dinner at her apartment with a packed house (about fifteen people in all). She had made a conscious choice to reach out, and she was blown away by the enthusiastic response of people in all stages of life. No one ever would have imagined this group of people under one roof, but now that they were all here, it was perfect. As Lori prayed for the meal, she thanked God silently for helping her through her own loneliness and for giving her the opportunity to help others through theirs.

Finding Purpose Beyond Your Loneliness

As you consider your own struggles with loneliness and your desire to find purpose beyond it, use these practical application points to guide you into deeper relatedness with those around you.

1. *Find the balance.* We all need time alone to ourselves and time interacting with other people. Depending on our personalities, we are more likely to drift toward one or the other extreme. If we spend too much time alone, we will starve ourselves of meaningful relationships that could have helped us in our times of loneliness. If we spend too much time with other people and do not make time for solitude, we will feel very uncomfortable with silence. We need a healthy balance of both (Ps. 46:10; Prov. 17:1; Heb. 10:25).

2. *Clear away the obstacles.* We all have barriers that keep us from relating to others. Many of them are superficial and unjustified. We need to identify them and then clear them away before we can go deep with others. Make a list of ways you can prioritize your relationships and practice scheduling time during your week to relate. That way the pain of loneliness will be less likely to catch you off guard (Matt. 7:7–12).

3. *Satisfy your over-longing with Christ.* If you have a void inside that you have been trying to fill with other people, chances are you will never be satisfied. People let us down. They cannot always be there for us, but Christ can. Make your relationship with Him the number one priority in your life so that you will never really be alone (Prov. 18:24).

4. *Know yourself.* Your life story is important in how you relate to people you meet. When you face conflict in your relationships, use it to learn more about your own emotions, desires, weaknesses, and strengths. Use what you learn to work at changing the negative and implementing the positive in your relationships. Allow God to smooth out your rough edges as you bump into others every day (Ps. 139:1–2; Prov. 27:17, 19).

5. *Know others.* You do not have to be a psychiatrist to make the study of people a priority in your life. Invest in the lives of others and seek to know them well. This will strengthen any current relationships you have and will make it easier to form new ones (Prov. 18:2).

Set aside some personal time to consider your own situation in the light of these truths. Then answer the following questions truthfully in order to establish the groundwork for overcoming the loneliness in your life.

1. Are you an introvert or an extrovert? What scares you the most about one or the other, and what are some ways you can break from your comfort zone to practice a healthy balance between solitude and socializing?

2. What obstacles are preventing you from developing relationships with people, and how can you clear them away? Who are the most difficult individuals with whom you feel you cannot relate? How can you bridge the gap between them and you?

3. Jesus wants to be your closest companion. How can you spend more time with Him and make it feel more like an intimate relationship rather than a religion?

4. Think back to the last conflict you had with a close friend. As you think about the circumstances of the problem, what can you learn about yourself and how you handled the situation? (Remember, be honest!)

5. How well do you know your friends and family? Can you name their favorite restaurants, their pet peeves, their most sensitive memories, or how they feel loved? If you do know, how can you use that information to show them love and acceptance? If you do not know these things, how can you find out?

Part 4

LOSS

"For the Son of Man has come to save that which was lost."

—MATTHEW 18:11

13

Beyond Loss

Garrett Chase never liked those sad country songs, but he had a morbid sense that his life was turning into one. If you had told him five years before that, come 2008, he would be unemployed, broke, and on the verge of a divorce, he would have laughed in your face, but there he was. As an engineer for General Motors, his job had never been the most secure, but he was one of the hardest workers at the company and had a great relationship with his manager, so he never worried about it . . . at least not until the recession hit. Each successive wave of layoffs left Garrett frazzled and irritable. He began to lose his temper at home, and, without thinking, said hurtful things to his wife, Sybil, and their two daughters. Every argument left him feeling guilty and wishing he could take back what he had said. Life for Garrett started spinning out of control.

When his pink slip was finally issued, Garrett sank further into depression. He and Sybil had to put their house up for sale, wondering the whole time who in the world was benefiting from all that bailout money the government had promised. The arguments at home intensified as the Chases' financial situation worsened. Their home was one of about twenty in their subdivision for sale, and there was a new development going up just a few miles down the road. Garrett's unemployment check was barely enough to pay the mortgage. All his inquiries about potential job offers seemed to be dead ends.

It looked as if they might have to move out of state, but that meant leaving their church, the girls' school, all the friends they had made over the last fifteen years, and even Sybil's parents, who were a huge help to their family. That was more than Sybil could bear. After a lengthy shouting match that climaxed with Garrett's fist through the living room wall, Sybil grabbed the kids and left for her parents' house. Garrett was left alone, wondering how he had lost so much so quickly. In the face of such pain, he began to question if life was even worth living.

Have you ever felt like Garrett? Have you ever lost something so precious you wondered how you would ever survive, if you even wanted to survive? Maybe you are feeling that way right now. You may have lost a close friend, a parent or spouse, even a child. Perhaps your health is failing or you have missed out on an opportunity of a lifetime that may never come again. Have you lost your innocence due to an abusive past or your sense of security in a failing economy? Whatever our losses, the void they leave behind can hurt terribly. It is the kind of pain that keeps us awake at night and makes getting out of bed in the morning next to impossible. It is the ache that sits deep in our chests, making it hard to breathe; the confusion that keeps us from knowing where to go or what to do next. We wonder what possible good could come from such pain. Will the sun ever rise on our sorrow?

In the next few chapters, we want to help you answer that question with a resounding yes! God always has a reason for the things He takes from us and the things He allows us to lose. Because He is good, we can trust Him. Even when our losses result from poor choices we have made, our God is merciful and gracious. He can restore to us much more than we have given up if we are willing to learn from our mistakes and return to Him. Whatever the case may be, we firmly believe that no matter how dark the pain of our loss, the morning will come, bringing answers to our deepest questions, answers that will not only satisfy us but will ultimately cause us to thank God for the loss.

In this chapter we are going to discuss two hard facts that must be accepted before the sun can rise on your darkest losses: First, the pain of loss is inevitable. Second, the pain of loss is individual. Once we accept these facts, we can move beyond them, begin to evaluate all that we have lost, and compare it with all that we have to gain in the end. We are confident you will see that the gains far outweigh the pain.

The Pain of Loss Is Inevitable

The first fact that must be accepted before we can experience great gains through the pain of loss is that the pain of loss is inevitable. Whether you want to or not, you cannot hold on to the things in this world forever. This is a temporal world we live in, a world that started decaying slowly the very moment the first man and woman disobeyed God's plan for His creation. When you think about that act, it was actually a blessing. With what you know about our world, would you want it to remain this way forever? We surely would not, and we know that the patients we see would agree. Sin has corrupted everything around us, even our bodies. God is not willing for us to remain in such a broken state forever, but in order to change, we must be willing to give up our broken possessions and allow Him to replace them with things that will last forever. That requires loss. Why is this so difficult? The reason is, we struggle between two desires: the desire for permanence and the desire for perfection.

Think about it. How often have you caught yourself thinking, *I wish this special moment would last forever,* when something good happened in your life, but when you were having a really hard day, you wondered, *Is this ever going to end?* As human beings we all have an ingrained desire for permanence, but not just for permanence's sake. We want things to be permanently perfect! Unfortunately, nothing is perfect right now, so permanence must be postponed. Something has to change. We must give up what is imperfect to attain what is perfect. See the problem? Sometimes we are not willing to sacrifice for the permanent goodness we desire, so we just settle for plain old permanence instead.

People in abusive relationships do that all the time. They are used to being abused. It is what they know. The thought of giving up their old lives and doing things differently scares them into complacency. They do not know what healthy relationships look like, so they assume it cannot be worth the sacrifices they must endure to attain them. So what do they do? They stay where they are and never experience what good relationships are like. The cycle of hurt and pain continues.

God, however, so loves us and wants what is best for us that He will often take what we are unwilling to let go and force us to look for something better, something we cannot lose. When we find that special something, we will thank Him in the end. The pain of loss may hurt worse than anything we have ever experienced, but ultimately the purpose is worth the pain.

At times in our lives, we feel invincible. The pain of loss seems irrelevant. Usually this is true with young people. It takes the pain of loss to awaken them to the fact that life will not continue the way it has forever. This feeling of invincibility is why many young people get involved with drugs, alcohol, promiscuity, and other reckless behaviors. But the pain hits home when someone they know loses his or her life or mind.

For those of us who are older, we know loss intimately. We begin to lose things as we age. Hair falls out, muscles turn to fat, jobs are lost, savings dwindle, and friends and family move away or pass away. As the reality of loss comes closer and closer to home, sometimes we can become obsessed with preventing it. We buy expensive life, disability, house, and car insurance policies. We work hard to diversify our portfolios to avoid financial losses. Some people spend thousands of dollars on plastic surgeries to maintain their physical beauty. When death comes calling for our parents, our spouses, or even our children, we cannot let go. We have seen family members of dying patients force doctors to perform every life-saving procedure available, no matter how painful, trying desperately to hold on to a loved one for just a few more months, weeks, or even days. None of the above activities are necessarily bad. We should be responsible with what God has given us, and use wise judgment with these personal decisions, but when we become obsessed with avoiding loss, it is like trying to hold back the ocean's tide.

So if we cannot escape the pain of loss, if we must face it sooner or later, then how can we prepare for when it comes? The first step is to ask the following questions:

- What do I have to lose in this life?
- What do I have to gain in this life and the next?
- Are the gains I have listed worth the sacrifice?

We will discuss these questions in the following chapters, but for now, just consider them. Once we have asked them and wrestled with the implications of our honest answers (the impact they have on our plans in life, our goals, dreams, motivations, relationships, and purposes), we can begin to find tremendous power through the pain of loss. When we let go of our invincibility and accept the inevitability of loss, God can fill the void with something lasting: a total dependency on His unfailing presence.

The Pain of Loss Is Individual

The second fact of loss that we must accept before being able to move on is that the pain of loss, just like any kind of physical or emotional pain, is individual. It is personal. Some of us have lost more than others, but each of us has felt the acuteness of the pain that results. That pain cannot be measured or quantified except by the person experiencing it. It is completely subjective. In medicine we use a "pain scale" with each person we examine. The scales for young children have pictures depicting levels of emotions ranging from a smiley face, representing no pain, to a crying face, representing severe pain. For older children and adults, we use number scales from zero, representing no pain, to ten, representing severe pain. These scales are important in that they help doctors determine if they are adequately treating the individual's pain. We cannot compare pain scales for different individuals for the simple reason that one person's ten may be another person's five, and vice versa.

In an outpatient clinic a young boy, who had cut himself deeply while climbing a tree, came for evaluation. The boy was trying to be tough, and he was doing a good job of it. When the doctor asked him how bad his pain was on a scale of zero to ten, tears welled in his eyes, and choking back his sobs, he whispered, "A ten."

At the same moment a college student, who had just been in a car accident, was lying in an emergency room with a shattered pelvis, several broken ribs, and a large gash in her forehead. Everyone could hear her screams ten rooms down. There was no need to ask her what number she would assign to her pain. It was a ten as well.

Someone might be tempted to compare these two individuals and say, "Obviously, the teenager's pain was much worse than the boy's." That might be true, but try telling that to the little boy: "Son, it could be worse. You could have been in a car accident and broken all your bones. Now, that would really be something to cry about." Would that comfort him? Would it comfort you? Of course it wouldn't. That little boy's suffering is just as real as that of the teenager in the emergency room. Things could always be worse, but the pain that hurts the most is the pain that hurts right now.

The same principle applies to our losses in life. If you have never lost an immediate family member (a spouse, a child, a parent, a sibling), then you can only imagine what that feels like, but that should not trivialize in any way the pain you have experienced at the loss of a close pet, a job, a physical ability, or a talent you once had. In fact, those losses may have more significance to you than the loss of a family member who might not have been involved in your life. For this reason trying to comfort ourselves by comparing our pain to others' never works. It either makes us feel guilt for whining, or it fills us with pride in a masochistic sort of way. The real starting point for experiencing light through the darkness of loss is to take the focus off of others and be honest with ourselves about our own pain.

Comparison Is Unhealthy

The Bible clearly tells us, "Judge not, that you be not judged" (Matt. 7:1). This would apply to our losses in life. There are several reasons why comparing our losses to others' is unhealthy.

Pride

The first reason that making comparisons is unhealthy is that it can lead us to become proud. Yes, it may seem strange, but pain can lead to pride. Like kids on the playground comparing their scars, we brag, "Aw, that's nothing. Check this one out!" We think, *I've lost more than you. My pain is a lot worse. Therefore I deserve more attention, more praise for my perseverance, or even special treatment because of all I've lost.* This not only diminishes our ability to sympathize and comfort others who may have lost less, but it sets us up for disappointment when others either fail to appreciate the depth of our own losses or become tired of hearing about them.

We see this a great deal in marriages. Many couples love to play the comparison game, always haggling over which one deserves more sympathy or special treatment for the sacrifices he or she has made in the relationship.

"I worked two jobs to put you through graduate school."

"Oh, yeah? Well graduate school was no cakewalk, and I did it to make more money so you could stay home with the kids!"

"You think staying home with the kids is easy?"

"I didn't say that, but you have no idea what it's like to put up with the people I work with, and then I have to come home and immediately start helping around the house. I never get a break!"

These people cannot sympathize with one another because their pride keeps getting in the way. They each want a break, but neither one will get it, because they are too busy playing tug-of-war. If, instead, they both dropped their ends of the rope and met in the middle, they might find the sympathy and encouragement they were looking for all along.

Though our pride sometimes causes us to brag about our losses, it may also do the opposite, fostering dishonesty as we seek to minimize our pain. There are some instances when we do not want people to know how badly we hurt. We do not want to admit to ourselves or to others that the pain is excruciating. It would mean admitting weakness, and our culture has taught us to hate weakness: weakness in others and in ourselves.

When my close friend Mike and I (Dr. Henderson) get together, the story of the "basketball accident" always comes up. The two of us were playing twenty-one with our friend Ben. You must understand how ridiculous we looked. An Ultimate Fighting Championship (UFC) cage match could not have been more violent. At one point in this game, I reached up to grab a rebound when Mike's hand came flying toward me and connected, full force, with my right pinky finger. The pain was immediate and explosive. I felt nauseous and light-headed as I looked down at the mangled piece of flesh that was once my finger. He had dislocated it in such a way that the bones were overlapping each other. I tried to pop it back in place, but the pain was too great, and I was too weak, so Mike obliged me instead.

Our friend Ben had run down to the other side of the court, mortified at what was happening. He told us later that from where he stood he heard the snap of my finger popping back into joint. To this day I like to brag about the fact that, instead of going to the emergency room to get an X-ray, we went to the local CVS drugstore, bought some popsicles, and used the sticks to create a splint for my finger. We then continued our game. My friends, however, are quick to remind me that I was screaming like a baby in the midst of the pain. Somehow my pride had caused me to block that part of the story out of my mind. Instead of being honest, I tried to make myself out to be stronger than I really was.

We do this with others all the time. Our pride will not allow us to admit that we are hurting, so we cannot be healed. Our pride tells us that God can be glorified only through stoic grinning and bearing. So we put on our game face and tell everyone that things are great, but the healing never comes. The pain continues to surface, and each time it becomes worse.

Lots of people stuff their feelings and bury their emotional pain—sometimes for fear that they will never stop crying if they get in touch with it, and other times because they feel as though it is a failure of character to admit it. Unfortunately, they still feel the emotional pain they are denying. They just displace it with what becomes a variety of illnesses, aches, and physical pains.

My (Dr. Meier's) own mother suffered from such a problem. She developed back pains after my father died, so I took her to her family doctor. I was concerned when, as he examined her lower back, she cried out in pain. Then I was amazed as he began to distract her with a conversation about politics. As he did he began mashing on the same spot, and she remained calm. He explained to me afterward that the real problem was her need to deal with her loss, not with her back. I am a psychiatrist, so I should have figured that out myself, but I was too close to the situation emotionally to think about it clearly. As I got Mom to talk more about Dad's death and cry over her loss, her back pain disappeared. She had to let down her guard, swallow her pride, and admit the emotional pain of loss she was feeling, and when she did, healing resulted.

False Guilt

If pride is not the problem, sometimes guilt is! Comparing our losses to others' may drum up feelings of false guilt. We feel guilty for our perceived weakness or lack of faith. We feel that we have no right to complain about our own little losses when others have suffered so much. It is true that the suffering we see around us should make us appreciate the blessings God has given us. If God has been merciful or gracious to you by sparing you from pain, thank Him for that. But never feel guilt about being honest with Him when you do hurt. The pain you are experiencing may seem small compared to others', but He wants to hear about it. You will always find someone who has suffered more, but that is no excuse for stuffing your own pain or feeling guilty about expressing it appropriately.

Fear

The comparison game can also cause us a great deal of unnecessary fear. We look at the losses of others and say, "I could never deal with that. If that happened to me, I would just die." Many people spend their entire lives in fear, worrying unnecessarily about the future.

I (Dr. Henderson) once counseled a young woman who listened to the news addictively. She obsessed over the losses of others and tried desperately to avoid them herself. Every time she got word of a particular illness going around, she refused to shake hands with anyone, carried hand sanitizer everywhere, and avoided people she thought might be sick. Once, she heard a story about a man who had been robbed while waiting in his car at a red light. From that time on she did her best to avoid hitting any red lights on her daily commute to work. Her determination to avoid the losses of others led her to take unnecessary, even obsessive actions that robbed her of the joy of life instead.

Bitterness

Finally, playing the comparison game has led many people to become bitter. This is what we call the "Why me, God?" syndrome. There is a big difference between honestly expressing your emotions to God and becoming bitter with Him. In one instance we question His purpose with a genuine interest to know His will. In the second instance we question His motives and character. We lose our faith in His goodness and turn our backs on Him. Many people even use the losses of others as excuses to deny God's existence. "Look at all the starving children in Africa. Look at all the homes destroyed by Hurricane Katrina. Look at all the people dying of AIDS, cancer, and heart disease. How can there be a loving God who allows children to die in school shootings or the elderly to waste away from Alzheimer's disease?"

Here is what's interesting: if these doubters were to speak with the suffering people they mention, they would be surprised to find those whose faith in God had actually been strengthened through their losses. Many people who go on short-term mission trips to Third World countries come back feeling humbled, blown away, even ashamed. They return with stories about people who, having next to nothing, not only believe in God but praise and worship Him amid great suffering and loss. If the comparison game really worked, then one would expect these people, who have suffered the most, to be the bitterest or the proudest, but it just does not work that way.

The comparison of our pain to others', not the pain itself, is what leads to pride, false guilt, fear, and bitterness. Cleanse yourself of these unhealthy emotions by consciously choosing to avoid the comparison game. As you read the next two chapters, put out of your mind everyone else around you and focus on your own pain for a moment. What have you lost, or what are you afraid of losing? Have you considered all that you have to gain? Let God shed some light on those questions as we explore the realities of loss.

14

What Have You Got to Lose?

Once we have been honest about the reality of loss in our lives, we must take a close look, no matter how painful, at all we have to lose. This helps us to put things in perspective, allows us to determine what we value most in this life, and enables us to put in place a plan of action for healing and recovery, if what we value is taken from us. In this chapter we will identify some of the most common treasures we have to lose in this life: time, significance, love, luxuries, and control over our circumstances.

As you read consider how important each one is to you personally. Then be honest with God about what you discover. Realize that the purpose of this chapter is not to instill fear over the potential for loss. Even Jesus told us not to worry about tomorrow (Matt. 6:34). It is, rather, an opportunity to face the fears that most of us already have deep inside of us. When hidden, these fears cripple us, robbing us of the fullness of life God wants us to have. The time has come to bring them to the forefronts of our minds and place them in God's hands. With a proper perspective and a lot of help from the Holy Spirit, even our greatest losses can lead to our greatest gains.

Lost Time

Why does so much of life have to be wasted on what seem like meaningless activities? Someone once estimated that if we live to be eighty, we will spend twenty-six of those years asleep and four of those years in a vehicle. Who knows how many of those years we will spend standing in line, talking to telemarketers, going to the bathroom, or changing diapers? Even with all our modern conveniences to maximize our time, life still seems so short and waiting so unbearable.

Because of the constraints of a physical universe, we have to make choices every day on how to spend our time. Activities we would much rather pursue, such as recreation, relationships, or altruistic endeavors, are often pushed aside for the more pressing issues: paying bills, doing laundry, going to work, sleeping. Life gets really complicated when, for whatever reason, we fail to manage our time wisely. Once we get behind, the sense of helplessness is overwhelming. At times like this we really do wish we could stop the world and just get off. The apostle James was right when he said our lives are like "a vapor that appears for a little time and then vanishes away" (James 4:14). How frustrating it can be then to feel as if we have wasted what precious little time we do have.

Many people are plagued with guilt from a past filled with "wasted" time. All of us have wished at some point that we could go back and redo what has already been done. We have missed out on opportunities and experiences, either because we have chosen to pursue higher priorities or because our sinful choices have, as the saying goes, taken us farther than we wanted to go, kept us longer than we were willing to stay, and cost us more than we were willing to pay. At moments like this we must remind ourselves that with God no time is wasted. Remember how long Joseph spent in prison before he was released and given the opportunity to save Egypt from famine: at least two full years! (Gen. 41:1, 14). Moses spent forty years in the wilderness before he was given the job of delivering the people of Israel from slavery in Egypt (Acts 7:29–30). What about Jesus? Our finite humanity tempts us to wonder why God waited thirty years before allowing Jesus to begin his earthly ministry. Did God waste time? No, God's timing is perfect! He waited for the perfect moment in history to reveal His plan to save the world from its helpless state. "When the fullness of time had come, God sent forth His son" (Gal. 4:4).

Perhaps you are mourning over lost time. Be encouraged, knowing that God does not operate under the constraints of human scheduling. He can use even "wasted time" for His glory if we give it over to Him. He can bring meaning and purpose to our lives, no matter what time we have left on this earth.

Maybe you find yourself in a season of waiting right now. You have dreams and goals that have yet to be fulfilled, and you are growing impatient with the monotony or uncertainty of your life. Remember, to God one day is as a thousand years and a thousand years is as a day (2 Peter 3:8). This verse may not be comforting until we consider its true meaning. It does not mean that God ignores time or thinks it is unimportant. Quite the contrary. God sees the whole picture, all at once. He knows what will happen a thousand years from now because He exists there in the future just as He exists here in the present. With God as the "author and finisher of our faith," timing is everything. That means our waiting times are never wasted times. They have purposes we cannot afford to miss. Knowing this allows us to trust that a seemingly insignificant day is still a "day that the Lord has made" for a purpose. No matter how uncertain, we can "rejoice and be glad in it" (Ps. 118:24). Ask God to help you use this time to prepare for the future. Continue to trust Him and He will make known to you the true meaning behind the mundane . . . in His time!

Lost Significance

Factory employees working long hours for low wages, nurses taking care of angry patients and arrogant physicians, neglected children abandoned by their parents, women who cannot conceive children, table servers who get stiffed by disgruntled or stingy patrons, students tucked away in secluded cubbyholes at their college libraries, elderly nursing home residents with no family to visit—all of these and countless others have felt the pain of insignificance. One of our biggest fears as humans is being forgotten. Time not only passes us by, but it robs us of our significance as it goes. People are searching to regain some semblance of significance in a world that values fame, popularity, wealth, talent, and youth. Reality television gives wannabe celebrities the illusion that they might actually mean something to the millions of viewers who tune in to watch their broken lives, but most of these celebrities are forgotten after a few years, months, even days after the show is over.

Scott Hamilton, the world-famous figure-skating champion, understands how easily the significant can become insignificant. After winning the 1984 Olympics in Sarajevo, he described the emotions he felt, knowing that he had finally reached the top. "It's a feeling of triumph that you've won the day [but it is also] a feeling of loss and emptiness. . . . Everything that was my identity had now come to an end." For seven years after his win, Scott kept his medal hidden away in his underwear drawer until he finally donated it to the World Figure Skating Hall of Fame. "[The 1984 Olympic Games] was a moment that I will keep in my heart, but it was just that. A moment. To look at that medal every day would have inhibited me from growing beyond it." Instead of clinging to the significance that medal represented in his life, Scott chose to give it away in order to inspire other skaters who would one day come behind him.[1]

Solomon, the wisest and most respected king of all times, said it best when he wrote during a time of great loss and suffering, "For there is no more remembrance of the wise than of the fool forever, / Since all that now is will be forgotten in the days to come. / And how does a wise man die? / As the fool! . . . For the living know that they will die; / But the dead know nothing, / And they have no more reward, / For the memory of them is *forgotten*" (Eccl. 2:16; 9:5, emphasis added). Are you thoroughly depressed now? The good news is coming, we promise, but pause for a moment and ask yourself, *What is the source of my significance? Is it my job, my family, my intelligence, my accomplishments? What would happen if I lost what currently defines me? Would life still be worth living?* It can be if we chose to replace our temporary significances with the lasting significance of knowing and being known by God. That is why Jeremiah said, "Those who wish to boast should boast in this alone: that they truly know me and understand that I am the LORD" (Jer. 9:24 NLT). When we use our accomplishments, our unique abilities, and those traits and characteristics that define us to point others to God, our significance will always last, no matter what we may be involved in at any point in our lives.

Lost Love

Losing someone we love dearly can be very hard to bear. Many young brides and grooms have been left standing at the altar, wondering the reason for the sudden change of mind. Parents watch with a twinge of sadness as their children grow up and start families of their own. Best of friends grow distant because of changing circumstances, interests, or ideologies. Broken promises and harsh words leave people scarred, realizing that the relationships they once treasured will never be the same. Medical illnesses or accidents can destroy or reverse the roles we performed in relationships. The caregiver can easily become the caretaker after a stroke or diagnosis of cancer. Even personalities can change over the years. The man or woman you know today may not be the same person ten years from now.

Death and divorce are the two biggest contributors to lost love. The Bible says that when two people get married, they become "one flesh" (Mark 10:8). It is no wonder then that many spouses say that after their loved one dies they feel as if they have lost a part of themselves. The willful abandonment of a spouse in divorce can feel even worse, because the individual who leaves makes a conscious decision to stop loving the one they left.

Lost love, however, does not just involve relationships. It can also include losing our passions in life. Whether because of financial constraints, the loss of time, loss of physical abilities, or prior commitments, we may no longer be able to pursue the things we used to enjoy. In other instances we just get bored with life. The newness of certain hobbies or passions wears off. Many depressed people experience this to the extreme with a symptom called *anhedonia*, the inability to experience pleasure. Others with bipolar disorder or attention-deficit/hyperactivity disorder (ADHD) struggle to finish what they have started because they become distracted by bigger and better enticements. Medications can help these people, but their disorders can still be difficult to overcome.

In the face of lost love, we must make time to mourn. Grieving is an essential process for living in a temporary world. The longer we wait to do it, the harder time we will have letting go of the past and focusing in on the new loves in our future. Grieving gives us the chance to acknowledge our pain and receive comfort from others. It allows us time to reflect on both the good and bad memories, to bring closure to the time we had, and to determine what we will and will not take with us into the new loves we find. Finally, the grieving process keeps us searching for that perfect permanence for which we were made but have yet to attain. Remember, we do not mourn without hope (1 Thess. 4:13). We count our losses, but we also look to God to replace them with greater gains.

As circumstances change, we must also remember that love is an act of the will, not of the heart. It is easy to fall in and out of love, even in our relationship with God. In fact, God scolded the church at Ephesus for this very reason, saying, "You have left your first love" (Rev. 2:4). We must remember to recommit each day to loving those around us, or else we will lose that love. If we are going to have healthy, meaningful relationships in this life, we must be willing to work through the misunderstandings, the differences of opinion, and the conflicts that will inevitably arise. We must also learn how to be sensitive to our own feelings and the feelings of others as we relate to each other. This takes work. Sometimes we feel as though love is a lost cause; but if we continue to endure, we can regain a deeper love than the one we may have lost.

Lost Luxuries

When we take things for granted, we lie to ourselves. We tell ourselves that the things we own are necessities that will and should always be there. There was a time when food, clothing, and shelter were considered the necessities of life, but every invention we have can start out as a luxury today and turn into a necessity tomorrow.

My wife and I (Dr. Henderson) had a used clothes dryer that was given to us almost ten years ago. Recently it broke down. Before I thought about what I was saying, I prayed, *Oh Lord, why did you have to let this happen now?* For ten years that junky old thing had done its job faithfully and did not cost us a dime on repairs. While the dryer worked, I never appreciated it, but now I was upset over the loss instead of being grateful for the use we had gotten from it.

In 2006 the Pew Research Center confirmed that an American's idea of a necessity was vastly broader than in other parts of the world. Close to 80 percent felt that clothes dryers were a necessity, 64 percent said that televisions were, and 68 percent put microwaves on the list. Cell phones (49 percent) and home computers (50 percent) were also included. Three years later, as the economy has quickly taken a turn for the worse, most of those numbers have dropped significantly.[2] People are now watching in horror as their retirement accounts and investment portfolios dwindle to the size they were ten years ago. People are cutting back on their spending in order to retain those necessities they may have taken for granted.

The stock market does not have to crash, however, in order for us to experience the loss of luxuries. Theft and natural disasters not only rob us of our luxuries; they leave us feeling violated and vulnerable as well. When our losses are the result of carelessness or forgetfulness, we feel sick with our own stupidity. Luxuries do not have to be lost physically either. They can simply turn into liabilities (things that tie us down and rob us of our freedom), such as the boat bought by a man who realized shortly thereafter that he had to find a mechanic to service it, buy a truck to tow it, make space in his driveway to store it, and oh yes, find a lake on which to use it. The hardest luxuries to lose sometimes have very little monetary value. A stolen laptop can be replaced for several hundred dollars, but the family pictures you saved to it cannot.

With all the things we have to lose, we can respond in one of two ways. On the one hand we can become obsessed with avoiding loss, but this is the very mentality that turns luxuries into liabilities. Our obsessing robs us of any joy the luxury might afford and then amplifies our frustration when our efforts to hold on to it fail. The other option is to accept the inevitability of loss before allowing yourself the luxury you want. Then hold on to it loosely, ask God to make you truly grateful for it while it is there, and seek out opportunities to use it for more than your own gratification. Then, if the time comes to lose it, you can at least take consolation in the fact that you used it wisely while you had it. If you are taking care of the possessions God has given you and using them to glorify Him, then the Lord will bless you, whether you have a lot or a little. That is what the Bible means by "storing up treasures in heaven where moth and rust cannot destroy" (Matt. 6:19).

Lost Control

William Ernest Henley developed tuberculosis of the bone at the age of twelve. As the illness progressed, doctors had to amputate his leg just below the knee. They wanted to remove his other leg as well, but he refused despite the fact that he might die as a result. He persevered, however, survived the illness, and was discharged with a prosthetic limb. While in the hospital, he wrote his famous poem "Invictus," which claimed that he was master of his fate and captain of his soul.

Unfortunately, William Ernest Henley, as much as he stayed death by his own motivation and perseverance, still died. No one can maintain control of his or her life forever. All of our other losses in life culminate in this one universal problem of human existence: our inability to control the uncertainties of life and death. When we go to funerals, we often weep, not only for the loss of our loved one but also for the reminder of our own finiteness. Both of these are painful blows.

Though the Bible is clear that while there are things in life we can and should control—our emotions and actions toward others (1 Cor. 13), our choices when tempted to do wrong (2 Tim. 2:22), our emotional responses to the uncontrollable circumstances of life (2 Cor. 12:7–10), and our acceptance or rejection of God's gracious offer of salvation (Josh. 24:15, Heb. 2:3)—the ultimate outcome of life is out of our control. If you meet someone who tries to sell you the perfect formula for total success and security, put your hands over your ears and walk away. There are no material guarantees in this world. When life seems most out of control, we must simply do what we can and trust that God will take care of the rest.

15

What Have You Got to Gain?

Now that we have reviewed all that we have to lose, it is time to consider the following:

1. What do we have to gain as we endure the pain of loss?
2. Are those gains really worth the sacrifice?

To answer these questions, we will look at the lives of several individuals who lost much but gained much more. Perhaps we can learn from them as we evaluate our own answers to the above questions.

Gaining Christ

When Carrie Prejean entered the Miss USA competition as Miss California, she knew she had what it took to win: looks, poise, talent, and experience. Up until the question-and-answer portion of the competition, she was favored to take home the crown, but when she was asked a politically charged question about legalizing same-sex marriage, Carrie had a split second to decide her own fate. Should she give the politically correct answer to win the competition, or should she stay true to her faith and lose everything else? What would you have done?

It is a rare instance when we would find ourselves in such a dramatic moment of truth, but we do face smaller but no less important decisions every day of our lives. Do we tell a little white lie to a customer in order to seal the deal, or do we save our integrity and risk them walking away. Do we teach our congregations the truth of God's Word even when it is unpopular, or do we stick to the mainstream issues to attract as many people as possible? Should we have sex before marriage and indulge our desires, or should we wait and risk being called a prude, backward, or even psychologically repressed? The Christian Medical and Dental Association is fighting a law right now that may deny physicians the right to choose against performing abortions. If the law passes, will they then leave the practice they have spent years to build? These and countless others are questions we are forced to answer. Is gaining Christ worth the other losses we have to endure?

The apostle Paul thought so. He had it all (education, religious authority, Roman citizenship, a good tentmaking business), but he chose to give up everything and follow Christ. He summed up his reasons in just two short verses: "I once thought these things were valuable, but now I consider them worthless because of what Christ has done. Yes, everything else is worthless when compared with the infinite value of knowing Christ Jesus my Lord. For his sake I have discarded everything else, counting it all as garbage, so that I could gain Christ" (Phil. 3:7–8 NLT).

He counted them all as garbage? Come on, is that not a little harsh? After all, it is not wrong to have a nice house, a good job, or a prestigious position. When someone we love dies, we do not take their ashes and throw them into the trash can out back. Right? Hold on. Paul is making a very important point here, just as Jesus did when He said, "If anyone comes to Me and does not hate his father and mother, wife and children, brothers and sisters, yes, and his own life also, he cannot be My disciple" (Luke 14:26). God does not actually want us to hate anyone, and He is not saying that we cannot enjoy life. Jesus' point was that He must be the first, the most important, the most central figure, entity, or possession in and throughout our brief existence here on earth. Why? Because God is eternal, anything that is in Him will be eternal as well. "People are like grass; their beauty is like a flower in the field. The grass withers and the flower fades. But the word of the Lord remains forever" (1 Peter 1:24–25 NLT). "Every good gift and every perfect gift is from above, and comes down from the Father of lights, with whom there is no variation or shadow of turning" (James 1:17). Anything we gain in this life that is not firmly built upon the foundation of our relationship with Christ will be lost. Why, then, would we want to hold so tightly to things that will eventually slip through our fingers when we could grab hold of the One who will grab us back and never let go? The gifts He has to give us will last forever.

Have you given your life over to Christ? Is He the Lord of everything you have? As psychiatrists, we are convinced you will never know power through your losses until you find the One you can never lose. "Can anything ever separate us from Christ's love? Does it mean he no longer loves us if we have trouble or calamity, or are persecuted, or hungry, or destitute, or in danger, or threatened with death? . . . No, despite all these things, overwhelming victory is ours through Christ, who loved us" (Rom. 8:35–37 NLT). It is only when we lose everything that we realize we need nothing but Christ.

We know what many people are probably thinking: *that is so easy to say, but living it is another matter.*

Just as in any relationship, it takes an act of faith and complete trust to give what we have to God. That is why Jesus said, "I tell you the truth, if you had faith even as small as a mustard seed, you could say to this mountain, 'Move from here to there,' and it would move. Nothing would be impossible" (Matt. 17:20 NLT). You do not need much faith, but whatever you have, give it to Him. His Word promises you will not be disappointed.

Although some may claim otherwise, we know that Carrie Prejean's answer at the Miss USA Pageant cost her the crown. Not only that, but it made her the target of the mainstream media, political activists, and Internet bloggers who wanted to peg her as a bigot, a blonde ditz, or a hypocrite. In a strange twist of Providence, however, all the attention gave her a platform to advance truth, more so than winning the competition itself. We cannot even remember the name of the actual winner without looking it up, but Carrie will be remembered for her commitment to her beliefs, not just here on earth but in heaven as well.

When we are challenged with the pain of loss, we may need to be honest with God about our lack of faith and ask Him to give us what faith we need. He promises that He will. Sometimes we can only pray, *Lord, You know what I can handle. As much as I hate to give up what I have right now, if You really require it from me, if it is really for the best, then go ahead and take it. But please give me the strength to be able to endure the pain of the loss. I can't do this on my own. Please be with me through the whole process. Don't take Your eyes or Your hands off me for one second. I've got to know that You are with me before I can let go.* Can you trust Him? Be prepared to move mountains!

Gaining Confidence

The book *Miracle on Ice* tells the story of the 1980 U.S. Olympic hockey team. Herb Brooks, coach of the team, set out to lead a group of talented but headstrong players to victory over the seemingly invincible Soviet Union team, who had won every ice hockey gold medal but one since 1956. To do this Coach Brooks had to turn a group of individual hockey players, many from rival schools, into a united team. Though his players often wondered about his unorthodox and often harsh coaching style, they were grateful for it when they finally took home the gold in one of the greatest upsets in sports history.

Sometimes we wonder whether God's methods for accomplishing His purposes for our lives are really the best. Sometimes we hear people say that God does things to us just "for His good pleasure," as if He were sitting in heaven, relishing our suffering. Nothing could be further from the truth. That is what Satan does, not God. We may not always know or understand God's purpose at the time of our loss, but we can be sure He always has a reason. We will never gain confidence in the way He works, however, if we are never put to the test.

Bethany Hamilton was just a teenager when she faced that test. While surfing off the coast of Hawaii, a fifteen-foot tiger shark attacked her, severing her right arm from the rest of her body. Her chances of becoming a competitive surfer seemed lost, but Bethany's confidence was not in her physical body; it was in God. Despite the pain of her loss, she pushed forward, continued to pursue surfing, and won the 2004 Excellence in Sports Performance Yearly (ESPY) award as Best Comeback Athlete. But through her loss she gained more than just recognition as a surfer. She became an author, a motivational speaker, and a television celebrity. With every opportunity she gets to tell her story, Bethany tells people about her love for Christ and His faithfulness to her throughout the whole ordeal.[1] That kind of confidence comes only from someone who has lost much but gained much more.

Sometimes the end of the story is not immediately made known to us. Sometimes we have to wait until we see God face-to-face before He will reveal the true purpose beyond our pain. That should not keep us from speculating. When God asked Abraham to sacrifice his son Isaac, Abraham was really confused. After all, God was the one who promised Isaac to Abraham in the first place, and the promise was more than just a son. God had promised that He would make Abraham a great nation through Isaac. So God's command surely seemed as if He was going back on His word. Instead of arguing, Abraham did what he was told, but the book of Hebrews gives us a clue into his thoughts at the time: "It was by faith that Abraham offered Isaac as a sacrifice when God was testing him. Abraham, who had received God's promises, was ready to sacrifice his only son, Isaac, even though God had told him, 'Isaac is the son through whom your descendants will be counted.' *Abraham reasoned that if Isaac died, God was able to bring him back to life again.* And in a sense, Abraham did receive his son back from the dead" (Heb. 11:17–19 NLT, emphasis added).

The book of Romans is clear: "Abraham never wavered in believing God's promise. In fact, his faith grew stronger, and in this he brought glory to God. He was fully convinced that God is able to do whatever he promises. And because of Abraham's faith, God counted him as righteous.

And when God counted him as righteous, it wasn't just for Abraham's benefit. It was recorded for our benefit, too, assuring us that God will also count us as righteous if we believe in him, the one who raised Jesus our Lord from the dead" (4:20–24 NLT).

We can have confidence that everything He does is for our ultimate good and that He will give us the strength to endure the pain in the meantime.

Gaining Clarity of Purpose

Many times in life we lose in order to gain a clear direction or purpose that we might not have discovered otherwise. Richard Stearns, president of World Vision (the largest relief organization in the history of the world), had been an extremely successful businessman. He rose to the top of the corporate world as the CEO of Parker Brothers, but it was not until he was fired from two consecutive positions within a nine-month period of time (Parker Brothers and Franklin Mint) and then spent fourteen months unemployed that God began to make clear to him his true calling in life. In his book, *The Hole in Our Gospel*, Stearns described the one lesson he learned through his loss. "[I learned that] no matter where I was or what my circumstances were, I was made to love, serve, and obey God. I could do all three whether unemployed or as a CEO—my situation didn't matter. When I was eventually offered a job, I took that lesson with me and began each day asking, how can I love, serve, and obey God today, in this place with these people?"[2] It was this newfound purpose that gave him the strength to leave the corporate world and join World Vision, an organization that has helped millions of children, families, and their communities to reach their full potential by tackling the causes of poverty and injustice.

Not all of us are called to lead international relief organizations, but fulfilling your purpose in life is no less important to God. He wants you to be fulfilled mentally, emotionally, and spiritually, but in order to do that, you may need to give up that to which you hold most tightly.

"Yes," you say, "I believe that happens sometimes, but there are plenty of examples even in the Bible where God allows people to suffer for no reason. Take Job, for instance."

As we read the book of Job, Satan and God do seem to be playing a game of chess, using Job as the unsuspecting pawn. It did not make much sense to Job either, but in his case God chose to remain silent about His purpose. "You are just going to have to trust me on this one, Job," God said, in essence.

When we were kids our fathers often told us, "Because I said so!" That was usually enough to silence our pestering, but it did not remove the questions from our minds. Sometimes there was not enough time to answer them. Sometimes we were not old enough to understand or handle the truth, and sometimes our earthly fathers just did not know the answers themselves. Not so with God. He always has a reason even for His silences. Though He may not reveal the answers to our questions, we can trust that He is purposeful and good.

So can we speculate about the real reason for Job's suffering? The Bible says Job was a righteous man. "He was blameless—a man of complete integrity. He feared God and stayed away from evil" (Job 1:1 NLT). Even though he still had a sin nature, Job lived a righteous life; but because this world is fallen, the righteous must suffer along with everyone else. We can easily be tricked into believing that the more faith we have, the less we will suffer. Many in Christendom seem to have forgotten this fact. We conclude that any pain we experience has to be the consequence of sin in our lives. Countless Christians, therefore, have been plagued with false guilt, thinking, *If I had only been a better parent, God would not have taken my child from me. If I had only prayed harder, God would not have allowed me to get cancer. If I only had more faith, I would not be struggling with depression, anxiety, schizophrenia, or bipolar disorder.* Has anyone ever said such things to you?

God knew these false kinds of accusations would occur, so He gave us the example of Job to teach us that not all pain is of our own doing or within our control. Could Job have understood this at the time of his suffering? Would it have comforted him? Maybe, maybe not, but God did not feel it was necessary to explain at the time. Even His silence had a purpose: perhaps it was to remind us today that even when we cannot hear His voice, He is still there and cares about what we are going through.

God always has a purpose for our losses, and His purposes are motivated out of a genuine longing to see us gain what is greater. Job was given more children, more possessions, and better health than he had had before, but the real power of Job's losses was displayed in God's ultimate goodness to all humankind. Job's losses were horrific and extremely painful. We would not wish them on anyone, and neither would Job. Yet Job is having a great time up in heaven right now, perhaps reflecting on his earthly life and thinking, *Wow, it was worth all that temporary pain to have a book of the Bible written about it that has helped millions of sufferers to learn from their pain and quit guilt tripping over it.* If you knew your current losses and pain would one day accomplish great things, not just in your life but the lives of many others, would a life of loss be worth living to you?

16

Was It Worth It?

There is always something to be gained through our losses if we look hard enough. Many people do not even try. They spend their entire lives in bitterness instead of seeing the power that losses can create to accomplish greater, more lasting opportunities and rewards. We have talked about some of these rewards already as we looked at the stories of people touched by loss. Through their experiences, all of them gained a deep sense of security in knowing we can never be separated from God's love. They gained an unspeakable appreciation of God's own sacrifices for us and a confidence in His ability to take tragedy and turn it into triumph. In the end they discovered a clear purpose for their pain that made life worth living even in times of loss. On top of all of that, they gained a legacy that would last in the hearts of those people who have heard and will hear their stories.

But the gains for us do not stop there. God replaces everything we have lost with eternal equivalents: eternal time on a new earth, eternal significance in a heavenly kingdom, eternal love from His precious Son, eternal luxuries or treasures in heaven, and an eternal opportunity to discover His perfect control over a universe we cannot even fathom. As sons and daughters of God, we have an inheritance waiting for us in heaven that is beyond our wildest imaginations, an inheritance that is, as the apostle Peter said, "pure and undefiled, beyond the reach of change and decay" (1 Peter 1:4 NLT). He is capable of doing "exceedingly abundantly above all that we can ask or think" (Eph. 3:20), and He is waiting to give us a life worth living here on earth if we will let Him. But first He wants us to let go of what we cannot keep anyway. The question we must ask: Is it worth it?

Rebecca Brabrook had to answer that question. She was born in the early 1800s in Bedfordshire, the smallest of the "shires" in the southeastern part of central England. As tradesmen of lace and shoes, her family suffered badly from the rise of machine labor during the Industrial Revolution. Instead of moving to a larger city, such as London, to find work, Rebecca and her husband, Samuel, decided to take their family to America, "the land of opportunity." As she and her husband boarded a sailing ship with their four sons (ages eight, six, four, and two), they were filled with excitement over the prospect of a better life. Little did they know it would prove to be the most difficult journey of their lives.

The trip took six weeks; and during that time, the Brabrooks' youngest son caught scarlet fever and died in his mother's arms. In those days, it was not uncommon to burn the personal effects of a person afflicted with scarlet fever to help prevent its spread. In this case, the crew took every keepsake and reminder the Brabrooks' had of their son and threw it overboard. As if their loss was not painful enough, the Brabrook's four- and six-year-old sons also died from the disease shortly thereafter.

I (Dr. Henderson) have always wondered what Rebecca's response would have been if asked, "Was it worth it? Was the loss of three children worth the trip to America?" If she had had the chance to look into the future and see all the incredible opportunities their painful losses had provided for not just their remaining children, but their grandchildren, great-grandchildren, and great-great-grandchildren, I think she would be surprised. Their descendants have become schoolteachers, farmers, dressmakers, carpenters, college professors, medical doctors, homemakers, engineers, nurses, corporate executives, and ministers. (There is even a quirky psychiatrist in the mix!) But most important, their faithfulness to Jesus through all their struggles left a legacy their descendants will not soon forget.

I (Dr. Meier) have a similar story. In the late 1700s many Germans, some of whom had Jewish heritage, moved to the Volga River Region of Russia because they were offered free land to develop into their own farms. Cities cropped up near Saratov, Russia. One of the cities was Franzosen, where some French families also joined the Germans. In the 1860s two missionaries came to that city to mend the soles of shoes. They also conducted Bible studies to mend the souls of men and women and children. About a third of the city became devout Christians as a result of those efforts. After a year the two missionaries went on elsewhere and were never heard from again. The wealthiest man in that city at the time of the revival was Jacob Meier, who owned not only a large farm, but a factory of sorts that built farm equipment. He was chosen by the revivalists to be the pastor of their new evangelical Christian church. They may have selected him for spiritual or intellectual reasons, but it sure helped church attendance to have the largest employer of the city as their pastor. His son became pastor after him, and this tradition continued.

Alex and Elizabeth were nine-year-old neighbors in that German city in Russia when the communist revolution took place in 1917. Alex was one of the grandsons of Jacob Meier and had inherited great wealth. The czar of Russia even visited their large home, and thirty servants lived in the quarters behind it. But all was lost in the revolution, and their friend, the czar, was killed along with all of the czar's family. Many relatives of Alex and Elizabeth were also killed for refusing to fight in the Red Army.

After escaping, hiding, and nearly starving, Alex and Elizabeth made it to Germany and eventually onto a ship to America. The ship struck another ship and almost sank, but Alex and Elizabeth survived, and their families settled in different states. Years later they ran into each other again, remembered each other with fondness, and soon became engaged and got married. They went to Michigan on their honeymoon, and because it reminded them of Germany, they moved there and raised four children, including a third-born son named Paul. Their suffering made them greatly appreciate their faith and their country.

Alex and Elizabeth were the most patriotic Americans I (Dr. Meier) ever met, and they ingrained that into me as well when I grew up as their child. I am sorry for their suffering but thankful for the many lessons I have learned from them as well. I still start to cry with joy and pride every time I hear America's national anthem. I am a psychiatrist, but I also followed family tradition by obtaining a seminary degree and becoming an ordained minister, although my congregation is one patient at a time.

Those are just two examples of the impact that perseverance through loss can have. The apostle Paul was right when he said, "What we suffer [lose] now is nothing compared to the glory he will reveal to us later" (Rom. 8:18 NLT). When we have the perspective of eternity, we discover yet again that the purpose beyond our losses is always worth the pain.

The Rest of Garrett's Story

We would be remiss in not updating you on Garrett, the man whose story we told at the beginning of this section. He is still working through the pain of his losses, but life has not been as bleak as it had been, despite some very hard times.

When Sybil left that night with the girls, Garrett realized that something inside of him needed to change. He had been desperately trying to hold on to the life he knew, but the more he tried to control his circumstances, the worse they seemed to get. With an uncharacteristic show of tears, he knelt down on his living room floor and began giving all he thought he owned back to God: his house, his family, his job, even his sense of self-worth. There were no fireworks afterward, no miraculous changes in his circumstances. He knew the road toward greater gains was going to be long, but he was sick of the status quo and ready to commit to the challenges that lay ahead.

Over the last year, Garrett has seen God do some incredible things through the pain of his losses. Through therapy he has made great strides in controlling his temper. He is still working to convince his wife that the change is genuine, but they are at least living together again, and trust is slowly being restored in their relationship. Instead of taking control selfishly, Garrett is trying to take control spiritually by leading his family in prayer, especially in regard to their financial situation. They did have to foreclose on their house, but instead of moving out of state, they decided to rent an apartment, and Garrett, after broadening his definition of acceptable job opportunities, found a position with a manufacturing company in Chicago that allows him to work from home. Though the salary is significantly less, the new job gives him more time to invest in other activities. He has even started leading a small group Bible study on Wednesday nights at church.

The Chases are sticking to a tighter budget and cutting out some of the frills they were used to, but this has actually helped them spend more time together as a family, talking, playing games, and being creative. Their neighbors at the apartment complex are missionaries to Africa, home on furlough. After several get-togethers with them, Garrett is talking to Sybil about budgeting some money to visit their country in what may be the first of several trips to help design and build a new activities center for the orphanage where their neighbors work. Garrett is living proof that God can replenish us with eternal rewards when we give up on avoiding the pain of loss. He can do the same for each of us, but do not expect the process to be easy. The sacrifices will be great, but if we allow it, God's power will prove greater still.

Finding Purpose Beyond Your Losses

Having discovered all that God can do through even our most painful losses, we want to give you five practical application points you can use the next time you experience the pain of loss in your life.

1. *Change is not the enemy.* First Corinthians 15:51 says, "We shall not all sleep, but we shall all be changed." This perfecting process can begin now in our hearts, if we can overcome our fear of loss. We should yearn for change, not run from it, especially if the change is for our ultimate good. Ask God to help you let go of those things that are holding you back from perfection, and trust Him to lead you through your losses toward greater gains (Eph. 4:22–24).

2. *Avoid comparing your losses.* Much of the pain of loss comes when we compare our circumstances to those around us. Instead, focus your mind on what God wants to teach you through your own losses (John 21:20–22).

3. *Be honest with God about the pain.* Honesty with God is not a sin! He knows the emotions you feel right now because of your losses. Express them to Him. Write them down in a journal so that when God does reveal the purpose behind your loss, you can use the journal as a reminder of how far you have come and as an encouragement for future pains (Ps. 120:1).

4. *Prepare for future loss.* It is wise to spend time and energy to avoid unnecessary or avoidable losses, but no system is foolproof. That is why we must also prepare ourselves emotionally for the inevitability of loss. One way to do this is to consciously maintain a daily spirit of thankfulness for the blessings God

has given us, asking Him for the strength to be content whatever our circumstances (Phil. 4:6–7, 11–13).

5. *Invest in eternity.* We are eternal beings, but so often we operate from a temporal perspective. All investors keep records of their losses and gains. God guarantees if you invest in eternity, any losses you experience in this life will be well worth the returns. Even your painful life experiences can be used to invest in the lives of others for eternity (2 Cor. 1:3–4).

Set aside some personal time to consider your own situation in the light of these truths. Then answer the following questions truthfully in order to establish the groundwork for overcoming the losses in your life.

1. In what areas of your life are you holding on to the status quo, desiring permanence over perfection? What would help you surrender those areas of your life to God? How can you begin to do this even today?

2. What comforts, concerns, or confuses you when you compare your losses to others, and why? How do you think your attitude would change if you kept the focus on your own life's story and what God is trying to teach you personally?

3. Between you and God, what emotions and questions would you like to share with Him regarding your loss? Are you willing to wait on Him for answers?

4. What can you thank God for this day, right now? What past losses have you seen Him use in your life for greater gains, and how can you use those experiences to encourage yourself and others for the future?

5. What treasures have you stored and are you storing up in heaven? How can you use your earthly treasures as the capital for future eternal gains?

Part 5

DISCIPLINE

"He who endures to the end will be saved."
—Matthew 10:22

17

Beyond Discipline

I 'm sorry, Mrs. Caldwell, but your lab work doesn't look good."
Donita Caldwell sat across from her family physician, Dr. Gupta, and braced herself for the bad news.

He continued, "Your fasting blood sugars are well over the normal range, your total cholesterol levels have also gone up since your last visit, and the results of your sleep study show that you are having several episodes at night when you stop breathing, what we call obstructive sleep apnea. This not only keeps you from getting restorative sleep, but it also increases your blood pressure during the day. With your family history of heart disease and diabetes, I'm afraid you are at high risk for a number of serious medical problems."

As if she didn't know the answer, Donita asked, "So what should I do?"

Dr. Gupta's gaze dropped as if he was reviewing something important in Donita's chart, but she knew better. She had felt this awkward tension with her family and friends whenever the subject of her weight came up, and now it was happening again. "We have several options for treatment, but none of them will be as effective without you making some significant lifestyle changes." His gaze returned to hers, and with a grim expression he said, "Donita, you have to lose some weight or else it's going to kill you!"

As she left the doctor's office, the weight of her depression and helplessness seemed harder to carry than the physical weight of her body. At three hundred and twenty pounds, Donita had come to the place where food was her only source of comfort. She had tried every fad diet and weight-loss program imaginable, but every time she became stressed or upset, she found herself making excuses for why she needed food. It was an addiction that had taken hold of her slowly over many years, and she knew the road back would be long and extremely painful.

How many people do you know who wake up one morning and say, "I'm going to work hard to weigh three hundred pounds, blow my perfect credit score, get fired from my job, destroy my family by cheating on my spouse, or addict myself to drugs and alcohol"? The answer is, no one does. We might be tempted to say, "It just happens," but that is not true either. The second law of thermodynamics says that, left to itself, the universe is constantly going from a state of order to disorder. The same is true for our lives.

Pilgrim's Progress is the famous allegory written by John Bunyan in 1678. In this book Pilgrim's (or Christian's, as his name became) journey is analogous to the Christian life. We set out searching for something more than what we see around us in this physical world in which we live. When we find Christ, He removes the burden of sin from our backs, gives us our passport for heaven, and protects us along the way from the perils, snares, and enemies that try to rob us of our heavenly inheritance. One of the deadly snares of Pilgrim's journey is depicted as a place called the Enchanted Ground. This was an area through which the King's Highway passed. Its air made travelers want to stop and sleep. If someone happened to fall asleep in this place, he would never again wake up.

The moral of the story: complacency is dangerous to our spiritual journeys in life. Just as the Enchanted Ground almost ensnared Pilgrim, complacency lures us to relax, let down our guard, and become comfortable with less than what God wants us to have. If we become too comfortable with sin, it will eventually destroy us. God is not willing to let that happen to His children. Though He loves us unconditionally just the way we are, He cares about us too much to let us remain that way. That is why He wants us to discipline ourselves to finish strong in this race of life and why, sometimes, when we start to get too comfortable, He will discipline us Himself.

The Need for Discipline

When most of us hear the words *discipline* or *punishment*, our minds immediately drum up images of Dante's *Inferno*, people suffering unbearable pain for messing up in this life. But this is not the essence of God's discipline. People who spend eternity apart from God have chosen to do so by deciding not to submit themselves to His loving discipline. They have instead chosen to be left alone, and that, sadly, is exactly what they will become—alone. This is in essence what hell is: eternal separation from God. The apostle Peter tells us that "God does not want anyone to be destroyed, but wants everyone to repent" (2 Peter 3:9 NLT).

His discipline is not the kind of punishment used to gain control or enforce obedience. He is not standing in heaven waiting with anticipation for us to mess up so He can whack us over the head with a two-by-four. In the 1600s and 1700s, Puritan churches did exactly that. A parishioner was designated to stand in the back of the church and watch for "nodders." If they saw anyone falling asleep, they would pop them on the head with a stick that had a hard round knob on the end. That is not the way God operates.

The more accurate definition of God's discipline is His developing our character by instruction, practice, and real-world experience of the natural consequences for our actions, since the only way to prepare for anything of value in this life is through practice and discipline. This is what loving parents try to do with their children, and this is exactly what God does with us—except that He does it perfectly. As God's children, we can trust that His discipline is always in our best interest and intended for greater purposes for our lives.

There are times discipline hurts more than we would like it to, but you can be sure that it is far better than the ultimate pain that complacency brings. Think of it this way: imagine yourself as a student, falling asleep in history class as your professor gives a dispassionate presentation on the Seven Years' War. Suddenly he begins to review the test questions for the final exam. What is the most loving act your friend sitting next to you could perform: allowing you to sleep through the review or waking you up in time to take notes? Hopefully you agree that the latter of the two is the more loving. Now, let us say that you are a very sound sleeper. A gentle nudge or neck massage might feel a lot better than an elbow to the ribs, but if you do not wake up, those acts of gentle kindness would be wasted. Your friend's "loving" pinching or poking may not be pleasant, but it will save you from the far worse pain of failing your exam and having to repeat Professor Snore's class all over again. As flippant as it may sound, the deeper our complacency, the harder the jolt we need to keep us out of harm's way and spur us on toward bigger and better things.

What if your family is falling apart because of your complacency at home? Would you prefer a friend who lies to you and tells you everything will be all right, or do you want someone who lovingly "gets in your face" and gives you the wake-up call you need, even if the criticism makes you uncomfortable? If you were suddenly diagnosed with a deadly but treatable form of cancer, would you want a surgeon who refused to operate because the procedure might be painful? What about money? As hard as it is to budget our finances, without it the consequent debt we accumulate will be ten times as stressful.

As much as we might try to avoid it, discipline is absolutely necessary for our survival here on earth. Some people do not need much. Just the thought of potential consequences or punishment keeps them on track. Others, like the prodigal son who sat wallowing in the mud, eating pigs' slop in a foreign land, may need to lose everything before they are willing to change. Either way the goal is the same: positive growth and change.

What happens if we completely fail to respond to discipline in our lives? The first book of Corinthians gives us a good idea: "But on the judgment day, fire will reveal what kind of work each builder has done. The fire will show if a person's work has any value. If the work survives, that builder will receive a reward. But if the work is burned up, the builder will suffer great loss. The builder will be saved, but like someone barely escaping through a wall of flames" (3:13–15 NLT). God does not just want us to escape punishment. He wants us to thrive in life, but complacency can rob us of God's higher plans.

The Destructive Nature of Complacency

There are many examples in the Bible regarding the destructive nature of complacency, but none is as powerful as the life of Lot, the nephew of Abraham and Sarah in the book of Genesis. His father, Haran, had died while the whole family was still living in Ur, a city near the mouth of the Euphrates River. When Abraham was called by God to leave that city and head for the land of Canaan, Lot decided to follow his uncle, who, most likely, had taken him under his wing as a boy. Lot shared in the wealth of his uncle Abraham. The land they settled on could not support both of them, so they decided to part ways. Abraham gave Lot the first choice of any section of land he wanted, and Lot was quick to decide. The Bible gives us insight into the motivation behind his choice:

> Lot took a long look at the fertile plains of the Jordan Valley in the direction of Zoar. The whole area was well watered everywhere, like the garden of the LORD or the beautiful land of Egypt. (This was before the LORD destroyed Sodom and Gomorrah.) Lot chose for himself the whole Jordan Valley to the east of them. He went there with his flocks and servants and parted company with his uncle Abram. So Abram settled in the land of Canaan, and Lot moved his tents to a place near Sodom and settled among the cities of the plain. But the people of this area were extremely wicked and constantly sinned against the LORD. (Gen. 13:10–13 NLT)

Lot saw all the things we tend to focus on in our society. He saw "all the plain of Jordan" (13:10). Its wealth and magnificent beauty invited him to a life of comfort and ease. The land also reminded him of Egypt, the land from where he had just come. He had gotten used to living in Egyptian society. Maybe he was even a little irritated with Abraham for making them leave. This place would allow Lot to return to the familiar—the comfortable.

There was only one problem. The Bible tells us that the people of the land were extremely wicked, constantly sinning against the Lord without fear or consideration. Like watching the suspense of a modern-day natural disaster movie, we want to shout at the scene playing out before us, "Don't stop there, Lot. Keep moving! Can't you see what's coming?" But Lot was slowly being lured into complacency, just as Christian experienced in *Pilgrim's Progress*, falling asleep on the Enchanted Ground. Something painful was going to have to happen in order for him to wake up.

Before we find out what happened to Lot and his family, let us consider for a minute the desires that got Lot into this mess. There were three.

Security over Sanctification

The first was a desire for security over sanctification. Sanctification is the process of being set apart for a special purpose. Discipline is the means by which we achieve this special purpose. A valedictorian of a large high school challenged her fellow students to "dream big." For most people that is not the problem. We all want to make a difference in the world, to know God in a deep and personal way, to achieve success in our professional and personal lives, but if we do not practice the discipline necessary to achieve these dreams, they will never become reality. That is why most people need someone or something to shake them out of their safety zones and remind them to keep moving forward. Our security is not in our circumstances but in the active pursuit of God's purpose for our lives. When we settle for anything less, we will never find lasting security or success.

Position over Purity

The second thing Lot desired was position over purity. Genesis tells us that instead of just settling in the surrounding area, Lot decided to take his family and live in the center of Sodom and Gomorrah. Genesis 19 tells us that Lot "was sitting in the gate" (v. 1), a place where political leaders often congregated to discuss matters of state and business.

God wants His children to be involved in politics and governing in our respective spheres of influence, but we must be extremely careful to keep those positions from destroying our purity or weakening our moral convictions. As we seek to make the world better, we must take care that it does not make us worse. Many people have been corrupted by their desire to climb the social ladder to success. If you doubt this, try counting how many famous actresses have made it to the big screen without stripping for the camera. Consider why politicians are stereotyped as dishonest and ruthless. Remember all the stories we have heard of ministers abusing young children or having sexual affairs. If your goal in life is to become famous or powerful, you are in for serious trouble. The consequences of Lot's compromise were devastating. Instead, pray for purity in all areas of your life, and let God worry about where He places you in society.

Conformity over Commitment

Finally, Lot desired conformity over commitment. Peer pressure is extremely difficult to withstand. Psychologists have proven this time and again with a number of experiments, the most famous of these being the Asch conformity experiments. These experiments were published in 1953, and they involved taking one volunteer, who thought he or she was going to take a vision test, along with a group of other "participants." In reality the others in the room were asked to purposely give the wrong answers to the so-called vision tests. Thirty-two percent of the real participants chose to give the same phony answers as their counterparts, even though they knew their decisions were wrong. Most of those who still answered correctly reported extreme discomfort in doing so because of the pressure to conform to the others' responses.

As kids we performed much simpler versions of the Asch experiments with various kinds of peer pressure. And we do this as adults all the time but in subtler and more dangerous ways. We must comply with the ever-changing styles we see on television and in magazines. We must change our understanding of truth to make it more acceptable to those around us. We must conform our ways of talking to make others feel comfortable about their sins. Before we know it, we have been lulled to sleep by the Enchanting Ground of conformity.

Lot subjected himself to the subtle influences of the culture in which he lived. This affected not only himself but his family as well, especially his daughters, who ended up marrying men of Sodom. Sadly, things have not changed much since that time. In fact, they have gotten worse. It has become harder and harder to stay set apart for pure commitment to our relationship with God and others when the world has made security, position, and conformity so much more attractive. We need discipline more than ever if we are to hold out for bigger and better things.

In the following chapters, we will discuss the pain of discipline and its importance for finishing strong in this life and the life to come.

18

A Wake-Up Call

L arry Dixon, author of the book *When Temptation Strikes*, lost his house in a fire a few years ago. It happened while he was away on business. In the early morning hours, as the family slept comfortably in their beds, Linda (Larry's wife) was suddenly awakened by an eerie sound resembling the noise of a small child zipping toy race cars back and forth in the attic above her head. She opened her eyes and stared up at the ceiling in the dark. Concerned by the noise, she got up to open the attic door and take a look. As she did, heat and flames burst out like dragon fire. Amazingly she was not hurt. She rushed to get her children and escaped within five minutes of the roof collapsing onto the bed where she had been sleeping such a short time before.

Though Linda and her family had escaped physical harm, the emotional discomfort (to put it mildly) was heartrending. The Dixons stood outside their home with literally nothing but the clothes on their backs, watching everything they owned, all the comforts and sentimental valuables that tied them to that place, burn in front of their eyes. They mourned the loss, but they would also use this test of their faith to discipline their hearts and minds to be more like Christ. Because of that, God set them apart for something greater.

Today a beautiful new house stands on the exact spot where the old one burned. Because of their tragedy and the godly discipline they developed through it, Linda and Larry have learned a secret that few people know:

the joy and freedom that comes from holding loosely to the temporary things of this world. And because of it they determined to use their new house to store up eternal treasures. Their doors are always open, allowing visitors to hear and be reminded of God's goodness and faithfulness in even the most painful circumstances. Their home is so much more than a place of shelter and comfort for the people who know them. It has become a safe haven for anyone seeking selfless hospitality, loving-kindness, light-hearted fun, and spiritual encouragement. The Dixons, through the power of the Holy Spirit, have taken a tragedy and set it apart for bigger and better things. That is the power of a disciplined life!

The Dixons' story is a physical example of a spiritual truth. Linda believes that God woke her up just in time to escape the fire. Her experience that night is an illustration of God's loving protection over our lives. Just as Linda and her family were protected physically from the fire, God protects us spiritually when we get too comfortable where we are, failing to recognize the dangers around us. He wakes us up through the act of discipline and then leads us away from the fire before it is too late.

When we finally do get up and get out, we may turn back and look at how much we have lost: wasted time, missed opportunities, and broken relationships. We wonder how in the world we are going to be able to pick up the pieces of our lives and move on, but if we allow the light of God's love to shine on our circumstances, if we remain diligent in seeking His purposes and use the tragedies we face to grow stronger and more disciplined, God's reward for our pains will be greater than we ever could have imagined. This is why the apostle Paul tells the Roman believers: "We can rejoice, too, when we run into problems and trials, for we know that they help us develop endurance. And endurance develops strength of character, and character strengthens our confident hope of salvation. And this hope will not lead to disappointment. For we know how dearly God loves us, because he has given us the Holy Spirit to fill our hearts with his love" (Rom. 5:3–5 NLT).

As psychiatrists we encourage our patients to keep a journal, often during the darkest periods of their lives. We do this because we firmly believe that at some point they will be able to return to it and see how God took everything they faced and used it for good. This conscious awareness requires discipline. The knowledge gained becomes like spiritual muscle. The more we begin to recognize God's intricate and detailed workings throughout our toughest times, the more willing we are to live as He wants us to live in the face of future problems.

Chris Remer did more than keep a journal. After giving in to temptation and having an affair, his psychiatrist had him sit down in front of an empty chair and write a letter to his future self, describing the pain he was experiencing at that very moment. Then he tucked it away in a drawer next to his bed. It took two years of counseling and a lot of hard work for Chris to restore the trust he had destroyed in that one moment of pleasure. Looking back, he saw how much he had grown in his maturity and his love for Morgan, his wife. Their relationship with the Lord, with each other, and with their kids had reached a depth they had not thought possible even before the affair.

Chris forgot about the letter he had written for several years until one day he was introduced to a fellow professor at the university where he taught. Young, attractive, and used to getting her way, she set her sights on Chris and would not back off. Chris tried to talk with his department's chair about the situation, but he saw nothing wrong in her behavior and dismissed it entirely. As Chris prayed for strength, the Lord reminded him of the letter he had written seven years before. A strange feeling came over him as he read his own words to himself, "Chris, please listen to me. You gave up everything you had for an illusion of pleasure. Remember how sick you felt the moment it was over. Remember the nights without sleep before you told Morgan and then the look of horror on her face when you did. I don't care what the cost, if you ever find yourself tempted to relive this hell, RUN! Don't do this to me or my family ever again." That week Chris resigned from a tenured position at a prestigious university and never looked back. With all he had gone through in the past, he knew God would honor his faithfulness and commitment to purity, even if it meant changing jobs.

This is the "character" Paul talks about in Romans 5:3–4. As our character becomes more like Christ's, we become more confident of His power within us. The future, instead of looking bleak, looks more and more exciting!

One question that still remains for those of us who have faced tragedy like Linda and Larry is, "Did God start the fire in their house?" This is a question that has been asked by skeptics and theologians alike throughout history. Some Christians might say, "Yes, God started the fire, but He meant it for good when others would have meant it for evil." Other Christians might say, "No, but He allowed it to happen because He wanted to use it for our good." We do know that God never tempts us to sin, but in Chris's case, He did teach him through it.

The truth is we may never know the answer to that question until we get to heaven, but we do know, as clichéd as it may sound, that Romans 8:28 is still inspired by the Holy Spirit and is the absolute truth! "And we know that God causes everything to work together for the good of those who love God and are called according to his purpose for them" (NLT). Claiming this promise may require godly discipline and resolve, but He promises that sooner or later our faith will become sight. At that point the end result will be so amazing that the cause probably will no longer matter. In the meantime we need not lose our hope in His goodness and love.

For those who like to attribute other people's suffering to the direct consequences of sin in their lives, we would warn you to be careful! You are sinning as soon as you do. As Christians we are called to judge blatant and obvious sin and avoid it or speak against it, but we are never called to judge the perceived consequences of sin. We are only harming our effectiveness in demonstrating the love of Christ when we attribute natural disasters like Katrina, terrorist attacks like 9/11, and diseases like AIDS to God's righteous judgment on sinful people. It may very well be true. He does often use these things to discipline people, but who are we to say the people who lost their homes in the flood, or the family members of those who died on 9/11, or even the man or woman diagnosed with HIV are being punished for their sins? If that is the case, then we all deserve the same fate. Let us instead use those moments of intense suffering to focus on the mercy and compassion that Christ had on sinners suffering in His day. Let us reach out our hands and help those who have fallen on the track and encourage them not to give up in the race of life. Let God do the judging in these matters.

As our heavenly Father, God is invested totally in our growth and maturity. As His children, we are given the opportunity to participate in the process. As with all children, parents start by enforcing discipline. As their children grow older, however, parents move toward encouraging discipline in activities such as homework, sports, and relationships. Finally, as their children reach adulthood, parents finish by entrusting discipline completely to their children. God works with us in the same manner as we grow into spiritual maturity. The apostle Peter explained the end result this way: "These trials will show that your faith is genuine. It is being tested as fire tests and purifies gold—though your faith is far more precious than mere gold. So when your faith remains strong through many trials, it will bring you much praise and glory and honor on the day when Jesus Christ is revealed to the whole world" (1 Peter 1:7 NLT). We will begin to discuss this process of discipline in the remaining portion of this section. As we do, remember that God's discipline is unlike any other's. If we submit ourselves to it, He will reveal the purpose for it in his time.

19

Because You're Loved

Why does God discipline us? The real reason is that He loves us too much to let us remain as we are. Most parents love their children, but if they are smart parents, they realize that continuing to treat children like three-year-olds when they are four, ten, or eighteen can create serious problems for their kids' mental and emotional health. (After all, sucking your thumb at a job interview does not bode well for good first impressions. Lying on the floor kicking and screaming will not get your boss to give you a raise, and wearing diapers to the office—well, you get the idea!)

In all seriousness, there are many adults who have failed to mature beyond their adolescence for lack of discipline. Some do not even make it that far. Physically they grow older, but in all other respects they remain children. Their actions are childlike—they hit or scream or manipulate when they do not get their way. Their attitudes are also childlike—they expect others to cater to their wants and needs but are unable to share what they have with others. Because they are unable to care for themselves, they are driven by fear: fear of abandonment, fear of the unfamiliar, and fear of the weight of responsibility. The normal stressors of life (stressors that any mature adult has been trained to carry) weigh them down like a ton of bricks. Rather than struggle with the load, they throw it off and live for the moment without any concept of postponing pleasure for greater good. Their universe remains small, manageable, until some unforeseen tragedy robs them of their security and leads them to wander like a child lost in the mall, directionless and crying out for help. It is a bleak picture, but it happens every day. That is why discipline, both self-driven and externally imposed, is essential for our survival in life.

God does not just want us to *survive* this life, though. He wants us to thrive here on earth. To do this we must see the world through the eyes of its Creator. The motivation behind His discipline in our lives is to see us mature and become more like Him, our perfect heavenly Father.

When we were kids, most of us wanted to grow up to be just like our parents in some way. They knew everything and could do anything! I (Dr. Henderson) can remember as a little boy sitting on the bathroom counter, "shaving" with my dad, only he had the razor and I just had a butter knife. I was not old enough yet to be able to do the real thing, but I could not wait until that day came. I used to love that scratching noise his razor made as it scraped along his chin. The first time I used a real razor and cut myself, I realized that being like my dad was not going to be as easy as I thought. Now I can grow facial hair and shave it (if I want to), just as he did. We look a lot alike, in fact (stubble in the morning and all), but only because I went through that most horrible experience called puberty.

God wants us, His children, to be just like Him. He has great and awesome jobs for us to do, but it requires a maturing process that takes time and discipline before we can handle them. This discipline can be annoying, frustrating, and downright painful, but the writer of Hebrews tells us not to despise it:

> Have you forgotten the encouraging words God spoke to you as his children?
>> He said, "My child, don't make light of the LORD's discipline,
>>> and don't give up when he corrects you.
>> For the LORD disciplines those he loves,
>>> and he punishes each one he accepts as his child."
> As you endure this divine discipline, remember that God is treating you

as his own children. Who ever heard of a child who is never disciplined by his father? If God doesn't discipline you as he does all of his children, it means that you are illegitimate and not really his children at all. Since we respected our earthly fathers who disciplined us, shouldn't we submit even more to the discipline of the Father of our spirits, and live forever?

For our earthly fathers disciplined us for a few years, doing the best they knew how. But God's discipline is always good for us, so that we might share in his holiness. No discipline is enjoyable while it is happening—it's painful! But afterward there will be a peaceful harvest of right living for those who are trained in this way. (12:5–11 NLT)

Ray Saint was a father whose fifteen-year-old daughter had been admitted to the hospital for depression and oppositional defiant disorder. He was distraught. Though it was obvious that he loved his daughter, he had no clue as to what he should do. He was a hard worker at a local factory, put in long hours, and could not be home as much as he wanted. When he was home he tried every trick in the book to discipline his rebellious daughter. Most of his tricks, however, were things he had learned growing up in a dysfunctional home. He was never physically abusive, but he often yelled out of frustration and was inconsistent in taking privileges away for poor behavior. It was obvious, however, that Ray showed a genuine desire to do what was right. He just did not have the training.

At one point during an interview with the two of them together, he turned to his daughter, almost pleading, and said, "Cindy, I know I've messed up, but you *have* to know that I've done these things because I love you."

With tears in her eyes, she said, "Of course I do, Dad. I'm so sorry."

Cindy had a chemical imbalance that caused her to struggle with depression and irritability, a chemical imbalance that her father had passed on to her from his father. When we treated her with medications, her mood and even some of her oppositional personality traits began to improve. She later admitted to us that, as much as she said she hated being disciplined, deep down her dad's constant persistence made her feel that he cared. Both Cindy and Ray agreed to see a counselor together to work on their relationship. Through therapy Cindy made a conscious decision to submit to her father's discipline, and Ray worked hard to practice consistency in the way he raised his daughter.

If Cindy could feel love and respect for a father who, though trying hard to do his best, had made a mess of good, healthy discipline, how can we not help but love our perfect heavenly Father who knows exactly what will work with each of us to help us become like Him?

The relationship between parents and children is a symbol of how God deals with us as human beings. Unfortunately, because of the fall, our earthly parents may have distorted God's perfect way of disciplining. They often discipline out of untempered anger, frustration, or a selfish desire for peace, but we cannot let their faults influence our attitudes toward God's active involvement in our lives. Too often we believe that God's discipline is unfair or random. If we allow it, this mentality can cause us to lose faith in His purposes, even His existence.

Sigmund Freud, because of the faults he saw in his own father, developed a theory that all humans wish for a greater, God-Father to fill the emptiness they feel when they first realize their earthly fathers are flawed. Unfortunately, he postulated that this "wish" could never be fulfilled. It was, rather, proof that God is a figment of our imagination. That was a faulty conclusion. Science fiction novelists have proven over and over that often our wishes can be realized. Space travel, for instance, was the stuff of fiction until Neil Armstrong set foot on the moon. What was once thought impossible suddenly became accepted as fact.

We must be careful, however, that our *wish* for God to be like or unlike our earthly parents does not mask His true identity. Honestly and wholeheartedly searching for God includes accepting Him exactly as He reveals Himself to us. He has given us His Word to study so that we can get to know our true heavenly Father and how He disciplines His children. Let's discuss the two ways He does this.

Active Discipline

There are two major ways God disciplines us as laid out in Scripture. One way is through active discipline. He brings certain trials into our lives to train us and make us stronger. Like a coach who pushes an athlete to train on more and more challenging courses, God allows circumstances and people into our lives to build spiritual muscle, endurance, and agility: a new job, a rocky relationship, a loss, a rejection, a season of loneliness or failure or injustice. We grow as we go.

He may also deal out specific disciplines to help us overcome sinful actions: an arrest for possession of drugs, a devastating divorce due to infidelity, a ruined reputation for false advertising, or missed opportunities due to laziness. More often than not, our own internal suffering is punishment enough for our sins: the guilt that gnaws at our chest or the overwhelming anxiety as we live a lie.

God's active discipline can be seen throughout Scripture. It is swift and fitting, but it is also usually merciful compared to what the offender deserves. King David knew this to be true. That is why when God gave him a choice of punishments for his sin of numbering the people of Israel, David said, "Let us fall into the hand of the LORD, for His mercies are great; but do not let me fall into the hand of man" (2 Sam. 24:14).

When I (Dr. Henderson) was living in South Carolina, taking out the garbage was my least favorite chore. We lived in an apartment complex that had only one dumpster. I had to drag our trash a hundred yards or so every night. My son, Christian, who was two years old at the time, liked to accompany me on these treks. Anyone who knows me understands that I hate making more than one trip to do anything. Instead, I will insist on hanging bag after plastic bag on both arms and then struggle, sweat, and groan the entire distance down the stairs, across the parking lot to the dumpster.

That day the garbage bags were especially heavy. I told my son, who was tagging along behind me, to stick close, but the freedom and excitement of the great outdoors called his name, and like a Mack truck, he bolted toward the parking lot. Instinctively I stuck my leg out to block his way, and he bounced off it like a rubber bullet, falling hard to the ground. With tears in his eyes and a pouty bottom lip, he looked up at me with sadness and frustration. I dropped the bags I was carrying, knelt down, and held him close.

I told him, "I'm sorry, buddy, but you could have been *really* hurt if I hadn't stopped you." I felt bad that I had hurt him, but I was also glad I had prevented him from running into the street. Now when we go outside, he always reaches up for my hand as we cross the street, and I make sure I have a hand free for him to hold.

That experience made me wonder how many times God has protected me from serious harm by not letting me get away with sinful choices in my life. Proverbs 19:18 (NLT) says, "Discipline your children while there is hope. / Otherwise you will ruin their lives." I can imagine that if God shows us the replay of our lives someday, we will be amazed at how much His loving discipline kept us from ruining things completely.

Passive Discipline

God's active discipline is always more merciful than what can happen when we disobey and seemingly get away with it. Unfortunately, our stubbornness as children can keep us from heeding His active discipline, so God employs passive discipline. He gives us what we want and lets us experience the consequences. We call this the "hot stove tactic." Sometimes we have to get burned in order to understand that God knows better than we what is best for us.

Earthly parents have a hard time letting go of their children and practicing passive discipline, because they cannot see the big picture. Releasing their children means letting go of control and facing the unknown. "What if I don't intervene and something terrible happens? What if the damage is irreparable? I could not live with the guilt, the shame, or the embarrassment." Parents who cannot let go often become what psychiatrists call "enmeshed" with their children. They cannot cut the strings and let their children be their own persons. This either breeds helplessness or rebellion. God does not suffer from this fear. He is perfectly willing to practice passive discipline, knowing that there is no better way to conform us to His image than to allow us to experience the consequences of our own sinful choices.

Jesus taught His disciples this truth with the story of the prodigal son in Luke 15. When the younger son asked his father for his share of the inheritance, his father did not say, "You go to your room, you ungrateful kid. I don't want to hear another word about this. You're grounded!" No, he gave him the money and the son took off.

Initially it seemed that the son had made the right decision. He found lots of friends who were willing to spend his money with him, and they probably had an awesome time, but then his money ran out. Soon his "friends" left him, and he was stranded in a foreign land in the middle of a famine, forced to work as a hired hand, so hungry he wanted to eat the slop of the pigs he was charged with feeding. Then the lightbulb went on. *Dad was right*, he thought. *What am I doing here? Dad's servants live ten times better than this. I bet if I went back and begged for forgiveness, he would at least let me be a slave in his household.*

The prodigal son found more than that, though. When he returned home he found a father so filled with love and acceptance that he sprinted down the lane to take him back into his arms. The son had learned his lesson, and the father had his son back. When you find yourself in a situation you have created because of poor choices in life, do not blame God for it. If He had stopped you, chances are you would have resented Him even more. Instead, let the consequences you've suffered humble you. Admit your mistakes and run back home to Him so He can welcome you back with open arms.

The Consequences of Avoiding Discipline

God gives us many examples in the Bible of the consequences of an undisciplined life. King David's son Adonijah lacked discipline. The Bible says that his father "had never disciplined him at any time even by asking, 'Why are you doing that?'" (1 Kings 1:5–7 NLT). Consequently, he developed into an arrogant, self-centered adult, who thought he knew better how to run his father's kingdom. He set up a coup to take over, but he was murdered by his brother Absalom. This was a miserable day for David as a parent.

What about the sons of Eli, the Israelite priest who raised the prophet Samuel? They were so wicked they cheated people out of their sacrifices, taking the best cuts of meat. They were getting fat on the offerings that were supposed to be given to God. Finally, God had had enough of them both: "I am going to carry out all my threats against Eli and his family, from beginning to end. I have warned him that judgment is coming upon his family forever, because his sons are blaspheming God and he hasn't disciplined them. So I have vowed that the sins of Eli and his sons will never be forgiven by sacrifices or offerings" (1 Sam. 3:12–14 NLT).

Ask any therapist or psychiatrist or pastor, "Who are the hardest individuals to help?" and they will tell you they are the people who are undisciplined. They include:

- patients who will not consistently take their medicines and then blame the doctor when they do not get better
- addicts who do not see their use as a problem or refuse to do all that is necessary to avoid their triggers
- church members who complain about every service but refuse to use their time, money, or spiritual gifts to make it better
- wives who manipulate their husbands relentlessly until they get their way
- husbands who refuse to take responsibility for their families
- students who always think they know more than their professors
- employees who are always trying to get out of any work they can

The list could go on and on.

Antisocial is the descriptive term we use in psychiatry to describe the severest kinds of people who grow up actively trying to avoid proper discipline or scoff in the face of authority. People with antisocial personality disorder become very good at breaking the law and getting away with it. They use deceit and lying to con people for their own selfish profit and pleasure. When people try to tell them what to do or how to behave, they become irritable and aggressive, often to the point of physical violence. They show laziness when it comes to financial and work responsibilities. With dripping sweetness they will smile and charm you and then stab you in the back as soon as you turn away.

On top of all of this, antisocial people have no remorse for their actions. When they have ignored their consciences long enough, the consciences remain silent in the face of evil. These individuals are the ones we see on television—cold-blooded murderers and serial killers, drug dealers, pimps, gangsters and mobsters, and black-market salesmen who roam the dark recesses of the underworld. These folks also believe that, because they act this way, everyone else around them must be just as dishonest and devious, so they trust no one but themselves. Many parents who raise such children without proper discipline have committed the sin of "provoking their children to wrath" (Eph. 6:4 KJV). Amazingly enough, the very first example of an antisocial was the first son of the first parents who ever lived. His name was Cain!

Think about it. Adam and Eve had no experience in raising children before they had Cain. They both had the knowledge of good and evil, but they had no understanding of how to apply that knowledge in raising children. When Cain was born Eve was overjoyed (Gen. 4:1 NLT). What a shock it must have been when Cain started showing signs of the sin nature his parents had begun in the garden of Eden. Perhaps their guilt kept them from disciplining their son when he sinned. Whatever the reason, Cain grew up doing his own thing and disregarding the rules of his parents and the laws of God (Gen. 4). When he faced the consequences for his actions (namely, God's rejection of his offerings), he became very angry.

As he brooded, the Lord approached and questioned him: "'Why are you so angry?' the LORD asked Cain. 'Why do you look so dejected? You will be accepted if you do what is right. But if you refuse to do what is right, then watch out! Sin is crouching at the door, eager to control you. But you must subdue it and be its master'" (Gen. 4:6–7).

The analogy God used was exact. Cain had to control the beast inside him, or else it would devour him. That is precisely what happened. Cain's anger turned into a violent homicidal rage, and he murdered his brother, Abel, out of jealousy. Because of his sin, he lost everything: his job, his home, and eventually his entire family, who were destroyed in the great flood. Hebrews 12:7 (NLT) asks, "Who ever heard of a child who is never disciplined by its father?" We have. And it is not pretty!

We need to be grateful for God's discipline in our lives. Without it we will become complacent and lazy, never fully experiencing the power of God in our lives. The next time you feel as if God is being too hard on you, remember that His love is what drives His discipline. Do not settle for less when God has so much more waiting for those who obey Him.

20

A Personal Training Plan

Lance Armstrong is the famous cyclist who has won the Tour de France, not once, but seven times! The Tour is a bicycle race that has been described by some as the equivalent of running twenty marathons in twenty days. In order to reach peak performance, Lance must have every ounce of fat, bone, and muscle measured and accounted for. A reporter once asked Lance if he felt it was necessary to endure not only the daily prodding and poking, but also to adhere so rigidly to his strict training schedules. "Depends whether you want to win," he replied. "I do. The Tour is a two-thousand-mile race, and people sometimes win by one minute. Or less. One minute in nearly a month of suffering isn't that much. So the people who win are the ones willing to suffer the most."[1]

As Christians we have an opportunity to run in a much bigger race than the Tour, with a far better prize than a little statue for the mantel at home or the fame and fortune we lose so quickly. The Bible tells us how we should run in this awesome race called life: "Don't you realize that in a race everyone runs, but only one person gets the prize? *So run to win!* All athletes are disciplined in their training. They do it to win a prize that will fade away, but we do it for an eternal prize" (1 Cor. 9:24–25 NLT, emphasis ours).

As we grow into spiritual adults and realize the magnitude of this "eternal prize," we become more motivated to discipline ourselves to attain it, even though we know the training will be grueling. We become less like wayward children and more like hardened athletes, driven by the prize rather than the punishment, fearing not the pain but the possibility of missing out, being benched, or standing on the sidelines as observers.

My (Dr. Henderson's) wife, Angela, is an avid runner. In Charleston, South Carolina, they have a run every year called the Cooper River Bridge Run. Thousands of people come from all over the United States and the rest of the world to participate. Several years ago I went to watch Angela run in that race. Because of the huge number of people participating, it can take ten minutes or more after the gun is fired for the last of the runners to reach the starting line. People from all walks of life come out to participate. Some are serious competitors; others are just out to enjoy the fun. Everyone who crosses the finish line is met by cheering crowds and upbeat inspirational music amplified by a huge sound system.

Once everyone has finished the race, the real celebration begins. Hundreds of booths are set up with free samples and goodies, delicious foods, and grab-bag prizes. The award ceremonies are followed by more celebrations and music.

I remember standing near the finish line and cheering loudly as my wife crossed the finish line. Angela had a great finishing time despite the long wait at the starting line, and I felt proud of her. But I also felt another emotion: left out. There was something about being just a spectator that did not quite do it for me. I could not fully identify with the joy, the excitement, and the good kind of pride the racers felt as they crossed the finish line and heard their names announced. I made up my mind that day that the next race I went to would be one I was running in myself. But I could not just go out and run a race. I had to train for it, and that required a great deal of time and suffering, especially for how out of shape I was. What I witnessed that day at the Cooper River Bridge Run inspired me to push through the pain. By the following year, Angela and I were running races together and having twice as much fun!

Are you willing to suffer for the prize? Are you willing to discipline your body into subjection as Paul said (1 Cor. 9:27) not just physically, but mentally, emotionally, and spiritually? Are you ready to use the right training manual (the Bible), the right coaches (loyal friends and family, pastors, even Christian counselors or psychiatrists, if necessary), the right exercises (daily times of prayer and Bible study, church attendance, practicing the fruit of the Spirit), and the right clothes and equipment (the full armor of God, described in Ephesians 6) in order to win the ultimate prize? If you are, then it is time to begin your training, but first a word of encouragement.

Life is not a sprint but a long-distance marathon. In a sprint everyone lines up next to each other, side by side in comparative positions and stances. At the finish a picture is taken to see who came in first. In a marathon, runners start in waves and have no way to measure their performance against the runners around them as they negotiate the twists, turns, and uphill climbs through forests and mountains, on busy highways and solitary footpaths. The only thing they have to go on is their own personal stopwatch, which they have used throughout their own training, continually trying to beat their own times. In a sprint you can see the finish line; in a marathon you can't. In a sprint there is no room for mistakes—if you fall you are out. But in a marathon, you can stumble and fall, get back on your feet, and still win the race.

So we must discipline ourselves for a marathon, not getting discouraged because others might be ahead of us or because we cannot see the finish line or because someone running beside us looks better than we do. It is a race between you and the eternal time keeper, God Himself. And not only is He rooting for you, but He wants to help you win! So be encouraged. Do not quit because of the pain. Keep moving forward. The race will be over before you know it.

Getting Started

There are a number of things we need to run our race well, and the book of Hebrews gives us a good list with which to start:

> Therefore, since we are surrounded by such a huge crowd of witnesses to
> the life of faith, let us strip off every weight that slows us down, especially

the sin that so easily trips us up. And let us run with endurance the race God has set before us. We do this by keeping our eyes on Jesus, the champion who initiates and perfects our faith. Because of the joy awaiting him, he endured the cross, disregarding its shame. Now he is seated in the place of honor beside God's throne. Think of all the hostility he endured from sinful people; then you won't become weary and give up. (Heb. 12:1–3 NLT)

Who Is in Your Crowd of Witnesses?

What would a race be without spectators cheering us on? If you have ever competed in any kind of a sporting event, you know that the size of your cheering section makes a huge difference in how well you perform. In team sports we describe this as the "home field advantage." The same is true in life. It is easier to be disciplined in our walk with God when we know that people around us are watching and cheering for us. In long-distance races, those who have already finished will often return to the sidelines and cheer on other runners who still have a ways to go. Their words of encouragement mean more because they know the course and how much farther we have to go.

In the race of life, we have a huge cheering section. Hebrews 11 gives us a long list of racers who have finished strong, and we have their testimonies to teach and encourage us; but we can also look to others—more current heroes of the faith whose stories we read or even witness personally as they touch our lives in big and small ways every day. These will be the people to whom we dedicate our trophies at the end of the race before placing them at the feet of Jesus.

If you are struggling to live a life of discipline, you must find a group of people to hold you accountable in your training. Those who enter treatment programs for various addictions learn this lesson right off the bat. Their group meetings are not just for socializing. They establish a support network of people who can teach, encourage, and challenge each other in the struggle to stay clean. Along with attending these groups, we encourage patients to find a sponsor or mentor, someone who has been through the pain of addiction and has succeeded in overcoming it. They are the kind of people you can call at any hour of the day or night and will be there for you, challenging you to keep moving forward even when you fall. Christians need this kind of support as we seek to live lives that are honoring to God. Satan would like nothing more than to keep us isolated and alone. Do not let this happen to you.

Carry Only the Bare Essentials

In a long-distance race, every ounce of weight you carry affects your time. That is why it is essential to carry only what you need to win. In a triathlon you need a suit that is tight enough for the swim, padded enough for the bike, and breathable enough for the run. You also need the right goggles, shoes, helmet, and bike. Engineers and scientists have developed lighter and faster equipment to help racers beat their records, and these competitors often spend thousands of dollars on this equipment in order to take off just a few tenths of a second from their times.

In life sin weighs us down. No amount of medicine will heal a person suffering from depression or anxiety if he or she is actively living against God's rules for the road. That is why, as Christian psychiatrists, we consider an individual's spiritual well-being just as important, if not more important, than their physical or emotional well-being. If we see areas in their lives where they are giving in to temptation, we lovingly challenge them to throw off those weights and change their strides.

Sin is the heaviest burden we carry, but there are also other things that weigh us down. Reread the section of this book on loss, and you will find that any of the items listed in chapter 14 can become burdens if we do not hold on to them loosely: our time, our significance, our loves, our luxuries, and our control. We can also be held back by our emotions—guilt, anger, and fear. To throw off these weights, we must go to God each morning and ask Him to remove from our hearts and minds everything that will keep us from making it through the day, "Casting your cares upon Him for He cares for you!" (1 Peter 5:7).

How Is Your Endurance?

Once we have stripped down to the bare essentials for the race, we must build our endurance. Some of us have been training a lot longer than others, so our endurance levels are different. One of the best ways to build endurance is to allow enough time for your muscles to rest after a hard workout. Any personal trainer will tell you that you cannot do the same routine every day and expect results. You need to switch it up, challenging different muscles and letting others recover. In life we may overcome a particular challenge only to find a different sort waiting for us on the other side. That is okay. Do not become discouraged. God wants to strengthen us in all areas of our lives and build the kind of endurance that can withstand any potential obstacle confidently.

For some people, taking a break from the busyness of life may be the first area that requires more discipline, especially in our culture. Our modern technologies have not made life any more relaxing. They have simply sped up the pace of life.

If we wanted to, we could go the whole day with noise. Many of us do. Clock radios wake us up from our sleep. Those irritating morning talk-show hosts who burst out laughing at anything and everything keep us company as we get ready in the morning and drive to work. Nobody should be that happy at 5:30 a.m.! (Sorry, everyone has a pet peeve!) Once we get to work, we go from meeting to meeting, socializing at the water cooler, talking to clients, making phone calls, and cutting deals, all while subconsciously listening to elevator music strategically designed to make us more productive. The drive home is more of the same. At home we talk to our spouses, play with the kids, and watch the news before collapsing into bed, trying to catch a few hours of sleep before the cycle starts all over again.

Does that sound like a typical day for you? Maybe you need to work on the discipline of quiet meditation, letting God speak to you through prayer and reading His Word. Take a deep breath from the business of life and let Him nourish you with the spiritual food necessary to grow strong minds, muscles, and bones. "The Bible—it does a body good!" You cannot have endurance without it.

Keep Your Eyes on Your Hero

All of us have had heroes growing up, whether in the sports world, the music world, the entertainment world, the political or military world, even the spiritual world; but there is only one Hero we need to fix our eyes upon if we are to finish strong in the race of life: Jesus Christ. As we press forward, we should seek to emulate His technique, His training methods, and His instructions. In the 1990s, the phrase "What would Jesus do?" became popular with young people. Although the phrase's message was soon overshadowed by its marketing, we should not let that stop us from asking it. Hebrews says that Jesus endured the pain of the cross and disregarded its shame. Setting aside comfort, He reached out to humanity, knowing full well that many would be hostile toward Him. He endured it in order to obtain the glory that was waiting for Him in heaven and the relationship He wanted with us.

When we become comfortable in our relationships and avoid reaching out to others, we ignore Jesus' example. One of the saddest commentaries about the Christian church today came from a secular professor of psychiatry who could not understand Christian isolationism. "What irritates me about Christians," he said, "is the fact that they close themselves off from everyone else around them. It's like 'as long as you do things our way, we'll include you, but if not, we want nothing to do with you.' There are so many good things that these big Christian megachurches could be doing to reach out to people in their communities, but instead they just cater to their own. It's like you have to accept Jesus or else they won't help you."

In some ways we can understand his frustration. We have become so comfortable in our Christian churches, Christian schools, Christian small groups, Christian cruises, Christian resorts, Christian sports leagues, and so on (none of which in and of themselves are bad) that we have forgotten our calling to "go into all the world and preach the good news" (Mark 16:15 NIV). Notice that Jesus did not say, "Stand on the balcony of your ivory towers and shout to people to come in." He said we must go, get involved in people's lives, and share the love of Christ. On an individual level, this takes a lot of discipline, but the people we inspire to join us in the race will be well worth the sacrifices.

Fitness Inventory

Now that we know what is required to finish the race, the next step is to take a fitness inventory. What areas of your life need some good old-fashioned discipline? It is time to do some self-analysis and determine what spiritual muscles need pumping up. It is time to work up a spiritual sweat. And we need to ask ourselves some hard questions that, when answered, can give us power to experience the discipline of God with spiritual toughness. Here is a list of six basic spiritual disciplines. Take a look at the list and ask God to give you the motivation to do some spiritual "reps" with these weighty practices:

1. *Prayer*. As we have mentioned, prayer is essential for a healthy, powerful spiritual life. You have to talk to your coach when you are training for a marathon. This is where we get our motivation to keep going!

2. *Meditation*. This is like spiritual weight lifting. This form of meditation is not like what is taught by dialectic behavioral therapists and yoga experts. We are not to remove all thoughts from our minds during meditation. Rather, we are to replace those unhealthy or sinful thoughts with healthy, God-honoring thoughts. Think about Scripture; weigh it over and over in your mind; practice lifting it to your consciousness so that you can build endurance and strength during times of testing.

3. *Fasting or Abstaining*. This is not simply avoiding meat or other select products during Lent. Good athletes adhere to a strict dietary regimen with the essential balance of proteins, fat, vitamins, and carbohydrates. They avoid empty calories. There are any number of things from which we should "fast" if they are preventing us from experiencing a deeper, more intimate relationship with Christ. They might be television, Internet addiction, pornography, books or movies that fail to nourish us spiritually, draining relationships. The specifics are between

you and the Lord. Ask Him to make you aware of what possessions or activities are getting in the way of your relationship with Him, and fast from them.

4. *Submission.* During the race you have to follow the rules set up by the Creator. No athlete wins a race by doing it his or her own way, apart from the rules. You can certainly try to do it your own way, but you will get severely injured when you try to lift heavy weights without proper form.

5. *Service.* This is like practice runs. It is where you test your abilities and determine what is working and what is not. When we serve others our weaknesses are made clear to us: our pride, fears, impatience, unkindness, lack of love, and so on. After a hard day of service, it may be necessary to go back to the locker room and review with your Coach an area or two where you need to work a little harder. One area of service we often overlook is serving our families at home. If we are not careful, we can neglect our families for the sake of Christian ministries or charitable causes. We need to learn how to have a healthy balance.

6. *Public Worship.* Public worship is like pep rallies before the games. At pep rallies we cheer, praise, and "pump up" the athletes who are about to play, but for Christians the opposite is also true. We get together and cheer, praise, and "lift up" the Creator of the game, thanking Him for His presence throughout and worshipping Him for the victory that is already ours. As runners in this race, we can start celebrating before the race is even over, knowing that God has already given us "the victory through our Lord Jesus Christ" (1 Cor. 15:57). It takes discipline, however, to be reminded of this. Hebrews 10:25 tells us the discipline he expects in this regard—to not forsake regularly getting together with believers to study, fellowship, pray, sing hymns and spiritual songs—to be part of a team rather than loners.

As you read this list, you may be feeling overwhelmed. "I don't practice any of these disciplines," you may be lamenting. Do not get discouraged! Ask God to give you the strength to begin training and then start slowly, be patient, and remember that you are not doing this alone.

The Consequences of Complacency

As we finish the story of Lot, consider what happens when complacency and comfort take precedence in our lives. As we mentioned, Lot was more concerned about his comfort than about being set apart for God. Because of this, he and his family suffered greatly. He lost everything in the destruction of Sodom and Gomorrah, including his wife and his daughters' fiancés. The pain does not end there. Lot's two daughters, having become so enmeshed in the immoral culture of Sodom and Gomorrah, rationalized with each other that they both had to commit incest with their father in order to continue his lineage. The two nations that came from their seed were the Moabites and the Ammonites, two of the wickedest nations bordering the nation of Israel. The grim reality of complacency and comfort could not be clearer. The Bible says that Lot himself was a righteous man (2 Peter 2:6–8 NLT), but his complacency cost him everything he had.

This should be a lesson to all of us who think it is easier to sit back and live "comfortable" lives as Christians. The longer we do, the more tormented our souls become. Eventually we realize that the comforts of the world are no comforts at all. Instead, we need to realize that this world is not our final destination. We need to keep moving through the Enchanted Ground of this world to our final resting places. When we seek first the kingdom of God, "all these things" including comfort (or, more important, peace) in difficult circumstances and the security of being in the center of God's will for us will be added to our lives (Matt. 6:33).

The Need to Keep Moving

The results of her blood work and the frankness of Dr. Gupta's words hit home to Donita the seriousness of her situation. She knew now that this was a matter of life and death. She joined First Place, a biblically based weight-loss program at a nearby church where she found a group of women to hold her accountable. She began to replace her desire for food with a desire for the Word of God. She realized that her body did not belong to her, but to God, and He wanted her to take care of it so that she could use it to honor Him. As she began to experience His grace in her life, she was able to bounce back from her failures more easily and continue moving forward.

The first day she tried to exercise, Donita remembered only being able to make it down to the end of the block and back. She felt very discouraged, but something inside her told her to keep moving. Every day she went a little farther and a little faster until one day, to her own amazement, she started to jog. After two years of daily exercise and a commitment to healthy eating habits, Donita had lost a hundred and fifty pounds. Most of her medical problems had cleared up on their own, and she had more energy to give to others than ever before.

When I (Dr. Henderson) asked her what kept her going, she said she kept reminding herself of a story her grandfather told her years ago about growing up in Norway. "He said that in a snowstorm, someone who was lost would experience an almost 'enchanting' urge to lie down in the snow and go to sleep. It was in that moment that they were in the greatest danger of death, but if they just kept moving, no matter how slowly, they would stay alive. I knew the same was true for me."

Finding Purpose Beyond Your Discipline

Hopefully, after having read this section, you realize why God is so passionate about disciplining His children. So do not get too comfortable, and do not get upset with God if you notice Him pulling you back to Himself through the pain of discipline. Keep on moving forward on your life's journey, knowing that God will see you safely to your journey's end. Here are some practical points to consider as you do:

1. *God's discipline is grounded in love.* It may be hard to believe this while we are going through discipline, but it is still true. Everything He does for or to us as His children is for our good. Ask God to help you see your difficult circumstances through His eyes and not your own (Heb. 12:6).

2. *Your desires determine your attitude toward discipline.* If you want something badly enough, you will do whatever it takes to get it. First, ask God to rein in your desires to line up with His. *Then* ask Him to give you the desires of your heart (Ps. 37:4; Heb. 12:11).

3. *We all need a wake-up call from time to time.* It is human nature to become comfortable in a routine, no matter how destructive. Sometimes we need a loving nudge to get going! Ask God to keep you sensitive to His voice so that He does not have to shout to get your attention (Deut. 4:30–31).

4. *Develop a training plan of your own.* It is much easier to stay motivated when you have an established plan complete with checkpoints for achieving success. Make God the source of your strength and you will never burn out (Rom. 8:31; Heb. 12:1).

5. *Remember to keep moving.* We all have setbacks. During those moments the key is to avoid the urge to stop and lie down. Do not let discouragement cripple you. Keep heading toward your goal, no matter how slowly you think you are moving (Isa. 40:31).

Set aside some personal time to consider your own situation in the light of these truths. Then answer the following questions truthfully in order to establish the groundwork for growing strong through the experience of discipline in your life.

1. How has your experience with your own parents' discipline helped or hindered your view of God's discipline in your life? What do you think are the similarities and differences between the way He disciplines and the way your parents discipline? Can you back up your answers with any specific Bible references?

2. How can you stay focused each day on sanctification over security, purity over position, and commitment over conformity?

3. What circumstances are you going through right now that may be a wake-up call from God? How are you responding to it?

4. What goals do you want to achieve spiritually, emotionally, and physically? What steps are you taking on a daily basis to achieve them?

5. What are the kinds of setbacks during the day that make you want to give up on your goals? (For example, not going to the gym today because you forgot yesterday or not doing your

Bible study because you are already four chapters behind.) What do you tell yourself in those moments? How can you change your attitude to get yourself back on the bandwagon quicker?

Part 6

FAILURE

"I have overcome the world."

—JOHN 16:33

21

Beyond Failure

Mind-numbing pain: there was no other way to describe it. He had been running for hours, first in a frenzied sprint, then at a forced march, and now a desperate stagger. Having started out to escape his circumstances, he had kept moving in a vain attempt to find distance from his own feelings of worthlessness and shame. There was no final destination in his mind. He just wanted total isolation, somewhere he could lie down undisturbed to die. As evening came, the last of his will to move faded with the setting sun, and he collapsed in the lengthening shadows. He had brought no food. No water. What man who wants to die does? Now, however, his body groaned for nourishment. This was not going to be easy.

"God," he whispered, "please . . . please, just let me die. I am nothing . . . a failure. I can't live with myself like this. I just want to go to sleep and never wake up."

He waited for an answer, but none came. Even God, he thought, must have been embarrassed by him. How had it come to this? The agony of the question would keep his mind racing even after his body found rest. Not even sleep could free him from this living nightmare. The pain of his failure was too great.

Failure comes to all of us. We fail to live up to the expectations of others or ourselves and then suffer the disappointment. We fail to accomplish childhood dreams and then feel empty and directionless for the future.

We fail to recognize the dangers of our poor choices and then find ourselves stuck in a mess of our own creating. Sometimes we do everything right and everything still turns out wrong! When that happens, it is hard not to feel like the brunt of one big cosmic joke. No matter what circumstances may have led us there, the barren wasteland of failure always looks the same. We find ourselves at the bottom of things looking up.

Elijah knew what that was like. Though he is known as one of the greatest Old Testament prophets who ever lived, one of his finest moments was followed by his darkest ever.

During a terrible drought that had plagued the nation of Israel for three and a half years, Elijah stood on Mount Carmel, a coastal mountain range in northern Israel, and participated in one of the biggest upsets history has ever known. He stood toe to toe with 850 heathen prophets of the false gods Asherah and Baal, challenged them to a battle against his God, Jehovah, and won! It must have been an awesome rush, but the feeling was not going to last.

Just a short time later, when Elijah realized that his moment in the spotlight had done nothing to change the hearts or minds of Israel's leaders, he found himself running to save his life and at the same time wishing he could die. How did this happen? We believe that, like many of us, Elijah had the wrong perspective on failure and success.

In this section we want to take an up close and personal look at what it means to fail and what it means to succeed in the eyes of God. We believe you can find just as much purpose beyond the pain of your failures as you can in a lifetime of successes.

The Upside—Success

Life often seems like a roller-coaster ride. Most of us have had top-of-the-world experiences: a marriage, a job promotion, a prestigious award, the birth of a child, a memorable vacation, or a service opportunity. These experiences can lead to a tremendous sense of accomplishment and fulfillment that we should celebrate. They give us purpose and direction for our lives, as well as hope for the future, but they can also create greater responsibilities and challenges, even subsequent pain and sadness when the novelty or good feelings wear off.

I (Dr. Henderson) can still remember the day I was accepted to medical school. I had applied without having yet obtained my bachelor's degree—something my advisers had told me was a foolish thing to do. But I felt strongly that the Lord was calling me to medical school, and I was attempting to cut some time off of what would already be a very long journey. Feeling down and discouraged by several disappointments, I knew the odds were stacked against me and that my chances were small.

One afternoon after finishing a challenging microbiology exam, I was lying on the couch at home when the doorbell rang. The postman handed me a certified letter from Wright State University, my first choice of medical schools. When I opened the letter and saw the word "Congratulations," I ran out the front door of my house and started sprinting back and forth, whooping and hollering. I could not believe it! I give God all the glory for that special moment in my life. The lesson I learned was humbling: when God has something for you to do, nothing can stop Him!

The Downside—Reality

I was so excited, so happy, so ecstatic that I wanted the feeling to last forever, but it did not. The grueling reality of four long years in medical school hit me like a punch in the gut just a few short weeks after starting. This was going to be painful. Though I had praised God for His powerful presence in my life just a few months before, I now began to question Him. Had He really gotten this right? He had, of course, but He was teaching me a lesson just as valuable as the one I learned on the day of my acceptance: "I am as present in your failures as I am in your victories. You still need Me!" The hardest thing I learned in medical school was not gross anatomy, microbiology, neuroscience, or pharmacology. It was that my own human abilities had limits and I was susceptible to failure just as everybody else is. Whatever arrogance I had inside me was beaten out during those four years. It took a lot of work to continue trusting that God knew what He was doing with my life.

Maybe you are feeling the same way. You have had some great successes in life, and expecting the sense of exhilaration to last forever, you have been blindsided by greater challenges that hold more opportunities to fail. Where God once seemed totally in control, He now feels distant and uninvolved. Do not be discouraged! He can use even our greatest failures for His glory if we will turn them over to Him. It is all a matter of perspective.

A Matter of Perspective

There are two types of failures. The first is an event that does not accomplish its intended purpose. For example, Molly plans the perfect outdoor sur-prise party for her best friend, Eva's, fiftieth birthday, but Eva finds out about it three days early, it rains on the actual day of the party, and only ten of the thirty people Molly invited show up. These kinds of events, when they occur in our lives, may seem like failures, but by whose definition? Eva certainly did not care. She was so appreciative of her friend's efforts that she did not take any notice of the glitches. This is a classic example that failure is in the eye of the beholder. Failed events may not have accomplished *our* intended purposes, but could they have accomplished others'? Could they have accomplished God's? We shall see.

The second kind of failure are people who believe, because of a series of mistakes or sins committed or successes unachieved, that they are fail-ures, destined to remain stuck in their situations forever: an addict who has relapsed after ten years of sobriety; a mother who feels pressured by her church friends to homeschool but constantly loses her temper with a strong-willed child; a daughter who cannot seem to win the approval of a distant father; perhaps a friend who cannot go deep in his relationships because of what others will discover about his past. These individuals define themselves according to standards they or the world have placed upon them. Instead of allowing themselves the grace God offers them, they beat themselves up day in and day out because of their perceived failures. Eventually their thinking becomes self-fulfilling prophecy. The addict believes he cannot regain sobriety, so he never tries. The mother refuses to give herself a break from her child, so they tear each other apart. The daughter cannot separate her own sense of success from her father's and always doubts the praise of others. The insecure friend always feels abandoned and unlovable because others perceive him as cold and aloof. These people enter every situation believing they will fail, and so they do.

Many people achieve success in one area of their lives, only to realize that the sacrifices required to reach that standard have caused them to fail elsewhere in their lives. We have all heard stories of the successful business-man who has been broken by the pain of a failing family, the successful athlete who has been consumed by the power of drugs taken to enhance his performance, or the beautiful woman who has suffered from anorexia or bulimia in her quest for physical perfection. The list could go on. The pres-sures of society have made such stories more and more commonplace.

I (Dr. Meier) remember growing up in lower-middle-class America. As a kid, I used to feel like a nobody. My mother had a third-grade education, and my father was a carpenter. When Dad drove me to school, I used excuses to get him to drop me off where the fewest students would see me getting out of our old car. When I entered college, I studied hard and suc-ceeded greatly. I had the highest GPA out of five thousand students at my university, got a scholarship to a graduate program at Michigan State University, and went on to medical school and finished my psychiatry resi-dency at Duke University, one of the top two psychiatry programs in America. Each of these levels of success felt good for a moment, but greater challenges always loomed in the distance, along with more opportunities to fail. The bar was always being raised, and every step I took on the ladder of success had me looking over my shoulder to see how far I could fall. Not until I got some therapy, quit the rat race of life, and shifted my focus to loving and being loved, did I find the truest form of success, the kind that remains constant despite the natural ups and downs of life.

Our measure of success dictates our response to failure. If our mea-sure of success is based on worldly standards, then our emotional highs and lows will be bounced around by our circumstances like a basketball in an NBA playoff game. Christians would do well to consider this. If we are not all as famous as Billy Graham or Mother Teresa before we die, if we do not have a building or highway named after us, if people are not writing books about our lives, or if we have not made millions or reached millions for Christ, then somehow we believe we have failed—we must not have been good enough or faithful enough for God to use us. In reality this measure of success is based on worldly standards, not God's.

Do not misunderstand. We are not condoning mediocrity, especially when it comes to our quest for Christlikeness. We are to strive for excellence in everything God gives us to do, but even godly perfection does not guarantee worldly success. And even if we achieve it, it may not be all we expected it to be.

Oprah Winfrey has had guests on her show at various times discussing the pitfalls of sudden success, whether through business, the lottery, sports, or other venues. The most common complaints are centered on the changes that occur in relationships. People they once thought were friends became enemies, and new "friends" suddenly appear out of nowhere. If these "successful" people have not mastered the art of relationships, they will soon find their material successes have only created more headaches in their dealings with people. Many become disillusioned with human sincerity and find it difficult to trust others. Thus was born the saying, "It's lonely at the top."

Further, success often breeds entitlement, arrogance, and bitterness toward those who are unwilling to give in to our wishes or demands. Success in *one* area of our life fools us into thinking that we know the answers to *all* of life's questions, and we lose our ability to be teachable.

Failure is no picnic, but most people are resilient enough to recover from it and actually become better people as a result. They usually come out of failure more insightful, humbler, and more in touch with the meaning of true success. We all know stories of people who have found their true purposes in life through their failures. Dave Ramsey went bankrupt before realizing his calling to help others get out of debt.[1] He is now the author of several best-selling books on financial planning and hosts his own national radio and television show. Lou Holtz's average size and abilities on the football field drove him to the sidelines where he pursued coaching, a career path that would make him a household name in the sports world.[2] Abraham Lincoln, one of the greatest presidents in the history of the United States, failed at several attempts to gain political office before he finally succeeded.

Most of us will never have such high-profile experiences, but God is just as interested in our stories, such as these:

- He remembers the young girl who got pregnant out of wedlock and had an abortion, now volunteering at a crisis pregnancy center where she encourages other women to appreciate the life they have inside them.
- His eyes are on the inmate whose murderous hands now open the Word of God each day to teach his fellow prisoners about the forgiveness of Christ.
- He smiles on the businessman who never amounted to anything, except in the eyes of his wife of fifty years and their godly children and grandchildren
- He loves the missionary who died in a foreign land without a single convert of which to boast.
- He admires the musician who never fulfilled her dream of being a concert pianist, but whose arthritic hands still help lead the worship services at her church.

Our greatest failures can still hold purpose if we use them for Him.

Have you experienced failure? You may be at your wit's end. There are a number of questions running through your mind, such as, *Where did I go wrong?* or *How could I have fixed this?* or *Why, God? Why did you have to let this happen?* A loved one died of cancer when you prayed for healing. You lost your job when you wanted a promotion. A rebellious child has defied you despite all your efforts to raise him with love. Abusive parents were never satisfied with your attempts to please them and obey. If you have ever experienced the night season of failure, then you can identify with the disappointment, even depression. Yet God is not finished with you. He can take your perceived failures and turn them into a mighty power that will bring *true* success in your life. Let us discover the light of purpose beyond our failures as we take heart from God's dealings with us when we fail.

22

God's Gentle Touch

God is not like others when it comes to dealing with a failure. Everybody wants to be the star quarterback's best friend. Everybody loves a beauty queen, but a failure is nobody's buddy. Though we pity him, we are not inclined to spend time with him. After all, his failures might bring us down. We make excuses for him, try to ignore him, or even reprimand him, but we are not as quick to identify with his pain. God, however, responds differently. In His eyes, no event is a failure if it draws the individual closer to Him, and no person is a failure if he learns from his mistakes and moves on toward true success. Whether we have failed once or all of our lives, He will never count us out. He will never throw in the towel and say, "Enough's enough." He will continue to be faithful and will use our failures to bring great successes if we will place them in His hands.

Sadly, many of us isolate ourselves from God when we fail. We run from His wrath rather than run toward His mercy and grace. In doing so we drift further and further away until we can no longer hear His voice. We anticipate the kind of conditional love we have received from others, but His love for His children is unconditional. Remember Elijah? In the midst of his failures, God did not scold him or mock him. Instead, God sent an angel to touch him and provide the strength to keep moving forward.

When people are oblivious or refuse to admit their failures (especially with sin), it is important to correct them or allow them to experience the consequences of their poor choices. Most people who fail, however, know it. They feel guilty enough inside and do not need someone to remind them of how far they have fallen short. Yet how many of us know parents who have verbally abused their children when they fail? We have all seen the father who, trying to live out his sports dreams vicariously through his son, stands on the sidelines after a big loss, chewing him out, destroying any pleasure the boy might have had from the game itself. We counsel many couples who cannot seem to refrain from digging up their spouses' dirt during an argument and throwing it in their faces. There are those who hold on to the past in order to manipulate the future, but God does not operate that way. Nor does He gloat over our failings. He is not the kind to say, "I told you so." Some people love to see the man on top come crashing down. Their own jealousy over another's successes makes them happy to see these successful people finally trip up and "get what they deserve." No, God does not respond like that either. Finally, though He may seem absent during times of failure, He does not disappear as many of our friends do. He never feels awkward around us or wonders what to say or how to help. In fact, God often makes Himself known to us in times of failure by meeting some of our most basic needs.

The Need for Nourishment

Sometimes we tend to overspiritualize God's interventions in our lives, but there are plenty of examples in the Bible where God meets the physical needs of people who are suffering before He ever addresses their spiritual needs. For Elijah, God provided bread and water and a deep, restful sleep. For David, He provided caves for shelter and protection against Saul. Jesus provided food for five thousand, a large catch of fish for His disciples, and even wine for a party! In this day and age, we strongly believe that God has provided medications for our nourishment and relief. Sadly, there is still a great deal of stigma in the Christian community and elsewhere concerning the use of medications to relieve suffering. Despite the clear evidence that our emotions are regulated in part by physical processes in the brain, many have refused to accept the gift God has given us in medications that have the power to heal us physically so that we can grow deeper spiritually.

I (Dr. Henderson) had a patient many years ago by the name of Clive Holden. Clive had grown up all his life believing he was a failure. As a child he was always in trouble. As much as he tried, he could not keep his mouth shut or sit still for anything. He wanted to please his parents but was so impulsive that he usually reacted without thinking. The spankings got worse and worse as his parents' frustration mounted with what they saw as his blatant disregard for their authority. Just think of the frustration that began to fester in Clive's heart and mind, frustration with himself for his failures and frustration with others for not understanding that he really was trying his best. This went on for years. Teachers hated him and other students avoided him like the plague. He began to expect failure everywhere he went, and his anxiety slowly turned to helplessness. When Clive came to see me in my office, he was a grown man, but the little boy inside him surfaced as he wept over the story he had to tell. "I just want someone to believe in me," he said.

The diagnosis of attention-deficit/hyperactivity disorder (ADHD) was just starting to be treated in adults, and when I started Clive on a stimulant, he literally described it as a miracle! For the first time he could read a book all the way through. He was even able to go back to school and get a degree, something I am sure his teachers from elementary school thought impossible. What a rush it was for me to see the change. All I did was write a prescription, but God healed Clive that day. Do not let anyone tell you that God does not care about our physical needs.

God also nourishes us through His Word. Jeremiah 15:16 says, "Your words were found, and I ate them. And your word was to me the joy and rejoicing of my heart." I (Dr. Henderson) recently counseled a patient on the importance of memorizing Scripture. When we go through stressful experiences in life, it is so helpful to have God's Word in the forefront of our minds and on the tips of our tongues. This will not happen automatically. I often write a verse on a note card and practice saying it four times a day, almost like taking a prescription. When I have major successes or high points in my life, I write them with a permanent marker on small polished stones that I keep in a decorative box on my desk. Every so often, especially when I am feeling discouraged, I pull them out and read them one by one to remind myself of all that God has done for me. This gives me confidence that He will see me through the current trial I am facing. Music is another way God speaks to us. When we listen to music that is uplifting and positive, it sticks in our heads and comes back to us when we are feeling low. God can use all of these things to comfort us in our failures.

The Need for Touch

Another gift God provides for us in our failure is the gift of touch. Touch is an amazing thing. Many times it provides more than words of encouragement or advice. Touch demonstrates a caring heart, loving affection, and unconditional acceptance in the midst of great pain.

Unfortunately, we have lost much of our ability to use touch effectively in our society, men especially. Our culture has made a mess of the meaning behind touch. Passages in the Bible like the story of David and Jonathan "embracing each other" are distorted to represent a kind of homosexual relationship. We become uncomfortable with the thought of John, who referred to himself as "the disciple whom Jesus loved," "leaning on the bosom of Jesus" (John 13:23 KJV) during the Last Supper. In this way we have robbed ourselves of a very valuable form of encouragement and affection. We are still floored by stories of people who were never touched as children except while being abused, but it is never too late to experience the power of godly touch: a simple hug, a pat on the back, a two-handed handshake, an arm around the shoulder, or a squeeze on the neck. It does not take much to show someone without a word that you care.

Touch, however, is more than just physical. People who have experienced failures in their lives need to feel the presence of others around them, emotionally and spiritually. They need a gentle touch of sympathy, the closeness of people who are quick to listen and slow to speak

(James 1:19), to be bathed in prayer by someone who knows their struggle (5:16). They need to know that someone cares and is willing to help in any way possible.

The Need for True Friendship

One blessing God gives us in the midst of failure is the knowledge of our true friends. These are the people who continue to believe in us. They sympathize with our pain and give us hope when we have none. They gently pull us out of our misery by first crawling into the pit of failure with us, but they also do not let us stay there for long.

Nacho Libre is one of those movies you either love or you hate. It is filled with slapstick antics and random, senseless, out-of-nowhere comedy. Nacho is a Spanish monk living in a monastery and caring for a pack of mischievous but lovable orphans. Nacho dreams of becoming a professional wrestler, or *luchador*, as they are called in Mexico. The problem is he is horrible at it. He and his sidekick, Esqueleto, get beat in every match, but because of their passion for the sport, the crowds love them. When the other monks find out that Nacho has been wrestling on the side, they kick him out of the monastery. Depressed and alone, feeling the frustration of his continued failures, Nacho decides to head out into the "wilderness" to die. (In reality, he only ventures a few hundred yards out of town!) But Esqueleto will not give up on his friend. He searches him out in the wilderness to encourage Nacho.

As silly as the movie is, it teaches us a good lesson about how God expects us to deal with people who are suffering from the pain of failure. First, we need to search them out, because they often try to hide their failures in their own wilderness of solitude and secrecy. Then we need to encourage them with gentle kindness as they struggle through their guilt and weakness. Finally, we need to speak the truth in love, noting the good that still exists inside them, and help them to envision who they can still become. It also reminds those of us who are in the midst of failure that help is usually not as far away as we pretend. When we fail, it is tempting to isolate ourselves from the rest of the world, but this is the absolute worst thing we can do. Every Holmes needs a Watson. Every Batman needs an Alfred. Every Calvin needs a Hobbes. We like the idea of having at least one Paul (a spiritual elder who can mentor us), one Barnabas (someone who is on our own spiritual level for companionship), and one Timothy (someone we can mentor ourselves). The Bible tells us not to "[forsake] the assembling of ourselves together" (Heb.10:25), especially in times of failure. If you do not have at least one close friend who can minister to you in a time of great failure, then get on your knees before God right now and start praying that He will send you someone. Are you that friend to someone?

Just Enough

As we think about God's dealings with a failure, we must remember that He rarely just fixes or removes our problems. Usually He gives us just enough to keep us going. He is not like the anxious parent who is afraid to watch his or her child suffer. He understands that such interventions would prevent us from growing stronger in our faith and reliance on Him. Many patients with psychological and social problems come into our office wanting a "magic pill" that will take away all their pain and suffering, but there is no such thing and there never will be. Instead of avoiding pain altogether, we must work through it, growing stronger as a person because of it. If God never allowed us to fail, we would all become spoiled, lazy, and weak. Unlike earthly parents, however, whose goal should be to wean their children from their dependence, God uses our failures to increase our daily dependence on Him. He knows that if He gives us too much, we might get too cocky in our own abilities, forget the importance of His presence in our lives, and set ourselves up for an even greater failure in the future. That is why God did not remove the "thorn" in the apostle Paul's flesh—some kind of physical, emotional, or spiritual failing that was inflicted upon him by Satan. He tells us in 2 Corinthians 12:7–9 (NLT): "To keep me from becoming proud, I was given a thorn in my flesh, a messenger from Satan to torment me and keep me from becoming proud. Three different times I begged the Lord to take it away. Each time he said, 'My grace is all you need. My power works best in weakness.' So now I am glad to boast about my weaknesses, so that the power of Christ can work through me."

All of us need to be taught that our survival in life is dependent on daily nourishment from God. His grace is sufficient for us. That grace is often just enough to get us through a difficult day or week. In the midst of the darkness, we learn that if we just keep breathing, the sun will shine again. God gave Elijah bread and water, but it was sufficient to sustain him for forty days and nights. When you, personally, are suffering from the pain of failure, look for the miraculous in the mundane, not in the magnificent. The subtle gifts that God gives us are often the most powerful. They keep up our strength just enough to take one more step, and then another after that. Unlike God, as people we must be careful not to do too much or too little for others. This takes practice and wisdom to learn. When those we love fail, we are not called to take over. This breeds codependency, which is an overreliance on others to fulfill our needs and wants. Helping others through their failures takes effort, but it should not be overwhelming. It should flow naturally out of hearts that have been strengthened by God through our own failures. A listening ear, an honest commitment to pray, and a willingness to help may be all that are necessary to sustain someone. The Bible tells us to "bear one another's burdens, and so fulfill the law of Christ" (Gal. 6:2). The Greek here really says to share each other's "over-burdens." We are not to take their entire load and put it on our shoulders. Instead, we are to take just enough so that they can make it to the finish line.

For those of us who do too little, it is usually because we get caught up in our own problems and fail to notice the needs of others. Interestingly enough this shift in focus might be the cure for getting over our own suffering. The more we focus on others' needs, the less time we have to wallow in our own. Therapy can be a great tool for this. People have said that talk therapy breeds self-centeredness, but in reality, taking just an hour a week to focus on our own problems with a trained professional can give us more power to focus on others throughout the rest of the week. If that is what is necessary for you to help others in their failures, do not hesitate to find a Christian psychiatrist or counselor who can help you in yours.

Now that we have seen how God deals with a failure (the person), we should experience hope and encouragement, knowing that God loves us and can continue to use us despite ourselves. In reality, if God is for us, we will never fail! When we commit our lives to Him, our successes may not come in the form we expected, but they will come nonetheless.

23

Permission to Vent

Roger was an extremely intelligent Ivy League–educated individual, who was struggling with the pain of failure after losing a job he had held for more than a year. In therapy I (Dr. Henderson) explored his view of success, which he measured according to a standard his father had inadvertently placed upon him. The father had been an extremely influential politician and had been honored as a hero in his home state. Unfortunately, he had been sparse in his praise of his son, who grew up searching for ways to please him. When Dad eventually abandoned the family, Roger was devastated. As an adult he strove for perfection in his studies and in work, hoping that when he achieved it, those in positions of authority, who were like his father, would finally show him the praise he longed for as a child. At one point in therapy, I asked him to write a letter to his father expressing his emotions about Dad's treatment of him.

"Would I have to read it to you, or am I just writing it for myself?" he questioned.

"Why do you ask?" I wondered.

"Well, I could be more honest in the letter if I knew you weren't going to see it."

Roger wanted to be honest, but he felt too guilty, too embarrassed to open up to me. He was afraid I would treat him just as his father did.

The unbridled expression of frustration or insecurity with others can be damaging to a relationship. A therapist can create a safe haven where people who have never learned to express themselves appropriately can practice. Even in therapy, however, patients are often fearful of being completely honest because of what they imagine the therapist or physician might think of them. We never have to worry about that with God. He knows what we are thinking before we even think it. Why fool ourselves into believing we can hide our thoughts from Him? Realizing how gentle He is with us in the midst of our failures should free us to be honest with Him about how badly it hurts. He will always listen with mercy and grace, even if our expressions are based on multiple misperceptions of the truth. If our desire to understand His will is genuine, then He will reveal the real truth in His time. Meanwhile, there is nothing we can say that will separate us from His love.

My (Dr. Henderson's) church has small group meetings that get together at different times of the week. Our group meets on Wednesday nights. For the last few weeks, we have been discussing a book on prayer. One of the questions in our study guide asked, "What things about our earthly relationships have affected the way we talk to God?" It was interesting to hear all the responses, most of which were directly related to our differing relationships with our parents.

One person felt that God would get tired of us if we kept coming back to the same problems over and over. "I feel as if He'd say, 'Okay, we've talked about this enough. Let's move on.'"

Another person described feeling as though God was distant and dispassionate, not necessarily getting annoyed or angry with us but just being distracted by other things. Yet another individual shamefully admitted that God, though always willing to listen and genuinely seeming to care, seemed impotent to do anything about it.

We committed together as a group to start viewing God, not as the heavenly version of our earthly fathers but as the true and perfect Father of the Bible. When we realize what kind of Father He is, we can "come boldly to the throne of grace, that we may obtain mercy and find grace to help in time of need" (Heb. 4:16).

The three most common complaints people make after suffering from failure are as follows:

1. Look at what I have done.
2. Look at what others have done.
3. Look at what God has *not* done.

As we explore these common complaints, you will see that, as we level with God, He changes our perspective with time and leads us to a deeper understanding of His power in failure.

Look at What I Have Done

When we blow it and we know it, our first reaction is to fall on our knees and cry out, "What have I done?" But there are also times when we nail it and still fail it. That is when we shout, "Look what I have done!" We want someone (often God) to notice and just give us a break.

When Roger finished the letter to his father and read it to me, I was surprised at the depth of his anger. His lifelong goal was to win the approval of the father figures in his life, but his successes meant nothing because the one man he wanted to appreciate those successes had died of cancer ten years earlier. The letter listed all his accomplishments since he was a kid, and with furious symbolism he had written it in red ink, the very color he dreaded seeing on any of his homework assignments at school.

As Roger dealt with his anger and disappointment toward his father, he eventually forgave him. Through therapy he came to realize that the lack of praise he received as a kid was not the result of his failures but rather the result of his dad's. He was able to see that Dad was only human, just like all the other father figures in Roger's life to date. With that knowledge he began to put less emphasis on others' praises as his measure of success.

The prophet Elijah felt similar frustration with God, although God had done nothing wrong. After all that Elijah had done, he just could not understand what happened, and God graciously allowed him to say so. In 1 Kings 19:9 God asks Elijah, "What are you doing here?" and Elijah's response reveals his frustration. Expanding on the first part of 1 Kings 19:10, Elijah says, "I have zealously served you, God. Haven't I? Haven't I done every-thing You asked me to do? And I am the only human left in all of Israel who is doing Your will and has not bowed the knee to Baal. From the moment I faced Ahab and told him about the drought You were sending, I have been in hiding. I spent day after day alone at the Kerith Brook, and when the water dried up, I followed You faithfully to Sidonia, enemy territory, where I performed miracles for one lonely widow and her son, leading them to a relationship with You. Even at Mount Carmel never once did I doubt You. So I guess, Lord, the answer is, 'I don't know why I'm here.'"

Why am I here? Have you ever asked yourself that question? You look at everything you have done to serve God, to love people, and to do good work, and yet you feel as if you have nothing to show for it. Remember, it is okay to vent. Just be prepared to be silenced and brought to your knees with awe and wonder when God's ultimate purpose for your life is revealed!

Look at What They Have Done

Just as we do with our losses, we make a big mistake when we compare our successes and failures to the ones of those around us. We see people who appear to be cutting corners, shirking responsibilities, being dishonest and flattering, and we think, *Why am I the one failing right now?* Job, who had more right than anyone to complain, said, "Look at me and be astonished; put your hand over your mouth" (Job 21:5). That is exactly what we do when we see how far Job sank before God was finished with him.

When we suffer from the pain of failure, it can be easy to think that we are the only ones who do not deserve it. *I can understand why he failed. After all, look what he did! But me? I'm not so bad. This should not have happened to me. I don't deserve this.* By making such statements, we elevate ourselves above everyone else through our pride. We all deserve to fail. There is nothing that we can do so well or so meticulously that will pre-vent us from experiencing this pain at some point in life. Even Job, who was a righteous man, had to accept that he was not above failure. Without

God's blessing in his life, he was nothing. Elijah realized that by himself he was no more powerful than his ancestors, and even though that was difficult to bear, it was the truth.

Comparison not only incites bitterness over our own failures but also makes us envious of others' successes. *How can they get away with only a few hours of studying and ace the test, when I have to hit the books for weeks just to get a C? Why did he get promoted when I did all the work on this project? How can she be so rude and have so many friends, when I try so hard to be kind and always feel alone?* It is even harder to see dishonest, corrupt, or godless people succeed against us.

A minister once complained about the shift in our society's morality. "They have removed prayer from the public schools, taken God's name out of the Pledge of Allegiance, and laughed at Him on their television shows and movies. They see Him as nothing but an imaginary friend for those too weak to stand alone. They worship sports, money, sex, drugs, power, even nature, but not God. It makes me so mad."

It is sad to see the moral decay that is taking place in society, but there was a deeper layer to this minister's frustration. As upset as he was over society's general disregard for all things spiritual, he was even more upset with how it had affected him personally. He had preached a sermon several weeks earlier on the sanctity of life, and a local newspaper got wind of it, blaming him and others like him for the violence against abortion clinics. The bad publicity hurt the church and his ministry for a while. Things had gotten personal! Later the minister admitted:

In the beginning I was angry for the wrong reasons. I thought, *Look at what all this is doing to my reputation in the community! How dare they accuse me of such things. After all my church has done for this community, the least they could do is show me some respect.* Then God got ahold of me. It was as if He said, "Wait a minute, Simmons. Show *you* a little respect, or me, Jehovah? Who are you promoting anyway: Me or you?" Suddenly I felt like a little kid caught trying to pull a fast one on my parents. *Oh, right*, I thought sheepishly. *That's what I meant, Lord.* I realized later that it did not matter what other people did to me. God was in control, and as long as I was honoring Him, I did not have to worry about defending myself.

Look at What God Has *Not* Done

It is easy for us to feel disappointed with God when we fail. Why didn't He intervene? Why didn't He reward us for all the hard work we have put in? Logically speaking, if we follow God we should be successful, right? After all, Proverbs 16:3 tells us, "Commit your actions to the LORD and your plans will succeed" (NLT). This is absolutely true *if* you understand the definition of *true success*. When we choose to follow God, His success is the most valuable but also the most mysterious: peace in the midst of trouble, joy despite pain, and hope during desperate circumstances. The formula for this kind of success is straightforward: "He has shown you . . . what is good; And what does the LORD require of you / But to do justly, / To love mercy / And to walk humbly with your God?" (Mic. 6:8).

Walking humbly with God is a process, and each path we walk is different. The formula for eternal success is not like a mathematics equation that always has the exact same answer. God gives each of us success in different ways, and it is not always in the way we expect or hope. Thank God, it isn't. Have you ever hoped and prayed for something that in hindsight you realize would have kept you from a greater success or led you into greater frustrations? We will never know all the "What ifs?" of our lifetime, nor does the Bible promise we will be "successful" according to the world's standards. But we can be sure God's plan for our life will be totally unique and very special.

Reality Check

When we feel the pain of failure, it helps to stop for a reality check. Who is really in charge here? God's ability to empower and encourage us amid our failures is beyond measure. For the prophet Elijah, God demonstrated His magnificence, first with a great windstorm like a tornado, then a mighty earthquake, and finally a raging fire. If you have ever experienced any of these phenomena, you know how terrible and awe-inspiring they can be.

I (Dr. Henderson) remember living in Ohio, where we used to have tornadoes quite frequently. My family's house was surrounded by farmland, so I could see for a mile in all directions. We knew a tornado was coming because the sky would suddenly change colors: bright pink, purple, and orange hues. On one occasion I thought someone had put orange-tinted sunglasses over my eyes. The colors were that brilliant. In the distance we could hear the siren from town, a long, low wail warning all those within range that it was time to take shelter. Then huge, black clouds would cover the land in darkness. Everything outside became deathly quiet until, suddenly, you could hear a sound like a freight train slowly coming closer. The rain would begin to beat hard upon the roof, but not hard enough to muffle the sound of that terrible windstorm as it passed. Fortunately, I have only seen one tornado touch down. It was very small for a tornado, but it was nonetheless a beautiful and terrible sight. I did not know whether to run and hide from it or just stand there amazed.

With Elijah, God used a storm so powerful that it literally tore holes in the mountainside. Through the windstorm, the earthquake, and the fire, He demonstrated that His power was beyond comparison and that, with such power behind Elijah, he need not fear failure. God, however, was not actually in any of those mighty and terrible demonstrations. Instead, he spoke to Elijah in a gentle whisper.

The take-home point is twofold. First, God gets our attention in the storms of our lives (failures, injustices, losses, rejections, and loneliness), but His gentle, soothing voice can be heard amid the noise if we will just stop long enough to listen. Second, God sometimes blows us away with spectacular demonstrations of His awesome power in our lives (miraculous answers to prayer, momentous occasions, and top-of-the-world successes), but more often than not, His voice can be heard more clearly in the quiet, seemingly uneventful moments of our lives when we are not distracted. We do not need millions of dollars, a glamorous career or ministry, or superstar status to experience true success. Instead, it is like a hidden treasure that no one else can see. The question is, "Are you searching for it?"

24

True Success

What is true success? If we think long and hard, most of us will agree that true success is contentment in life. Understanding that contentment does not necessitate complacency, we strive for excellence in all areas of our lives with the mentality that "if the Lord wills, we will live and do this or that" (James 4:15), but if He does not, we will not be devastated. People have many different ideas about how to find this kind of satisfaction, but those who do find it are the envy of the world.

Think about this for a moment: if we could be satisfied with our lives the way they are, would our net income, the square footage of our house, or the number of vacations we took each year really matter? Would we need any more recognition, any more pleasures or perks, any more comforts beyond what we already have? Of course, the answer is no. Ask yourself, *If I could find the source of complete satisfaction, would I need or want to have anything else?* If your answer to this question is no, then you are well on your way toward finding true success.

The next step in the process is to determine what desires you have and if they are achievable. Let us give you a hint with this one. As you describe your desires, if they are preceded by the word *more* or end with the letters *er* then we guarantee that your desires are unachievable. John D. Rockefeller, the richest man on earth during the 1930s, when asked by a reporter how much wealth was enough, responded by saying, "Just a little bit more." How right he was. Unfortunately, no one ever achieves "more," because there is always "more" to be had beyond that. This is true for all areas of our lives. There is a big difference between wanting a good job, a good marriage, or a good friend, and always wanting a better job, a better marriage, or a better friend than the one you have. One desire has a potentially quantifiable end point. The other does not.

Here is a second hint: if your desires are not in line with God's design for your life, then even if you do achieve them, they will not satisfy you completely. James 1:14–17 tells us that we can be drawn away by desires that lead to death. He reminds us not to be deceived into thinking that any good or perfect gift comes apart from God.

So how do we determine our desires? It requires more digging than we might think. For instance, a young man who has just obtained his driver's license may tell his father that he needs a car that will get him to school on time. But if the specific car he wants is a Bugatti Veyron, one of the fastest and most expensive cars in the world, when a Toyota would do just fine, his father must assume that his son "needs" more from his car than just reliability and good gas mileage.

Likewise, an individual who continues eating long after his hunger has been assuaged may betray his deeper desires for pleasure or relief from boredom, anxiety, and depression. These desires go far beyond his need for nutrition. Other examples include people who cry for justice but really want vengeance, those who pursue sexual relationships but really long for emotional intimacy, or individuals whose desire "to be heard" is, in effect, a need for control.

Once we identify our desires, we can begin to examine the importance we have placed on them for our happiness and how effective we have been at satisfying them. Without this honest scrutiny, we could spend our entire lives striving for the wrong answers to our deepest needs or trying to satisfy the wrong desires altogether. True success comes when we know our deepest desires, work to align them with the will of God, and then satisfy them with a lasting source.

Why is finding this true success so difficult? It is because the world continually preys upon the desires we have that are either unachievable or unsatisfying. It is not in their best interest for us to be content, but of course, they cannot just come out and say so. Everyone, including the mainstream media, preaches to us that money is not everything, beauty is in the eye of the beholder, fame is fleeting, and power corrupts. So why do we not get the message? The reason is because our culture may say these things, but what they say and what they demonstrate are two different things. Subliminally they ask us to do what they do, not what they say. Modern advertising companies pay big bucks to psychologists and marketing experts who create commercials that will manipulate the minds of consumers in the subtlest ways. Insurance company advertisements use fear; beauty and clothing product commercials use seduction; comfort food industries appeal to our "right" to have them; modern appliance moguls prey on our desire for increased productivity and speed; the list could go on all day. In offering these things, however, these companies do not necessarily want our deepest longings realized. Often they want them to remain only partially fulfilled so that we will keep coming back for more! The source of complete satisfaction, and thus true success, is found in a relationship, not the realization of our material hopes and dreams.

Somebodies and Nobodies

There are now seven billion people in the world, and the vast majority of these humans go through life feeling like nobodies. They spend most of their lives trying to prove to themselves and to others that they are somebodies. This human condition is commonly referred to as the rat race. A wise person comes to realize that the rat race never gets us to a level of success that satisfies. A great adage says, "Even if you win the race, you're still a rat!"

Nelson Rockefeller, the son of John D. Rockefeller, had everything this world could offer: money, fame, prestige, position. He attained the second highest office in the land as vice president of the United States. Even today his name is recognized all over the world. In that sense he was and still is "a somebody," and yet David Broder of the *Washington*

Post wrote an article shortly after Rockefeller's death describing him as an "incomplete man." Nelson Rockefeller had always wanted to be U.S. president, but that dream was never fulfilled.

Contrast that epitaph to the one written about Abraham in the book of Genesis: "He died at a ripe old age, having lived a long and satisfying life" (Gen. 25:8 NLT). Abraham, in many respects, had been a failure. God had promised Abraham that he would become a great nation, but when Abraham died, all he had was an only son, Isaac. God's promise was left unfulfilled in Abraham's lifetime. So how could it be said that Abraham lived a satisfying life? The key was a matter of relationship! The source of Abraham's satisfaction was not in the promise itself but in the Promise Giver! Abraham knew God and knew that He is good and that He is faithful; and as long as Abraham had God, he was satisfied.

Which Would You Rather Have . . . ?

One way to determine what is most important to you in life is to ask, "Which would you rather have . . . ?" Many of us played this game as kids, imagining different scenarios that required us to make a choice one way or the other. It taught us a lot about what we really thought was valuable. Some of the questions we asked as kids were, "Would you rather have a girlfriend that was a supermodel or a gourmet chef?" or "Would you rather explore the universe with your own customized space shuttle or travel down the Amazon in a submarine?" "Would you rather have wings like an eagle or speed like a cheetah?"

As adults we ask more mature questions about finances, education, family, dreams, and goals. The choices we make will determine the direction of our lives and the level of satisfaction we find. The difference is that real life is not a game! Proverbs gives us a good list of choices as we consider the which-would-you-rather-have question. Let us look at some. You can use these to help determine if your measure of success is in line with God's definition for true success.

Worldly Knowledge or Godly Wisdom?

"Wisdom is more profitable than silver, / and her wages are better than gold. / Wisdom is more precious than rubies; / nothing you desire can compare with her" (Prov. 3:14–15 NLT). We, the authors, know many extremely intelligent people with Ivy League educations who have very little wisdom. These people are lauded as experts in their particular fields but have no common sense when it comes to the more important issues of life. We also know people who have not graduated from high school and those who may stumble when they speak yet have great wisdom when it comes to finding true success in life. They may not know how to negotiate a peace treaty between two countries, but they know how to experience peace in their own souls. They may not know how to cure disease with modern medicine, but they know the cure for a broken heart. They may not have all the answers to life's most difficult questions, but they have found a hope in the future that can never be shattered, regardless of the circumstances. What is the source of such wisdom? It is the relationship they have with God. Which would you rather have?

Immediate Sexual Pleasure or Intimate Sexual Pleasure?

Solomon taught in Proverbs 5:

> For the lips of an immoral woman are sweet as honey,
>> and her mouth is smoother than oil.
> But in the end she is as bitter as poison,
>> as dangerous as a double-edged sword. . . .
>> Don't go near the door of her house!
> If you do, you will lose your honor
>> and will lose to merciless people all you have achieved. . . .
> In the end you will groan in anguish
>> when disease consumes your body. . . .
> Drink water from your own well—
>> share your love only with your wife.

Why spill the water of your springs in the streets,
    having sex with just anyone?
You should reserve it for yourselves.
    Never share it with strangers. (vv. 3–4, 8–9, 11, 15–17 NLT)

Sexual addiction is running rampant in our culture. The advent of the Internet has created a threefold threat of sexual addiction that Al Cooper has termed the "Triple-A Engine": Accessibility, Anonymity, and Affordability.[1] But allure will never satisfy. Instead, it will destroy you and your family and have you lamenting, "This really wasn't worth it."

What if, instead, you could have complete intimacy with someone who knew everything about you and still loved you? You could be completely secure in his or her commitment and completely satisfied by his or her affection. I (Dr. Meier) once read a poll of many thousands of women, who were readers of a rather liberal women's magazine. The poll was on their sex lives. The editors of this liberal magazine were caught by complete surprise when they found that women who were close to God and prayed with their husbands also had the most outstanding sex lives. That is the way God intended it. In Proverbs 5, quoted above, God inspired King Solomon to also write to married men, "Let her [your wife's] breasts satisfy you at all times; / and always be enraptured with her love" (v. 19). God must think sex in the right context is pretty cool, since He invented it, but again, satisfying sex starts when a man and woman first develop an intimate spiritual relationship with the Creator of such pleasures. Which would you rather have?

Hard Work or Hard Time?

"Take a lesson from the ants, you lazybones. / Learn from their ways and become wise! / Though they have no prince or governor or ruler to make them work, / they labor hard. . . . But you, lazybones, how long will you sleep? / When will you wake up? / A little extra sleep, a little more slumber, / a little folding of the hands to rest—/ then poverty will pounce on you like a bandit; / scarcity will attack you like an armed robber" (Prov. 6:6–11 NLT). Some of the most miserable people have absolutely no responsibilities in life. Many of them are on welfare or social security, and instead of finding something, anything to do that is productive, they generally sit at home watching television and movies, smoking, and drinking. These same people feel angry, irritable, insignificant, and unmotivated. They are doing hard time in self-made prisons of boredom and worthlessness. Even the filthy rich become bored with all their toys. Humans were made to work. This was not part of the curse; it was a pleasure given to Adam by God to tend the garden and take care of the animals. Sin has made work more difficult, but it is still necessary to be happy. Why? It is because work fosters our rela tionship with God. That is why Colossians 3:23 (NLT) says, "Work willingly at whatever you do, as though you were working for the Lord rather than for people." Then you will be completely satisfied, knowing that "nothing you do for the Lord is ever useless" (1 Cor.15:58 NLT). Which would you rather have?

Unlimited Wealth or Unlimited Contentment?

Again from Proverbs: "Evil people get rich for the moment, / but the reward of the godly will last" (11:18 NLT). "Better to have little, with fear for the LORD, / than to have great treasure and inner turmoil" (15:16 NLT). Paul echoed this truth to Timothy when he wrote, "True godliness with contentment is itself great wealth" (1 Tim. 6:6 NLT). Would it not be won- derful to be able to look around at what we have, no matter how much or how little, and honestly be able to say, "I am happy"? Paul developed this power through the Holy Spirit. He said, "I have learned how to be content with whatever I have. I know how to live on almost nothing or with every- thing. I have learned the secret of living in every situation, whether it is with a full stomach or empty, with plenty or little. For I can do everything through Christ, who gives me strength" (Phil. 4:11–13 NLT). Without Christ no amount of anything can satisfy. With Him nothing else needs to! True success is all about relationship. Which would you rather have?

World Renown or God's Renown?

Proverbs 11:20 (NLT) says, "The LORD detests people with crooked hearts, / but he delights in those with integrity." Matthew 6:1–2 describes the man who does good deeds to get the praise of others. It tells us that it is all the reward he will get. Even well-known pastors and preachers who use their power and influence to build themselves up in front of others, to accumulate wealth and praise in this life, had better enjoy it while they can. It ain't gonna last. But the mother who cares for her children day after day without praise, the janitor who faithfully scrubs the floors, the pastor, teacher, doctor, or salesman who works diligently to seek God's praise will get what he or she is looking for not just in this life but for all eternity. I think we will be very surprised at how many "nobodies" are actually "somebodies" in heaven. Which would you rather be?

The Source of Our Satisfaction Is Christ!

The key to all of the above questions is based upon the source of our satisfaction. Psalm 37:4 says, "Take delight in the LORD, / and he will give you your heart's desires" (NLT). We often quote this verse thinking that God will give us something other than Himself, but instead He will usually take something away from us first to prove that we need nothing else but Him. Then and only then will He give us the desires of our hearts. In this way our failures become our greatest successes.

When Alistair Pineiro failed to get accepted to the college of his choice, he was devastated. Looking back now, however, he acknowledges that it was the best thing that ever happened to him. "I decided to take that year to work, and during that time I wrestled with God over His plans for my life and finally surrendered myself to Him. I remember praying, *Whatever you want from me, Lord, I'll do. If college is not for me, then I trust that You have something better.* That year, He changed my desires. I had initially planned to major in premed at college, but the construction job I worked that year got me interested in architecture. With a newfound peace, I applied again the following year and this time was accepted."

Alistair went on to start his own company after college and, among other things, helped build the Christian school his daughter now attends. But the story does not end there. "In my senior year of college, I met my wife, Sarah, who was a freshman. If I had been accepted the year before, I never would have met her. We've been married now for twelve years, and I would not trade that failed attempt to get into college for the world!"

Through that experience God taught Alistair about His sovereignty, even in failure. It was the year that Alistair spent wrestling with God that matured him enough to take responsibility for the blessings God gave him in his new career and his family.

When we get too focused on achieving human success, we miss out on the spiritual successes God blesses us with every day. When Alistair said that he wrestled with God over his failure, he meant that he was struggling to understand God. During that year, he memorized more Scripture than he had in his whole life. Knowing God was a matter of utmost importance, because it would determine the direction his life would take. He wanted to be sure his desires were in line with God's desires for him, and because of this attitude, God blessed him with more than just a good education and meaningful career. He gave him the blessing of a godly woman, who has continued to encourage him in his relationship with the Lord. With God's power and a little time, the seeming failures of our past can be transformed into the victories of our future.

But what if our failures are moral? What if we have spent our lives thus far chasing after our own desires and we find ourselves in a complete mess as a result? Is it too late to find satisfaction in Christ? The answer is, it is never too late.

Truth or legend, we love the story of the young boy who was given the job of transporting the first lightbulb from Thomas Edison's hands to the generator that would be used to test it. As the story goes, the young boy tripped on the way up the stairs and broke it. After hours of redundant labor to make another test lightbulb, Thomas Edison is said to have called the boy over to him, handed him the new lightbulb, and charged him with the same task. God never gives up on us. Give your desires over to Him and allow Him to change you for the best.

The Rest of Elijah's Story

Sometimes we fail to see how relevant the stories of men and women from Scripture are to our own modern-day struggles, but the book of James is clear: "Elijah was a man with a nature like ours" (5:17). It is amazing that despite Elijah's perceived failures of ministry, as well as his real failures of faith, personality, and emotional stability, God continued to use him, not just in his lifetime, but throughout the Scriptures and even today. His name comes up over and over in the Old and New Testaments. Remember it was the "spirit of Elijah" in John the Baptist who prepared the way for Jesus to begin his earthly ministry (Luke 1:17). Matthew 17:12 tells us that Jesus would be abused just as Elijah was. Elijah's suffering at the hands of a corrupt political system was a prophetic parallel to the suffering Jesus would face from the same system. In fact, it was Elijah who, along with Moses, talked with Jesus on the Mount of Transfiguration shortly before Jesus' own crucifixion (Luke 9:28–36). When people mocked Jesus on the cross, they said, "Let us see if Elijah will come to save him now" (Matt. 27:49). Finally, some scholars believe that Elijah will be one of the prophets who will come before Christ returns to earth for the second time.

Who was Elijah? He was a common, ordinary man with all the shortcomings and failures we struggle with today, but he was used by God to do great and wonderful things for eternity. If God can use Elijah, He can use us. When we find our satisfaction in Him and allow Him to take care of the rest, we will discover that success really is all about Who you know!

Finding Purpose Beyond Your Failures

Now that we have discovered all that God can do through even the most painful failures, here are five practical application points to strengthen and encourage you as you search for the purposes beyond your own failures.

1. *Failure is in the eye of the beholder*. What you deem a failure in your life may actually be the start of a great work that God can do in and through you. Ask God to give you His perspective on the situation, be patient with yourself, and look for the possible intended purposes beyond the failure, which you may have missed (Rom. 5:1–5).

2. *Don't hide your failures from God*. When we fail, God does not treat us like others do. Run to Him, not away from Him, and allow Him to touch you, nourish you, and provide you with the friendships you need to see you through the failure. Remember, help is usually not as far away as we pretend it to be (2 Thess. 3:3, 5).

3. *Take time for a reality check*. When we fail, it is easy to believe that the world is spinning out of control. If life feels like this to you, it may be helpful to get alone with God for some quiet reflection. We humans tend to catastrophize, but God and His counselors help you realize that nine out of ten things we fear never happen. And when they do, God's power to minister and encourage us is beyond measure (Ps. 27:1; Isa. 35:3–4).

4. *Know your true desires*. Many of us have never sat down and thought through what we really want out of life. Fewer still

have considered whether those desires are pure or reasonable. Our definition of success will dictate our response to failure, so make sure that you are clear in what direction you are headed (Ps. 27:4–5).

5. *Make Christ the source of your satisfaction.* It is so true that success is not about what you know but who you know. "Delight in the LORD and he will give you the desires of your heart." Don't lose heart in the midst of failure. Trust Him to make known to you the purpose beyond your failure in His time. In the meantime satisfy yourself with the fact that He is ever present, no matter how you may feel (Ps. 27:13–14).

Now set aside some personal time to consider your own situation in the light of these truths. Then answer the following questions truthfully in order to establish the groundwork for overcoming the failures in your life.

1. How has God taken failure and turned it into success in your life? (If you cannot think of a situation off the top of your head, ask Him to bring one to your mind this week or give a present failure over to Him right now and ask Him to use it for His glory.)

2. What are some of the reasons we want to hide from God and others in times of failure? How can you change that mentality and seek out the help you need?

3. What can you do to keep from feeling overwhelmed by failure? How many times have you worried about something that never actually happened? (Be specific.)

4. What desires do you have right now in life? Are they consistent with God's plan for us as human beings? If not, what can you do to change them?

5. What are the most important desires you have in life (the desire for love, the desire for acceptance, the desire for comfort, the desire for significance)? What have you been using to satisfy those desires? Is it working for you? How might Christ's presence provide more lasting fulfillment for you?

Part 7

DEATH

"O Death, where is your sting?"

—1 Corinthians 15:55

25

Beyond Death

Perhaps the happiest moment of Devon and Paige's marriage was the day their son, Hunter, was born. The Ollestads had been trying to have a child for several years, but even after two very expensive attempts with in vitro fertilization, they still had not conceived. Then, out of the blue, Paige began to have signs of morning sickness. Halfheartedly she bought a home pregnancy test and almost fainted when the result was positive. When Hunter was born, Devon and Paige were overjoyed, but not for very long. The doctors told them that Hunter had a rare heart condition that would require multiple surgeries to sustain his life. Over the next eleven years, the Ollestads lived with the fear that their son could die at any moment. They did everything they could to save him from death, but to no avail. He died a few months before his twelfth birthday, but not in the way his parents expected. They were driving to a routine doctor's appointment when a car heading in the opposite direction suddenly swerved and hit the Ollestads head-on. The entire family was killed.

The horror of that day sent chills down the backs of everyone who knew the family, but the saddest part of the story is not that the Ollestads died. The worse tragedy was how unexpected their fate was. Devon and Paige were so focused on saving the life of their son that they had no time to consider that their own deaths might also be close at hand. They were totally unprepared.

Awareness of Death Brings Power

Amazingly, many human beings depart from this life in exactly the same way. The departing may not be as dramatic, but it is no less tragic. Whether through sudden catastrophes, such as car accidents, or through chronic diseases, such as cancer, people fail to recognize when death is upon them. For those upon whom death comes suddenly, there is not time to contemplate its present reality. For those who are blessed with time enough to ponder it, they waste that time on pleasurable distractions, denying death's reality to the bitter end. Somehow they believe beyond reason that escape is still an option. They hope in vain that some miracle will save them from its pain. Even people who are chronically suicidal usually have not thought through the significance of the action they are contemplating. In failing to do so, they rob themselves of the power that conscious awareness of death can bring.

Consider Your Own Death

This will sound strange to many of you, but one of the most powerful experiences I (Dr. Henderson) have ever had was working at a hospice care facility. The great chasm between life and death was never so narrow as in that place. Every morning I entered that building with its peaceful gardens outside every window, its plush corridors echoing with the sounds of Mozart and Vivaldi, its soft but warm lighting like a Thomas Kinkade painting, and its reverent staff whispering like nuns in a convent. I felt as if I were standing at an eternal crossroads, watching as men and women passed by at every moment on the way to their final destinations. Everything was arranged to make the passing as pleasant as possible.

God Himself walked the halls, standing at the entrance to every room but never crossing the threshold unless invited. Some *had* invited Him, and you could tell. Their faces exuded the peaceful contentment they had in knowing they were almost home. Their loved ones sat holding each other, holding the dying, mourning the separation but not the loss. Their parting was truly "sweet sorrow," confident in a future meeting far more wonderful. They had faced the pain of death and come through it possessing a power beyond belief.

Not every room was like that. Angry siblings in one room argued over an unconscious patriarch. They were more concerned about their inheritance than the soon-to-be-departed's meeting with death. Even as their "loved one" passed away, they were too blinded by their greed to reflect on death's presence. In another room a despairing wife voiced what many have felt, "I'm never going to see him again. There was so much I didn't get to say." There was no sweetness in her sorrow, no power or hope beyond the grave. Yet in still another room, the saddest sight to see was a woman lying in bed all alone. Unconscious for several days and with no family to help ease the passing, hers was a lonely death. The section on her records designated for religious affiliation said, "Atheist." Not even God could comfort her now. The great gains that come through conscious awareness of death had passed by all of these people, never to return again.

I had to think a lot about my own death during my time in that hospice facility. It demanded consideration in a way I had never known. *When will it be? Will it hurt or be painless? Will the process be sudden or slow? Who will I leave behind, and will they be sad or perhaps glad to see me go? Will I be ready when the time comes? Am I confident of my final destination?*

I also thought a lot about my life. *How would I live if today were my last day on earth? What would be the most important priority on my "to-do list"? Would those be priorities that would have lasting effects on earth and in eternity? What about my relationships? Would I treat people differently, being humbler, more honest, kind, or loving? If God were to look at my life, what would He say about it? What would be the final review?* Death had forced me to do some much-needed self-reflection, and that reflection, in the long run, has shaped my focus and goals in this life.

If you have never considered death for yourself, then you are missing out on a tremendous power that can be yours. But it is not obtained without pain. It is probably the most difficult reality to ponder, because death is scary, to say the least. To think about it is like swallowing a bitter medicine, but it is the only cure for a life without meaning.

The Importance of Being Prepared

Solomon, the wisest man who ever lived, said, "A wise person thinks a lot about death, while a fool thinks only about having a good time" (Eccl. 7:4 NLT). That does not sound like a wise statement to most people. Should it not be the other way around? "A wise man maintains a positive attitude, always focusing on the time he has instead of focusing on something so painful and morbid as death. Only a foolish man or a severely depressed man sits around thinking about that. What a waste of precious time! How could that possibly give someone power?"

There are two ways. First, a conscious awareness of the ever-present possibility of death, whether through natural or accidental causes, motivates us to spend wisely what time we do have to live. The importance of priorities in our lives hits home. What is really important? We would all live life to the fullest if we could fully understand how short our time here really is. Tim McGraw expresses this fact in the song "Live Like You Were Dying."[1] In the song he describes a friend who suddenly finds out he has cancer and is going to die. Tim asks him what his life has been like since, and the friend's reply reveals his change of heart and his change in priorities. The song ends with the friend wishing that everyone could have the same experience. The truth is we can!

Have you ever been forced to consider how you might change your life if you knew today was your last day on earth? Would you do anything differently? Are there people to whom you would reach out? Attitudes you might change? This is the power in thinking through the ever-present reality of death.

The second way in which our conscious awareness of death can give us power for life is by providing us with a measure of our preparedness for eternity. If your first reaction to death is absolute terror, then you know you are not prepared. The amount of fear you experience is a gauge that must not be ignored. Though it is painful, the fear of death is like the warning light in your car that tells you there is something that needs to be fixed. Though taking your car to the mechanic may be a hassle, it will save you a lot of trouble in the long run when you avoid being stranded in the middle of a busy highway. If you experience unbearable fear when you consider your own death, asking yourself why could be the key to great gains in your life. Now is the time to work through that fear. Philippians 2:12 says, "Work out your own salvation with fear and trembling." If, by considering death, you are filled with fear, and that fear causes you to "work out your own salvation," you have gained more than you will ever know. The peace that follows is like no other.

People who contemplate suicide would do well to consider this further. The fact that they are considering taking their own lives suggests they do not fear death, but this is usually not true. It is just that their fear barometer is broken. They are so consumed with escaping the pain of this life that they cannot consider what pain they might experience on the other side of death. They fail to see the significance of their actions, even though they think about it all the time. I (Dr. Henderson) had a patient who talked constantly about killing herself, so I confronted her on it.

"So what do you expect to happen after your death?" I asked.

She quickly replied, "Everyone I know will regret how they treated me and finally understand all the pain they caused."

"No, I mean what will happen to *you* after your death?"

She hesitated. "Well, I don't know. I guess I won't have to suffer anymore."

"Are you sure about that?" I challenged.

"Well, not really. It's just what I've always believed."

"So let me get this straight. You have no idea what happens to you when you die, and what you *think* will happen you have no evidence to prove. Shouldn't that be the first item on your to-do list before contemplating suicide?"

It should have been, but for most people contemplating suicide, it is not. A healthy fear of death can be a good thing if it leads us to prepare for it properly.

So what do we fear about death? It is different for all of us. Some of us fear the process of dying (the physical pain, the long good-byes, the shame of losing our independence or being a burden to those we love). Others fear the permanence of death (the realization that we cannot come back). This is why the idea of reincarnation is so popular. Unfortunately, there are no do-overs. We fear how we will be remembered, if at all. Still others fear the purpose beyond death. There are those who believe death is meaningless, but we would argue that if there is no purpose in death then there is neither any purpose in life. Those who do believe in a purpose beyond death may fear some form of eternal judgment or penance. What is important to realize with all of these fears is that they are perfectly valid fears to consider as you prepare yourself for death. The goal is to use them to drive us toward solutions based in truth. The answers are there if we search for them.

Not only does a conscious awareness of death help us prepare for our own passing, but it also helps us prepare for the passing of others we know and love. So much of the pain surrounding death exists because of our misconceptions about it. We experience guilt, believing that loved ones who died might be angry with us for moving on with life. We worry that they may be holding a grudge against us because of an unresolved disagreement or conflict. We experience regret because we believe they do not understand how much we loved them in this life. These emotions are our own, not the deceased's.

One helpful technique in grief therapy is to take empty chairs and have the clients imagine the dead family members or friends sitting in front of them. We have the clients talk to the people as if they were still alive and tell them all the things they did not get to say while the individuals were living. Then we ask them to imagine what the loved ones would say back to them in return. This can be very cathartic and help bring closure to the loss. We, as the therapists, work to change misconceptions and bring about healing, no matter what the circumstances that caused the death. None of this can be done, however, without experiencing and acknowledging the reality of the death.

Solomon likens death to a battle in his book Ecclesiastes. He says, "None of us can hold back our spirit from departing. None of us has the power to prevent the day of our death. There is no escaping that obligation, that dark battle" (Eccl. 8:8 NLT). It rages on with or without our participation, claiming us as victims or victors, depending on how we fight. We may not be able to escape the battle, but we can defeat it if we prepare for it ahead of time. Are you ready to know how? Are you sure? It could be that we will need to drive farther into the darkness before we see the light, but we are confident you will find that the light shines brighter on the other side of the pain!

26

The Battle

I (Dr. Meier) realized how unpredictable death can be when I woke up one night gasping for air. I have always been quite healthy, and all my ancestors have lived to one hundred years, so I had always thought that I would face death around that time of life. I knew I had "a little bit" of sleep apnea, but it turned out to be worse than I thought. Because I never consciously remembered snoring, I had no way of knowing how close I was coming to suffocating. I knew sleep apnea could be deadly. In fact, the famous defensive lineman for the Green Bay Packers, Reggie White, had died of this very disorder years ago. I, however, had used denial as a way of avoiding the annoyance of treatment, and so the apneic periods began to lengthen.

Finally, at the urging of my wife, I went to a sleep clinic where a specialist reviewed my sleep pattern. With wires attached all over my body and brain, I slept in a monitored bed where it was discovered that I was holding my breath for up to one minute and forty seconds at a time. My oxygen levels were falling into the sixties, just barely above death. It was only when I realized how close to death I had come that I agreed to be fitted for a sleep apnea machine, a device that blows moist warm air into your nostrils to keep your throat from closing. I feel great today. My friends like to joke with me that they are used to hot air coming out of my mouth, not going into it. The lesson of that experience has stuck with me. There I was, "safe" in my bed, never knowing, never expecting that death could reach me there. How wrong I was!

Where We Fight

The first step in conquering the pain of death is to acknowledge that the battleground on which we fight it can be anywhere. It can strike in the classroom of an elementary school just as easily as in the cancer ward of a hospital. It can ambush us with the suddenness of a heart attack, or it can pick off our bodily functions one after another like a distant sharpshooter. At any time and in any way, we must be prepared to meet this insidious enemy wherever it strikes.

We have fallen prey to a shrewd military tactic of the enemy if we believe we can meet death on our own terms. By doing so, we let our guards down. We become lazy and flippant about our lives, our health, and our actions, thinking there is always tomorrow to make matters right, but suddenly death appears and tomorrow never comes. Many people are left behind by loved ones who refused to take care of themselves or their families ahead of time.

For example, Mark was an attorney who failed to take care of his debt and left nothing for his wife and children to live on after his passing. Thomas was an old-school tough guy who refused to go to the doctor unless he felt as though he was dying. Unfortunately, he was dying of prostate cancer, and by the time he did feel it, there was nothing that could be done. If he had only gone to his doctor for routine physicals, he might have seen his grandchildren get married.

Debbie refused to forgive her sister for a slight in order to "give her some time to suffer first." Sadly, her sister died in an accident, and Debbie was the one who suffered for years instead.

Craig said he would ask the deeper questions about God and eternity after his retirement when he had time to think about them. That day never came. He died at the ripe age of ninety-two, but retirement had been busier than he thought.

The Bible warns us, "Today is the day of salvation!"(2 Cor. 6:2 NLT). "The devil walks about like a roaring lion, seeking whom he may devour" (1 Peter 5:8). We have to be prepared for death's coming at any moment.

How We Fight

Once we have accepted the ever-present possibility of death, how do we keep it from ruining the life we have?

First, live resiliently. Do not let the reality of death keep you from living an abundant life. Our preparation for death should relieve us of fear, not fill our hearts with it. The most famous Psalm quoted at funerals is Psalm 23, which says, "Yea, though I walk through the valley of the shadow of death [the battleground], I will fear no evil." Most people think the "valley of the shadow of death" is a particular moment or experience in time. It is not. If you understand the ever-present possibility of death, then you understand that we are all walking through the valley of the shadow of death every day of our lives. Even so, we do not have to fear any evil. Many people do. They spend most of their lives retreating, trying to dodge death's bullets by hiding in holes of false security and inactivity, but in doing so they have already been robbed. Death wins if we let it take from us through fear what God has given us to enjoy. (Yes, life on earth can be full of joy even in the face of death.)

Our response to the evening news is a perfect example of how fear can overtake us. In an effort to increase their ratings, news stations sensationalize violence and terror, hoping that they can prey upon our fears like little children watching a horror movie.

"Another seven people were killed today as they took their dogs out for a walk." So we stop walking our dogs. "A new study shows that butter increases your risk of a heart attack by 1.2 percent." So we start eating that disgusting margarine junk, not realizing that the amount of chemical additives and preservatives in margarine is enough to run a nuclear power plant for a year (okay, we cannot confirm that statistic, but you get our point).

Someday in the future we might all live in "virtual worlds" as in *The Matrix*. Many people already do, playing sports on the computer, shopping on the computer, having long-term relationships over the computer, all from the comfort of their easy chairs. Their fear of death and real living has caused them to settle for a cheap imitation. These activities are living in essence, not in reality. The dramatic rise in depression and boredom with life shows we are indeed robbing ourselves of life. Like zombies, we have become the "living dead."

A severe form of this kind of fear is termed *agoraphobia*. People with agoraphobia cannot stand being in public places, due to an irrational fear that something terrible will happen to them if they do. We now have medications that can help these people feel calmer and improve the quality of their lives. Talk therapy also helps by gradually exposing them to the situations they fear and talking them through the emotion. The more they expose themselves, the easier it becomes. The same is true for our fear of living. The more we understand death, the better able we are to live with the possibility of it.

So do not spend your life hiding from death. Take the opportunities to enjoy the life God has given you while you can. Do not let fear keep you from fulfilling His purposes for your life. Trust Him to protect you as you seek to do His will.

The second way to battle against death is to live responsibly. We should not let our fear of death keep us from living, but neither should we be reckless in trying to challenge it. We are not invincible, and we need to be sure we are seeking God's guidance for our lives. That way, if we *are* called home, we can be confident that it was a part of His will for us and not a result of our own foolishness.

No true soldiers go looking for trouble apart from the orders of their commanding officers. It is only the foolish soldiers who tempt the enemy by getting as close as possible to enemy lines. Many people treat death in this very way. In an effort to overcome their fears, they participate in reckless behaviors, seeing how close they can come to death and still escape it. This is irresponsible and dangerous and gives people a false sense of invincibility.

One of the most fascinating characters in world history was Charles XII, King of Sweden until 1718. A self-professed fatalist, Charles believed he would "fall by no other bullet than that which is destined for me. And when that comes no prudence will help me." This belief led him to charge recklessly into battles against armies vastly superior to his own, risking not only his own life, but the lives of his men. In one such battle, Charles emerged, bleeding from his ear, his nose, and his cheek, where bullets had grazed him. During an intense engagement, he almost lost his thumb after grabbing hold of an enemy's blade barehanded. His recklessness may have won him fame as a military general, but it cost him his life at the young age of thirty-six in a very unromantic way. A stray bullet hit Charles while he was carelessly inspecting his army's entrenchments. Charles may have believed that the bullet that killed him was destined for him, and maybe it was. Maybe God just got tired of his arrogance and decided enough was enough. Maybe if Charles had used a little common sense, he might have lived longer. The point is Charles was not invincible; and despite all his heroics, his life made very little impact on the world. Better to die while responsibly seeking God's plans for our lives than to live recklessly fulfilling our own.

Living and Dying Well

If we prepare for death, the rewards will be lasting. We can even set the example for those we leave behind, helping them to face death with bravery and dignity.

My (Dr. Meier's) mother, Elizabeth, was prepared for death. A strong believer for the vast majority of her ninety-seven years of life, she had experienced many of the joys and blessings of life, as well as the trials and tribulations it brings. Each of those experiences had prepared her to meet death with complete peace of mind, knowing that God had brought her this far and He would take her safely through this experience as well. She could truly say with the apostle Paul, "To live is Christ, and to die is gain" (Phil. 1:21). Even as she lay dying, she continued to make use of what little life she had left in service to the Lord. Her testimony even helped to lead one of the nurses at her nursing home to Christ. She reflected on that experience and said, "Well, I really wish God would let me come home to heaven, but I guess this is why He still has me here."

A few days later the time had finally come for my mother's last battle. I asked another psychiatrist at the office to see my remaining Day Program patients and rushed to be at her side for the final moments of her life. "Mom, your doctor just told me that your kidneys are failing and you will probably die within a few days." I had tears in my eyes, but my mom gave me a quick hug and said, "I sure hope he is right, Paul. I'm looking forward to it."

She immediately asked for her phone and, one by one, called each of her many grandchildren, telling them matter-of-factly, "I just found out I am going to die and be with the Lord in a few days, and I just wanted to be sure to encourage you to have a deep relationship with Jesus. I really want to see you there in heaven with me someday." That evening her kidneys failed and poisonous natural chemicals accumulated in her blood and put her into a coma. I stayed with her around the clock for the next two days. I was determined not to miss the glorious departure of one of God's daughters if I could help it.

As her breathing grew shallower and shallower and her skin grew increasingly pale, her hospice nurse informed me that she would probably pass in the next ten minutes or so. She had been in a coma for a couple of days, so it was unlikely she would wake up again. I prayed, however, "Lord, You know I am a sinner and I do not deserve any special treatment from You. But I pray that You will consider waking my mom up from her coma for the last ten minutes of her life so I can tell her good-bye in person."

The experienced hospice nurse almost went into shock when immediately Mom became wide awake and lucid. I asked her if she was ready to go home to heaven, and she said an enthusiastic, "Yes!" with a smile. With her last breath she whispered, "I love you, Paul," and her head dropped into my hands, with a big smile on her face. I wept openly with joy for her gain and grief over my temporary loss. She had fought the last battle and come out victorious. Victorious in life and victorious in death! Her example has given me confidence that I can do the same someday. We, too, can have that kind of victory if we take the time now to prepare for eternity.

27

Death's Only Weapon

Now that we have identified where and how we should fight the last battle against death, we must consider the weapons we are up against. In reality death only has one. It is a weapon that is both biological and psychological. It is not just physically destructive, but emotionally, mentally, and spiritually destructive as well. Ironically, we become infected with it the very moment our lives begin! Death uses it to wage war against us as soon as we are born. It is the weapon of sin. First Corinthians 15:56 says, "The sting of death is sin." This is what makes death so painful. It is from where death's power stems. To conquer death we must conquer sin!

I (Dr. Meier) have had clients tell me, "Sin is too much fun to give up!" But after spending some time examining how much fun they are really having, these same clients come to realize it is often their own sins that have contributed to the depression or anxiety that has brought them to our office in the first place. We must remember that all sins hurt someone. Sometimes the way it does it is subtle. At other times it is more obvious. Drawing on thirty-plus years of clinical experience, I tell patients, "Even if I did not believe in God or the Bible, knowing what I know from psychiatric research, I would still try to abstain the best I could from the very things the Bible addresses as sins. That is because every client I have seen who does not avoid these things ends up depressed, lonely, and often wishing for death."

Unfortunately, attempting to avoid sin is a losing battle when we fight it with our own human resources. The Bible is clear that "there is none righteous, no, not one" (Rom. 3:10). It says that "all have sinned and fallen short of the glory of God" (v. 23) and that "the wages of sin is death" (6:23). None of us has the equipment necessary to defend against sin, even though many believe they do. Like foolish knights, they ride toward the fiery dragon of sin (Satan himself) with a pocketknife for a sword and a burlap tunic for armor, thinking they will not be burned to a crisp.

Interestingly, Satan would rather we not know the true power of sin. Like Sadaam Hussein, he declares, "I have no weapons of mass destruction." There may or may not have been weapons of mass destruction in Iraq, but never let anyone convince you that there are no sins of mass destruction. Sin not only exists, but every sin, be it a tiny white lie or a brutal homicide, is deadly.

In psychiatry of all places, we must be extremely careful of this tactic to conceal. C. S. Lewis was right when he said that psychoanalysis (if performed from a secular worldview) can have "a profound effect on the public mind's awareness of sin."[1] In our efforts to help people understand why they struggle with certain types of sins, we must be careful not to excuse the sin or call it something other than what it is. Psychiatry has wrongly taken all pejorative terminology out of its diagnostic manuals and replaced them with euphemisms. No longer do we call criminals child molesters, but pedophiles. Sexual perversions, as they used to be called, are now paraphilias. Most people do not realize that homosexuality was once listed under this diagnostic category until it was completely removed in 1980. Slowly our culture, under the influences of a subtle but extremely powerful force, has sought to remove sin from our vocabulary. The consequences of such actions have been devastating to our understanding of what makes death so painful.

The "Unoriginal" Sin

There is nothing new about Satan's tactics to cause us pain, especially when it comes to the pain of death. To remind ourselves of the real consequences of sin and the subtle tactics death uses to convince us otherwise, we need to return yet again to the story of Adam and Eve. As you read the Genesis account, you will notice that the Bible makes specific mention of how shrewd Satan was in deceiving Adam and Eve. He gets the humans to question God in three areas: the accuracy of His word, the consequences of disobeying His word, and the motivations behind His word.

The Accuracy of God's Word

First, Satan tempted Eve to question the accuracy of God's word. He asked, "Has God really said . . . ?" Down through the centuries, Satan has used this tactic to confuse us over the issue of sin. By questioning the validity of God's Word, people have sought to distort His views on sin. Unfortunately, we do not have room in this book to provide evidence for the validity of the Bible, but if this is an obstacle for you in understanding God's views concerning sin, read His Word with an open heart and mind and see if it is not the most amazing, powerful book ever written. We would also recommend that you pick up Norman Geisler and Frank Turek's book *I Don't Have Enough Faith to Be an Atheist*,[2] Lee Strobel's *Case For . . .* series of books,[3] and Josh McDowell's *New Evidence That Demands a Verdict*.[4] You will see there is enough scientific, historical, eyewitness, and revealed evidence to allow you to confidently put your faith in what the Bible has to say about sin and death.

In the end, all aspects of life and death revolve around faith, as much as a secularist would try to deny it; and faith is not isolated to religion. To demonstrate this point to a group of second-year residents, I (Dr. Henderson) provided them with a copy of a controversial article on antidepressant medications and asked them to read it prior to a lecture I gave. Out of the six residents present at the lecture, only two of them had read the article all the way through. Those who did not described their reasons as (1) a lack of interest in the subject matter (even though it was attacking the core of their profession), (2) a lack of time (speaking to priorities), and/or (3) irritation with the conclusions drawn from the study. The two residents who had read the article admitted confusion over the statistical analyses used to draw the conclusion and a failure to review the references cited at the end of the study.

I then had a prominent researcher at the university come to discuss the article. She focused on the limitations of the study, which, according to the residents, "made them feel more at ease." None of them reported a desire to change their prescribing habits based on the results of the study. It was not until I pointed it out that they realized each of them had demonstrated faith in their handling of such a controversial subject. Never once during that lecture did they discuss religion, but the practice of faith was evident throughout.

Most people, when confronted with the reality of sin and death, choose to ignore it, whether out of disinterest, busyness, or irritation with the conclusions others have drawn. They would rather trust in their own worldview and avoid examining the evidence to the contrary. We need to have faith in God's Word, but it need not be blind faith. After examining the evidence, we will realize that sin is real. It is the power of death—a power Satan loves to conceal from us as he did with Eve.

Consequences of Disobeying God's Word

The second tactic Satan used with Eve was to get her to question the consequences of disobeying God's word. "You shall not surely die" (Gen. 3:4). By getting us to question sin's consequences, its relationship to death, or its power to separate us from God, he causes us to lower our guard so that he can secure his victory. "It's not as bad as it seems. Everyone else is doing it. God will understand. Nobody's perfect." But no amount of fancy catchphrases or cool slogans will change the reality of the final consequences for our sins. The sins of Adam and Eve not only brought physical death, but also emotional and spiritual death, in a variety of ways. Satan said that God's threat was an overstatement, when in reality it was the truth.

If you really want to ruin a conversation, start talking about hell. It is the ultimate "buzz killer." No one wants to be reminded that sin causes spiritual death. The world has told us that as long as we are not as bad as the guy next to us, God will be understanding and let us into heaven. "You shall not surely die." If you believe that, then you are that much closer to death, maybe not physically but spiritually. If physical death is separation of the soul from the body, spiritual death is separation of the soul from God. It is the ultimate darkness.

Talking about hell can be extremely painful. Those who cannot tolerate the idea usually tend to ignore it, but before you do, ask yourself this question: "Is my denial of hell the result of my own unwillingness to deal with something that might be painful?" Are you trying to avoid pain? Remember that sometimes we have to drive farther into the darkness in order to experience the real light of living.

Before we move on, it is important to notice that God never told Adam and Eve that if they touched the fruit, they would die. Eve added that one herself. This is another mistake we make as humans: adding to the words of God. When it comes to sin, human beings love to add things in order to manipulate others. Churches, families, organizations, and individuals make laws and traditions that have no biblical basis but are used to gain political, social, or relational control. People come into our office every day suffering from the false guilt that organized religion, family members or spouses, employers or teachers have placed on them. Such guilt often requires radical "psychological surgery" to remove. When people finally realize the deception, they often feel silly for having bought into it, but more important, they feel liberated from having to experience the guilt again.

The *Oakland Tribune* reported a story in July of 2007 about two brothers who committed three consecutive robberies in one night . . . using a toy gun! The first victim was a man robbed of his cash, cell phone, and backpack while waiting for a bus. The second victim was a fifty-six-year-old woman, who lost her purse to the toy-gun terrorists when leaving a gas station. The final victim, a thirty-year-old man on his way to meet his wife for dinner, not only let himself be robbed, but then submitted himself to a beating all because he imagined his life to be in danger from what he thought was a real gun.[5]

Sometimes, if Satan cannot hurt us with the real thing, he will use *toy guilt* to rob our lives of anything precious: peace of mind, joy, happiness in relationships, and the like. Seek and destroy—that is the plan. Anything he can use to make us feel dead inside, he will. Distinguishing healthy guilt from pathological guilt can be difficult, but with therapy and supportive relationships, we can win this battle over death.

Motivations Behind God's Word

The final tactic Satan used in the garden was to get Eve to question the motivations behind God's word. One of the best weapons of war is psychological. By inducing questions about the motives of our Commander, His government, or His cause, the enemy can seriously demoralize us. Just like all of Satan's tactics, this one is not new. During all wars, both sides have used propaganda to help spread despair and frustration. The very first example of this psychological warfare was in the garden of Eden when Satan told Eve, "You won't die! . . . God knows that your eyes will be opened as soon as you eat it, and you will be like God, knowing both good and evil" (Gen. 3:4–5 NLT).

In other words, "God just does not want you to be like Him. That is the only reason He told you not to eat this food. He is holding back from you. Don't believe His lies." Satan's reverse psychology worked. The Bible says, "The woman was convinced" (Gen. 3:6 NLT). Adam, however, who could not claim deception, knowingly ate the fruit with his wife and so infected all of humankind with sin. That very day Adam died both physically (the process of death began in him at the moment he sinned) and spiritually (he found himself no longer in the presence of God). Because of his sin, that death passed to all of us.

Unbeatable Odds

If sin as the weapon of death is so powerful to have infected us all, how can we possibly beat it? We have bad news: we can't! Psychologists are just starting to realize what the Bible has said all along: left to ourselves we cannot escape the power of our pasts. Sin is genetic, psychological, and social. It permeates every part of our beings, our minds, and our society. One need only to sit in therapy for a few short sessions to realize that so much of what we do in this life is unconsciously motivated by past experiences, personality, and genetics. Even acquiring that knowledge consciously does little to help us change. We are fighting an uphill battle wearing roller skates, climbing Mount Everest on skis, bailing water out of the *Titanic* with a silver spoon. In a word, it is *impossible*. Sure we can make strides, we can improve ourselves, we might even feel better for a time, but eventually we all get swept away by sin's power. It is not until we accept this reality that we can ever possibly find the hope of being rescued.

So how do we defeat sin? The only way is to find a power outside of ourselves, a power that has not itself been infected by sin. We cannot merely call in reinforcements from our own human resources. We must look for another army altogether, one that we can submit ourselves to in exchange for protection. That army is the real Army of One. The power comes from none other than Jesus Christ, the Son of God. The apostle Paul describes the desperateness of the situation and the cry for help we must all humble ourselves to make: "We were crushed and overwhelmed beyond our ability to endure and we thought we would never live through it. In fact, we expected to die. But as a result, we stopped relying on ourselves and learned to rely only on God, who raises the dead" (2 Cor. 1:8–9 NLT). Christ is the key to our victory. If you want to disarm death, you must disarm yourself. Drop your weapons of self-sufficiency and control and surrender your life to Jesus. You must realize that no matter how hard you fight, death will win unless you turn everything you have over to Jesus and let Him take command. He is the only One who has power over death. Read on to know why.

28

Resurrecting Hope

As psychiatrists we see people every day who have lost their hope of life. Many of these individuals contemplate suicide, and some even attempt it. Suicide is the natural act of hopelessness. Some find suicide as the ultimate vengeance, but most who commit suicide probably do so out of pure hopelessness. With no reason to live, death seems to be the only option. For some their lives are so painful they would much rather endure the pain of death and have done with it. *This is good!* The only way to resurrect hope in people's lives is by encouraging them to commit suicide.

Hold on a minute! We are not talking about physical suicide. We are talking about spiritual suicide. It is the hopelessness over a meaningless life that drives us to seek life elsewhere. Unfortunately, physically suicidal patients focus their attention on escaping the hopelessness of life through physical death, when in reality they should be focusing on escaping that hopelessness through spiritual death instead.

Instead of trying to conquer or escape death, go ahead and die . . . die to yourself. Give up your life! Commit not physical suicide but spiritual suicide. Give up control and hand it over to Jesus. Then watch what happens. Suddenly, in a strange twist of eternal providence, death loses all its power. It becomes nothing more than a passageway to an eternity of real living, not just in this life but for all of eternity. Jesus said, "I am the way, the truth, and the life" (John 14:6 NLT). The blessings of eternal life start as soon as "the Life" (Jesus) takes control of our own lives. The moment we give up our sorry excuses for lives and turn them over to Christ, He gives us lives we never could have imagined otherwise. What we once thought was life, we now realize was just a slow dying that began at birth. Jesus opens our eyes to so much more. As our trust in Him strengthens, we learn the kind of peace that does not waver, no matter how terrible the circumstance. We experience the kind of joy that cannot be stolen by anyone or anything, no matter how crafty or powerful the thief is. We find true purpose, serving a leader who knows us better than we know ourselves. He now protects us from death until His purposes are accomplished and then gives us strength to wrestle with it when it comes. As we pass through it, He takes us to a place where "There will be no more death or sorrow or crying or pain. All these things are gone forever" (Rev. 21:4 NLT). Our physical deaths may still be painful, but the victory will be that much sweeter on the other side, knowing that death has been defeated once and for all, not through our own strength, but through the power of our Savior, Jesus Christ. He died not for Himself but for us.

During the writing of this chapter, Easter has just passed. Easter's publicity will never compare with the strategic Christmas advertising that begins sometime in late August. The material gifts are not nearly as spectacular either: if you are lucky, you get a basket overstuffed with fake grass and a few plastic eggs that cannot hold more than a dime's worth of candy.

As low profile as Easter may be in our society, for those who know the truth, it is the most exciting and hope-filled holiday of the year! At Christmas people get that warm, fuzzy feeling. There is something about the birth of a sweet, innocent little baby that no one can resist. We sing carols and drink hot chocolate while sitting by the fire. It is awesome, no doubt. But most people stop their celebration after January first. They miss the true purpose for Jesus' coming. Some people make it *spiritually* to Palm Sunday, when they praise the human virtues Jesus possessed. They raise their proverbial palm branches in worship of Jesus' good moral character and saintly life. It gives them hope to think that they might be able to do the same. Some, spiritually, make it as far as Good Friday. They worship a Jesus who hangs eternally on a cross, a symbol of "the importance of self-sacrifice for the good of humankind" or "staying true to one's self and one's principles even in death." Some may even rightly believe that Jesus died on purpose to save the world from sin. But if we stop short of Easter, the third day, the resurrection, we have missed the point entirely.

A man named Sam told me (Dr. Henderson) he could not bring himself to watch *The Passion of the Christ* when it entered theaters. "I refuse to subject myself to the pointless, sadistic torture of such a good man. I just don't get how anyone can celebrate something like that."

His honesty was admirable. Many people like him do not understand because they do not believe in the resurrection. Yes, Jesus suffered for us, and it is important not to forget it. That is why we take communion. But without the resurrection all that suffering was pointless, just "sadistic torture of a good man." We cannot find hope from a Savior who Himself could not defeat death. If, however, the resurrection is the real deal, then we now know someone who has faced the reality of death and "lived to tell about it." His are the only words we can trust on the subject, because He has been there and He has won!

Victory over Death

Those who want to destroy Christianity must disprove the resurrection. If you can do so, Christianity is finished. All our hope of being saved is in vain. We might as well "eat, drink, and be merry" for tomorrow we die (Luke 12:19). First Corinthians 15 tells us how important the apostle Paul believed the resurrection was to the Christian faith:

> Let me now remind you, dear brothers and sisters, of the Good News I preached to you before. . . . I passed on to you what was most important and what had also been passed on to me. Christ died for our sins, just as the Scriptures said. He was buried, and he was raised from the dead on the third day, just as the Scriptures said. He was seen by Peter and then

by the Twelve. After that, he was seen by more than 500 of his followers at one time, most of whom are still alive, though some have died. Then he was seen by James and later by all the apostles. Last of all, as though I had been born at the wrong time, I also saw him. . . . If Christ has not been raised, then all our preaching is useless, and your faith is useless. . . . And if Christ has not been raised, then your faith is useless and you are still guilty of your sins. In that case, all who have died believing in Christ are lost! And if our hope in Christ is only for this life, we are more to be pitied than anyone in the world. (vv. 1–19 NLT)

Most people trying to advance an idea do not reveal a potential "weak link in their chain," but here Paul lays it out for all to see. If Christ, who was the perfect Son of God, untainted by the weapon of sin, could not defeat death for Himself, how in the world can we put our trust in Him to do the same for us? We can't!

But in fact, Christ has been raised from the dead. He is the first of a great harvest of all who have died.

So you see, just as death came into the world through a man, now the resurrection from the dead has begun through another man. Just as everyone dies because we all belong to Adam, everyone who belongs to Christ will be given new life. . . . Then, when our dying bodies have been transformed into bodies that will never die, this Scripture will be fulfilled:

"Death is swallowed up in victory.
O death, where is your victory?
O death, where is your sting?"

For sin is the sting that results in death, and the law gives sin its power. But thank God! He gives us victory over sin and death through our Lord Jesus Christ. (1 Cor. 15:20–22, 54–57 NLT)

We have victory over death and sin, we will have new bodies that will never die, Jesus Christ is our Savior, and God is our Father. Now, those are what we call "reasons to celebrate"! Those are reasons to hope!

Is There Any Other Way?

Jesus said in John 14:6, "I am the way, the truth, and the life. No one comes to the Father except through me." For many people this exclusive means of salvation is the most painful part of gaining victory over death. Giving up their right to live life their own way is so painful they would rather spend an eternity apart from God, paying for this right, rather than submitting to the authority of another person.

In some ways we all struggle with the urge to invent our own truth, instead of facing the hard discipline of searching for absolutes. We all want to feel we are in charge, that we are in control of our own lives and that no one else can tell us what to do. "Who can possibly know better than I what is best for my life?"

It can be difficult to submit ourselves under the authority of others, especially when they are sin-infected people just as we are, but we are deluding ourselves if we believe we need not do it. There are penalties for speeding, littering, stealing, failing to pay taxes, and the list goes on. Not only these, but there are laws of nature, relationships, and money. We do not jump out of airplanes without parachutes unless we are willing to pay for the deed with our lives or at least some broken bones. We do not abuse others unless we are willing to experience a divorce or separation of that relationship. And we certainly do not walk into a store and take things without paying unless we are willing to pay with jail time instead. We may, at times, be able to escape the immediate penalties for the infractions of these laws, but they are nonetheless our masters.

Christ, however, is the perfect Master. He knows us even better than we know ourselves—and that includes our every thought and action, what is best for us on this earth, what purposes will be most fulfilling for our lives, and what actions and attitudes will make us truly happy. If we are to have meaningful, productive, and fulfilling earthly lives, we must submit to the powers that be. More important, if we are to have meaningful, productive, and fulfilling spiritual lives, we must submit to the authority of Jesus, the One who gave everything to give us that life.

After all He has done, does He not have the right to be demanding of our allegiance, or at least to demand that we choose one way or the other? He will settle for nothing less than a dictatorship in our lives. Unlike most dictatorships, however, King Jesus really wants the best for His subjects. He proved how far He was willing to go to get the best for us by His own willing death on the cross. Now we, as subjects, have a decision to make. We can either bow before Him as loyal children of the King with gratitude in our hearts for all He has done, or we can bow to Him as His enemies, rebels of the heart who, having held on to our own false sense of power and control, will never partake in the blessings loyal subjects receive— namely, victory over death, the final enemy; an inheritance from the King's infinite storehouse; and an honored position in His kingdom for all eternity. Maybe for some readers sacrificing such gifts is worth the temporary illusion of self-control, but not for us!

Think about it this way: if we could truly reach heaven, our eternal kingdom, any other way, why in the world would Jesus die for us in the first place? Jesus asked the very same question in the Garden of Gethsemane when he said, "My Father, if it is possible, let this cup of suffering be taken away from me. Yet I want your will to be done, not mine" (Matt. 26:39 NLT). Consider the agony of that question. What a slap in Jesus' face when someone, knowing what Christ went through on the cross, says, "What you did was so nice, Jesus. Thank You. It is so good to know that I'm loved! If You don't mind, though, I'm going to follow my own path. I just like doing it this way better. You understand, right? It's not that I don't appreciate You and all, but I'm just not ready to make that kind of commitment." Like the dissatisfied girlfriend who is afraid to face conflict with a scorned lover, we say to Jesus, "Let's just be friends. It's not You. It's me."

No, the sadistic brutality Sam used to describe Jesus' death demands a yes or no answer to His kingship in our lives. The physical pain He suffered was just a glimpse of what Jesus went through to bear the full force of our sins, death's only weapon, the weapon that should have destroyed us. If He really is "The Life," then to deny Him entrance into our lives is to face the ultimate defeat against death. "Whoever has the Son has life; he who does not have God's Son does not have life" (1 John 5:12 NLT). It doesn't get any simpler than that!

Dying to Live

If you think about it, all of us are just dying to live. Some people will do anything to hold on to the illusion that they are really living apart from God. Others are willing to die to themselves in order to gain an eternal life that they can never lose. If you are dying to live, it does not matter how old or young you are—the choice is yours as long as you have breath.

Jerry was a man in the winter season of his life. He was a well-educated man with a PhD in microbiology and amazing talent as a pianist. For years he taught at well-known universities across the United States. With all his education, however, he refused to examine the validity of the Bible and its teachings on death.

One day during a routine physical, Jerry discovered that he had a rare, inoperable form of cancer. His prognosis was clearly explained to him, but he refused to believe he was dying, still holding on to the hope of a cure. As the cancer progressed, he slipped in and out of a coma. Doctors told his family he only had a few weeks, if not days, to live. Not wanting to squelch their father's hope, however, they refused to share the news with him and thus robbed him of one last chance to make things right with God.

When I (Dr. Henderson) first started working on this chapter, my daughter was only twenty-four hours old. At the moment Jerry was passing on, she was just starting to live. I had no idea at the time of all the problems she would have to endure in the first couple of years of her life. One night in particular something woke up my wife and prompted her to check on our little girl. She found her gasping for air, and we had to rush her to the emergency room. The doctors measured the level of oxygen in her blood and found that it was very low. Later we discovered that she had reflux, which had been irritating her lungs and causing them to constrict in the middle of the night. Though she is doing well now, the experience reminded me that her struggle against death has just begun. Her little eyes cannot at this point see the road she must travel. Her little ears have only heard the loving sound of her parents' voices. Her mind cannot conceive what battles will be hers to fight, but as long as she lives, the opportunity for her to conquer death remains just as it did for Jerry, and for you and me.

Interestingly, before I ever knew I would be writing this book, my wife and I chose to name our daughter Victoria. The name means "victory." I want nothing more passionately than for her to find true meaning in her name. As she begins this life's journey, no matter how long or short it may be, I pray that she will give her life to the only One who can make her Victoria in the truest sense of the word: "the victorious one in Christ."

We pray the same for you! "May the God of hope fill you with all joy and peace in believing, that you may abound in hope by the power of the Holy Spirit" (Rom. 15:13). "Thanks be to God, who gives us the victory [over death] through our Lord Jesus Christ" (1 Cor. 15:57).

Finding Purpose Beyond Your Death

Now that we have discovered all that God can do for us, even in the face of death, we want to give you five practical application points to strengthen and encourage you as you search for the purposes beyond your own death.

1. *Acknowledge your fear.* When it comes to our own mortality, most people live in denial. They repress any conscious consideration of death and thus rob themselves of the fulfillment and peace that comes after wrestling with its reality. Do not let this happen to you. Identify your fears, and then ask God to give you the truth necessary to assuage those fears. Then and only then will you be prepared to meet death wherever and whenever it strikes (Ps. 23:4).

2. *Live resiliently.* Once you have identified your fears and conquered them with the truth of God's Word, you will have the freedom to live a life that is resilient against the subtle attacks of death. Second Corinthians tells us that we do not have to lose heart, because even though our outward bodies are dying, our inward person (that part of us that is eternal) will be renewed every single day (2 Cor. 4:16–18).

3. *Live responsibly.* Reminding ourselves of the reality of death helps us to prioritize those aspects of life that are most important: sharing the love of God with others, honoring Him with the good things He has given us, and being grateful for every opportunity to serve Him. We have all of eternity to party! Let's use the short time we have here to make a difference that will last forever! (James 4:14–17).

4. *Disarm death.* The only weapon death has is sin, and we have all been tainted with it. We can, however, be free from its power if we will trust in Jesus' sacrifice on the cross as payment for our sin. In doing so, death loses all its power over us (John 3:16).

5. *Commit spiritual suicide.* Ironically, if you want to conquer death, you must die to yourself. You must give up control of everything, even the time and place of your death. The apostle Paul had the best excuse of anyone to be suicidal. He suffered tremendous pain in his life, and God even gave him a glimpse of heaven, the celebration that he had waiting for him after death. Yet Paul knew God was keeping him here on earth for a reason. He was confident of a purpose greater than himself, and so he stuck it out to the very end. We, too, must do the same (Phil. 1:21).

Now set aside some personal time to consider your own situation in the light of these truths. Then answer the following questions truthfully in order to establish the groundwork for overcoming the fear of death in your life.

1. What do you fear most about death? How have these fears been ruling the way you live your life?

2. What do you believe about death? What is the evidence you have to support your beliefs? What other beliefs are there about death, and how are the arguments proposed valid or invalid?

3. Who do you know who has died well? Who do you know who has died poorly? How have their deaths helped or hindered your own readiness to face death?

4. What is robbing you of true life? Is it false guilt, fear, resentment, dissatisfaction, or disappointments? The Bible says Christ came so we could have life and have it more abundantly (John 10:10). How can you make this happen practically on a daily basis?

5. What areas of control are you most afraid to relinquish? What would turning them over to Christ mean for you?

Conclusion

The Power of the Purpose

"For this very purpose I have raised you up, that I may show My power in you"

—Romans 9:17

This book started out as an intellectual idea: that pain, if handled with a proper perspective, can set us apart for amazing things in life. It has now become the prayer of our hearts. Just before the battle of Jericho, Joshua told the people of Israel to "consecrate" (set apart) themselves "because tomorrow the Lord will do amazing things among you" (Josh. 3:5 NCV). The same is true today! If you take the struggles you have faced in this life and allow them to set you apart for the unique opportunities God has in store for you, He will surely do amazing things in you also. And here's the secret: *the power to cope with the pain is in focusing on its purpose.*

We want to leave you with two important truths to hold on to while you focus on the purpose beyond your pain: (1) the presence of Christ is sufficient, and (2) the promise of heaven is secure.

The Presence of Christ Is Sufficient

Have you ever wondered why Jesus' disciples were able to endure so much pain and suffering in their lives following His ascension into heaven? The

Bible gives us two answers. First Jesus presented Himself to them *alive* after all of His suffering was over. The Bible says He did so "by many infallible proofs" (Acts 1:3 KJV).

In order for Jesus to prove to His disciples that He was indeed alive, He had to do so not just physically, but emotionally and spiritually as well. On a human level He had to demonstrate that the Jesus they knew *before* His excruciating crucifixion was the same Jesus they were now enjoying *after* His resurrection, only more brilliant and glorified. The power He used to endure the earthly pain of the cross was focusing on the eternal purpose of His death—the redemption of the people He loves.

Imagine that! The disciples had witnessed firsthand the anguish Jesus had suffered as He lived among them. They had seen Him verbally abused, hounded, and rejected by those who either hated His message or envied His power. His closest friends had abandoned Jesus in His time of greatest need. He had been stripped of every earthly possession He owned, arrested, humiliated, and beaten before being brutally executed. Yet here He was before them, undeniably alive and well in body, mind, and spirit. Jesus had endured every struggle this broken world could throw at Him, and He had come through it all triumphantly. Now, with His presence confirmed before their eyes and in their hearts, they knew they could do the same.

The Promise of Heaven Is Secure

The second act Jesus performed as He sought to strengthen His disciples' resolve in times of trouble was not a miraculous sign or wonder, but instead, a forty-day seminar devoted totally to the kingdom of God. Why is this significant? It is because pain is so much easier to bear if we know there is something to look forward to on the other side of it. By teaching His disciples all about heaven and the coming kingdom of God, Jesus gave them something amazing to which they could look forward. The disciples clung to His words during the darkest moments of their lives. Even in prison or in exile or awaiting their own executions, they wrote letters to each other reminding them to "comfort one another with these words"

(1 Thess. 4:18). No matter how bad life would get, they firmly believed the best was yet to come. They focused on the purpose of their lives, not the pain they knew they would have to face.

Perfected by Pain

Today we have amazing hope for the same reason. There is coming a day when pain will cease to be. Its purposes in our lives will be completed. We will not need it anymore, because it will have perfected us. In the meantime we must focus on the purpose God wants us to realize through our struggles.

My (Dr. Henderson's) dad, having just turned seventy, reflected upon the struggles of his own life. In a moment of complete candor, he said to me, "You know . . . sometimes I wish I could be a child again. I remember distinctly, as if it were yesterday, taking a walk with my father and uncle around the lake next to our house. I was only six years old. It was Christmas Day and World War II was almost over. My uncle, who was in the navy at the time, had just gotten back from active duty and was still in uniform.

"A light snow, which had started falling the night before, continued to cover the ground in a pure blanket of white. It was early in the morning, so there weren't many cars on the road, and the snow muffled the sound of those that happened to pass by in the distance. All was quiet except for the soft murmurs of my father and uncle talking about things I didn't understand. With their hands holding mine, I walked with who I thought were the two most powerful men in the world, feeling a total security and an innocent peace that I've never known since.

"I have faced a great deal of pain in my life since then, and I've often wished, even as a grown man, that I could hold my dad's hand as I did that Christmas morning, but now I know a different kind of peace. In every way it's better than the one before, because it is no longer innocent and naïve. It has been tested and it is true. I *do* have a hand to hold . . . and this time I'm not letting go until it pulls me into the arms of the most powerful and loving Father I will ever know."

The next time you experience pain, find the perfecting purpose it plays in your future—beyond the pain, and use that powerful knowledge to endure the pain today. It is always the deepest mine, the darkest cave, or the loneliest desert that holds the richest treasure for those of us determined to find it. As you search for the purpose, remember what Colossians 2:3 (NCV) says: "In him [Christ] all the treasures of wisdom and knowledge are safely kept." In Christ and Christ alone can you ever find the purpose beyond your pain. Don't give out; don't give in; don't give up until you have found it!

Notes

Introduction

1. Asa Cummings, *A Memoir of the Rev. Edward Payson, D.D., late pastor of the second church in Portland*. Published by Ann L. Payson. (Shirley and Hyde Printers, 1830), 413.
2. World Health Organization, http://www.who.int/mental_health/ management/ depression/definition/en/. Accessed April 22, 2009.
3. The National Institute of Mental Health, http://www.nimh.nih.gov/health/ publications/suicide-in-the-us-statistics-and-prevention/index.html. Accessed April 22, 2009.
4. Dan Allender and Tremper Longman, *The Cry of the Soul* (NavPress: Colorado Springs, 1999), 105.

Chapter 1

1. D. T. Miller, "Disrespect and the Experience of Injustice," *Annual Review of Psychology*, 2001; M. J. L. Sullivan, et al., "The Role of Perceived Injustice in the Experience of Chronic Pain and Disability: Scale Development and Validation," *Journal of Occupational Rehabilitation* 18, no. 3 (2008): 249–61; F. M. Blyth, L. M. March, M. K. Nicholas, M. J. Cousins. "Chronic Pain, Work Performance and Litigation," *Pain* 103 (2003): 41–7; R. Ferrari and A. Russell, "Why Blame Is Factor in Recovery from Whiplash Injury," *Medical Hypotheses* 56 (2001): 72–75; R. T. Gun, O. L. Osti, "Risk Factors for Prolonged Disability after Whiplash Injury: A Prospective Study," *Spine* 30 (2005): 386–91; D. C. Turk, A. Okifuji, "Perception of Traumatic Onset, Compensation

Status, and Physical Findings: Impact on Pain Severity, Emotional Distress, and Disability in Chronic Pain Patients," *Journal of Behavioral Medicine* 19, no. 5 (1996): 435–53; G. Mikula, K. R. Scherer, and U. Athenstaedt, "The Role of Injustice in the Elicitation of Differential Emotional Reactions," *Personality and Social Psychology Bulletin* 24 (1998): 769–83.

Chapter 2

1. C. S. Lewis, *Mere Christianity* (New York: HarperCollins, 2001), 32.
2. Friedrich Nietzsche, *Human, All Too Human*, 1878.

Chapter 4

1. Debbie Townsend, letter to a therapist.

Chapter 5

1. William Shakespeare, *As You Like It*, act II, scene vii.

Chapter 14

1. Scott Hamilton, "Olympic Optimism: Interview with Scott Hamilton," Olympic Hall of Fame (Sun Valley, ID), June 29, 1996 http://www.achievement.org/autodoc/page/ham0int-4.
2. Rich Morin and Paul Taylor, "Luxury or Necessity? The Public Makes a U-Turn," *Social & Demographic Trends* (Pew Research Center, April 23, 2009), http://pewsocialtrends.org/pubs/733/luxury-necessity-recession-era-reevaluations. Accessed May 12, 2009.

Chapter 15

1. Bethany Hamilton, *Soul Surfer: A True Story of Faith, Family and Fighting to Get Back on the Board* (New York: MTV Books/Pocket Books, 2004).
2. Richard Stearns, *The Hole in Our Gospel* (Nashville: Thomas Nelson, 2009). Used by permission.

Chapter 20

1. Michael Specter, "The Long Ride: How Did Lance Armstrong Manage the Greatest Comeback in Sports History?" *New Yorker*, July 15, 2002, 5.

Chapter 21

1. Dave Ramsey and Sharon Ramsey, *Financial Peace Revisited* (Harmondsworth, Middlesex: Viking Penguin, 2003), 325.
2. Lou Holtz, *Wins, Losses, and Lessons: An Autobiography* (New York: Harper Entertainment, 2007), 18.

Chapter 24

1. A. Cooper, N. Delmonico, R. Burg, "Cybersex Users, Abusers, and Compulsives: New Findings and Implications," *Sexual Addiction and Compulsivity* 7 (2000): 5–29; A. Cooper, ed. *Sex and the Internet: A Guidebook for Clinicians* (New York: Brunner-Routledge, 2002).

Chapter 25

1. "Live Like You Were Dying," words and music by Tim Nichols and Craig Wiseman. Recorded by Tim McGraw on Curb Records, 2004.

Chapter 27

1. C. S. Lewis, *The Complete C. S. Lewis* (San Francisco: Harper, 2007), 579–80.
2. Norm Geisler and Frank Turek, *I Don't Have Enough Faith to Be an Atheist* (Wheaton: Crossway, 2004).
3. Lee Strobel, *The Case for Faith* (Grand Rapids: Zondervan, 2000); idem., *The Case for Christ* (Grand Rapids: Zondervan, 1998).
4. Josh McDowell, *New Evidence That Demands a Verdict* (Nashville: Thomas Nelson, 1999).
5. "Police: Brothers used toy gun in robberies," *Oakland Tribune*, July 2007, http://www.earthtimes.org/articles/show/87837.html.

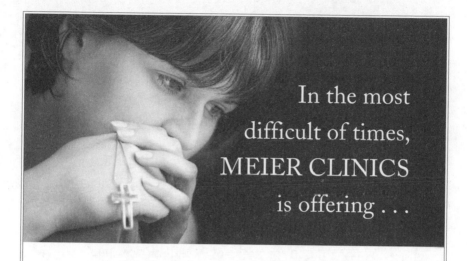

"Hope this side of Heaven…"

Dr. David Livingstone Henderson, MD is a board-certified psychiatrist, author, and speaker who is committed to helping people find purpose beyond their pain, be it physical, mental, emotional, or spiritual. His areas of expertise include:

- Mood problems (depression, bipolar)
- Anxiety disorders (panic attacks, obsessive-compulsive disorder, PTSD)
- ADD/ADHD
- Addictions (substance abuse, sexual, food, other people)
- Marriage difficulties
- Anger problems
- Personality disorders
- Crises of spirituality/worldview

Need a speaker for your church or organization?
Visit Dr. Henderson's website for event listings and contact information at www.drdavidhenderson.com.

"There is so much more to living . . . take the first step today!"